Silenced!

Silenced!

Academic Freedom, Scientific Inquiry, and the First Amendment under Siege in America

Bruce E. Johansen

Foreword by Matthew Rothschild

Westport, Connecticut
London

Library of Congress Cataloging-in-Publication Data

Johansen, Bruce E. (Bruce Elliott), 1950–
    Silenced! : academic freedom, scientific inquiry, and the First Amendment under siege in America / Bruce E. Johansen ; foreword by Matthew Rothschild.
        p. cm.
    Includes bibliographical references and index.
    ISBN 978-0-275-99686-4 (alk. paper)
    1. Academic freedom—United States. 2. United States—Politics and government—2001- I. Title.
    LC72.2.J64 2007
    378.1'21—dc22   2007008456

British Library Cataloguing in Publication Data is available.

Library of Congress Catalog Card Number: 2007008456
ISBN-13: 978-0-275-99686-4
ISBN-10: 0-275-99686-7

First published in 2007

Praeger Publishers, 88 Post Road West, Westport, CT 06881
An imprint of Greenwood Publishing Group, Inc.
www.praeger.com

Printed in the United States of America

The paper used in this book complies with the Permanent Paper Standard issued by the National Information Standards Organization (Z39.48-1984).

10 9 8 7 6 5 4 3 2 1

Those who would give up essential liberty to purchase a little temporary safety deserve neither liberty nor safety.

—Benjamin Franklin, 1759 (Maharidge, 2004, 203)

Truth is great and will prevail if left to herself, that she is the proper and sufficient antagonist to error, and has nothing to fear from the conflict, unless by human interposition disarmed of her natural weapons, free argument and debate.

—Thomas Jefferson, 1779 (Packer, 2006, 59)

Contents

Foreword

George W. Bush's presidency is nearly over, but the Bush Age may be with us for decades longer, if we let it. Many of the salient features of this epoch have already been duly chronicled: the messianic militarism, the debacles in Iraq and Afghanistan, the sanitization of torture, the redistribution of income to the rich, the cynical appointment of industry representatives to head the very agencies designed to regulate those industries, the criminal indifference to Hurricane Katrina, and the bizarre cohabitation of neoconservatives with far-right evangelicals.

But one aspect of the Bush Age has not received the attention it deserves, and that is the wholesale assault on our civil liberties. A chill is in the air, but we have been living with it for so long now that it is becoming dangerously imperceptible.

This is why Bruce Johansen's book is so essential. Focusing on academic freedom and scientific inquiry, he takes his readings. For the most part, they are not comforting. What they tell us is that those who dare to oppose government policy in an age of hysteria often put themselves at great risk. They can have trouble getting tenure or being hired at prestigious universities. If they have been sloppy at all in their work, they can lose their jobs. And sometimes worse. Johansen tells the story of Professor Paul Mirecki, who chaired Religious Studies at the University of Kansas. Mirecki, who in an e-mail had indelicately referred to religious conservatives as "fundies," planned to offer a course called "Special Topics in Religion: Intelligent Design, Creationism, and Other Religious Mythologies." The outcry was so great that he had to cancel it. Shortly afterward, two men beat him up with a metal object, sending him to the hospital. More notoriously, University of Colorado professor Ward Churchill received dozens and dozens of death threats. And the family of Jay Bennish, the high school teacher who compared Bush's rhetoric to Hitler's, also received death threats.

Johansen does a good job of showing how the ideological hazing and hounding proceeds, from right-wing student groups funded and organized by David Horowitz to local, hate-filled talk radio, virally through the Internet, up to the Billy pulpit of O'Reilly, and back down to the yahoos in state legislatures.

To his credit, Johansen also pinpoints how difficult the Bush Age has been for Middle Eastern scholars. "Where we once had witches, or bad Indians, or Communists, the hate-object Arab is now the generic barbarian at our gate," he writes. After 9/11, Arabs and Muslims in America have suffered from a qualitatively worse level of repression than anyone else here. Their experience in academia reflects that, and Johansen cites some cases. If you criticize U.S. policy or Israeli policy, you make yourself an especially easy target, he notes. He also describes how the government has denied visas to Muslim scholars and has even attempted to regulate the curricula of Middle Eastern studies.

Oh, there are some triumphs. James Hansen of NASA, whom Johansen aptly describes as "the Paul Revere of Global Warming," managed to outlast his Bush "minder." The advocates of so-called intelligent design, which the satirist Will Durst once described as "creationism with aluminum siding slapped on it," keep losing in court after court. And Johansen highlights the success of the scholar Mike Davis to show that you can be a radical critic and still make the big time.

Two final bits of praise for this vital book.

I applaud Johansen for his fairness. When he discusses complicated cases—such as Ward Churchill's or the controversy over Michael Bellesiles and his book *Arming America*—Johansen lays it all out. He does not blur the picture in favor of the academic under assault. Instead, he presents the negatives unadorned and lets the reader see the whole thing.

I also applaud him for writing in a breezy, playful, colloquial style. A journalist by trade, Johansen is a storyteller. Not for him the stuffiness of academic writing. While discussing the incendiary remarks of Columbia professor Nicholas de Genova, who, at a teach-in against the Iraq War, wished for "a million more Mogadishus," Johansen drolly added that some people were amazed that "de Genova could coin such a headline-grabbing phrase out of a general vocabulary so dense that even PhDs in his own field sometimes had trouble deciphering it." Johansen then quotes from Genova's Columbia biography to back up the claim deliciously.

While this book is about academics, it is not only for academics. It is for citizens. It is for people who cherish freedom of speech and freedom of inquiry. It is for people who worry about the fate of our democracy.

If you read this book and take its urgent message to heart—a message that embraces the Enlightenment and upholds the First Amendment—you will help bring the curtain down, finally, on the Bush Age.

Matthew Rothschild
Editor, *The Progressive*

Preface

This book had a very definite date of birth—November 15, 2005, as I was exchanging e-mails with Praeger senior editor Hilary Claggett, describing how a new committee assignment might crimp my style as an author. I had been asked to sit as one of the five professors who would recommend to the University of Colorado Board of Regents whether Ward Churchill, about whom you will be reading shortly, had committed research misconduct serious enough to consider termination of his employment at the University of Colorado.

The committee was assembled late in October, and made public on demand of Denver-area media under Colorado's open-records law very early in November. The other members were Marianne Wesson, CU law professor and an expert on employment discrimination, women and the law, and civil rights; Marjorie McIntosh, CU professor of history; Michael Radelet, CU professor of sociology and an expert on the death penalty; and Robert A. Williams, professor of law and American Indian studies, University of Arizona.

Very quickly, some Denver print and broadcast media, fed by an anti-Churchill Web site, Jim Paine's pirateballerina.com, busied themselves questioning Williams's and my impartiality because we had defended Churchill's free-speech rights in public, a matter that was not under investigation (Johansen, February 9, 2005, 7-B). The university had said that Churchill's comments associating victims of the World Trade Center atrocities with Adolf Eichmann was free speech protected by the First Amendment.

I lasted exactly two weeks in a rancid atmosphere during which some in the media surrendered their critical faculties to Paine and his blog, a raging partisan who was telling me I could not be fair. In Denver, a gaggle of Internet gossips, radio talk-show hosts, and editorial writers seemed to think they owned the university, despite the fact that it receives only 8 percent of its funding from state taxes. Churchill was wonderful cannon fodder in the audience-ratings wars, and they knew it.

By early November, I was spending large parts of my work days, evenings, and weekends defending my *own* research integrity, after pirateballerina (with no evidence) accused me of being a "stooge" of Churchill, as well as a "fabulist" and a "fabricator of research" who had a "quid pro quo" with Churchill. Paine's Web site had become the tail that wagged the media dog in Denver on the Churchill issue. Paine rang his Internet bell, sang "Ward Churchill, come and get it!" and the press came abounding like a pack of half-starved, naïve puppies. Surveying the situation, my wife, Pat Keiffer, summed up the situation in one word: "Cesspool."

When he is not baiting Churchill and his supposed "stooges," Paine, who was 51 years of age at the time, runs Appaloosa horses on his Wicked Pony Ranch near Denver, listens to old KISS records, and builds Internet pages for pay. The *Colorado Daily* (the university's student newspaper) called him the "go-to guy" on the issue. After a reporter at the Boulder *Daily Camera* interrupted our family's Sunday supper with a battery of accusatory questions (Clark, 2005), Paine's allegations about me spread quickly to the Denver dailies, as well as KHOW's virulently anti-Churchill Caplis-Silverman radio talk show.

Fortunately, I was not the biggest local news story on the Front Range that week. I was playing second fiddle to a 57-year-old man, who had sued Boulder Home Depot for $3 million almost two years after he sat on a toilet seat at the store that had been smeared with contact cement by Halloween pranksters. The victim alleged that Home Depot employees ignored his cries for help.

Paine's quid-pro-quo accusation was based on two items googled from the Internet: In Paine's mind, the "quid" was an endorsement by Churchill of a book I had edited (*Enduring Legacies*, 2004), solicited by the publisher without my knowledge several months before the controversy over Churchill's "little Eichmanns" remarks blew up. The supposed "quo" was a statement of mine posted on a Churchill defense site early in 2005 saying that Churchill had cited my work fairly. Paine's string of demeaning adjectives otherwise had no factual support.

I promptly fired off a note by e-mail offering Paine a 200-word seminar in libel law. A *quid pro quo* (Latin: "this for that") is a specific set of events leading to a mutually agreed-upon outcome, usually involving money. In this case, there had been no such agreement (I have never met Churchill personally). McCarthy-style, Paine had blown it all into a premeditated conspiracy, and the anti-Churchill media had come along for the ride.

Charlie Brennan, a reporter at the *Rocky Mountain News*, called me and reported that he had been reading Paine's Web site when the words "quid pro quo" vanished. He produced a fair news story. Soon, however, the *Rocky Mountain News*' editorial page, editorially jumped on Williams and me as "cheerleaders" of "the Ward Churchill fan club," calling for us to be removed from the committee in the name of impartiality ("Churchill Inquiry," 2005). Not that "the Rocky," as it is called in Denver, was itself bending over backward to be fair. The same newspaper's editorial page had called for Churchill's removal many times during previous months without any investigative process at all by the university.

I resigned, as did Williams. I requested and was provided op-ed reply space in the *Rocky Mountain News* (Johansen, November 10, 2005). I said, in part, that I was leaving the committee because the level of discourse on this issue in the Denver area had become nearly neurotic, and because my continued membership on the committee in such a toxic atmosphere was going to inhibit its ability to conduct a proper investigation. I also resigned because the rules of the committee prohibit *apparent* or *perceived* conflict of interest, as well as the real thing. Thus, by this test, imagination trumps reality. These rules beg one very important question in an incendiary conflict: *whose* perceptions govern? Paine certainly believed his did.

On pirateballerina.com, Paine said I had displayed remarkably good judgment by resigning—a supposed stooge fabulist, faker of research, and mutually back-scratching member of the Ward Churchill Fan Club with remarkably good sense—a *very* rare bird, indeed. The night the news broke that Williams also had resigned, my wife Pat and I celebrated our seventeenth wedding anniversary with a movie: *Good Night and Good Luck*, the story of Edward R. Murrow and Senator Joseph McCarthy, a fitting conclusion. Was I now, or had I ever been, a stooge of Ward Churchill?

The next day, on pirateballerina.com, Paine congratulated himself on having vanquished two of the five "stooges," and set his sights on the other three, broadening his ambit of evidence he considered incriminating: Marianne Wesson, for example, had been interviewed on National Public Radio (NPR). What she said did not matter to Paine; he regarded NPR as leftist enough to incriminate anyone on its airwaves. Michael Radelet opposes the death penalty. Paine had cracked that with him on the committee, death would not be an option for Churchill. Of Margorie McIntosh he said he could find nothing, perhaps because he had not looked hard enough. This was, of course, textbook McCarthyism.

At one point in December 2005, after I had left the investigating committee, I mentioned in an e-mail to Churchill that the United States had always had an "undertow of fascism." In his case, he replied, "It's been more than an undertow" (Churchill, December 10, 2006). In the meantime, this book was born.

* * * *

To fire a professor on freedom-of-speech grounds is akin to shooting a police officer—soon, hundreds of others will line up behind the offended party. Professors very generally take their colleagues' right to profess seriously. They are one of very few groups that take rights of free speech seriously enough to extend them to people with whom they disagree—in Voltaire's words, to disagree with what others say, but to defend to death their right to say it. It is a nicely honed principle; it is profoundly sad that a majority of professors with valuable (and often hardly popular) points of view today find their work exiled to a kind of First Amendment gulag—library shelves, where hardly anyone is looking. We do not burn books as much as we trivialize and ignore them.

Given the amount of hot rubber that they lay on the metaphorical and rhetorical road, editorial writers, talk-show hosts, and politicians might be more tolerant of dissenting opinions with which they disagree. With a few cherished exceptions, however, these gatekeepers have been too rushed for time, too ignorant of history, and too worried about collecting advertising revenue from large audiences to afford deep dissent much running room.

Dissent rides a rough road in our "land of the free." Ideological intolerance rides high in our time, an attitude that seems related, most often, to the worldwide embrace of religious fundamentalism. Who would have guessed that the fabled "bridge" to the third millennium would have an off-ramp to the thirteenth century, a reminder of crusades and inquisitions? At some point, all religious impulses to censor nonbelievers begin to sound similar. Thus, the beating of religion professor Paul Mirecki for having taunted fundamentalists in Kansas reminded me of Danish newspaper cartoonists, on whose heads bounties were placed by Islamic fundamentalists after the publication in February 2006, of a drawing of the Prophet Mohammed with a turban styled as a bomb (and another, of suicide bombers arriving in Muslim heaven as the Prophet warned them that the supply of virgins has been exhausted). The Danish embassies in Damascus and Beirut went up in flames, and various imams called for severance of the cartoonist's heads and hands.

The First Amendment, a gift of Enlightenment tolerance, grants us all the precious right to make fools of ourselves, and not to hang from the petard of someone else's narrowly drawn ideology, especially someone vested with official power. This is a very valuable right, best exercised in the face of its denial, when someone or some official agency, out of fear of terror, of communism, or just in the service of official zeal, enforces what it takes as a moral or patriotic imperative, usually invoked to protect us from intellectual contamination. The United States has a history of attempts to enforce such orthodoxies, official, political, or religious. We have a First Amendment for many very good historical reasons.

We are watching here the long-time tension between the forces of freedom of expression and America's enduring undertow of restraint, the central intellectual fault line in this book. The most vehement of critics in these cases tear into their targets as anti-patriots, ripping, roaring—and, in the meantime, diverting attention from the real issues. Whether it is Paul Mirecki (on intelligent design), Nicholas de Genova (on the Iraq war), or Ward Churchill (on why the World Trade Center was attacked), many of the critics cannot (or just will not) distinguish between jingoistic, imperialistic patriotism on the one hand and the kind of patriotism that loves a country for its potential and its ideals on the other. There is nothing more American than questioning authority in an atmosphere that allows disagreement with official policy and popular assumptions or beliefs without penalty.

This is the ideal. Reality, of course, often sings a different tune. In his *Age of Anxiety*, Haynes Johnson writes that scapegoating in the name of national security is hardly new in the United States: "McCarthyism is not a new phenomenon in

America, but a recurrent manifestation of a basic element in the American condition and character that keeps reappearing during times of national stress and
crisis" (Johnson, 2005, 95). Johnson mentions three epochs of ideological repression previous to the "War of Terror." The first was a reaction to the French Revolution, which spurred the Alien and Sedition Acts, passed by Congress in 1798,
including restrictions on immigration, provision for deportation of subversives,
and (echoing the Patriot Act of our own time) legal avenues by which to arrest
and imprison anyone suspected of opposing "any measure or measures of the
government of the United States" (Johnson, 2005, 98). Such language was broad
enough to virtually negate the First Amendment to the United States Constitution,
on which the ink was barely dry at the time.

The second epoch of reaction was a "red scare" after World War I, following
the capture of authority in Russia (and the creation of the Union of Soviet Socialist Republics) by the Bolsheviks. This wave of guilt by association was officially
sanctioned by the U.S. attorney general (and carried on long after by J. Edgar
Hoover and his Federal Bureau of Investigation). Reacting to the Bolsheviks' sei-
zure of power in Russia, the U.S. federal government's "Palmer Raids" (named
for U.S. Attorney General A. Mitchell Palmer, whose house had been bombed by
anarchists) rounded up suspected anarchists, socialists, and communists in a manner not dissimilar to the pursuit of suspected Islamic terrorists after the September
11, 2001 attacks. Nearly a hundred men were arrested in Bridgeport, Connecticut,
held for five months in jail, beaten, denied food, tortured, and threatened with
death in futile attempts to extract admissions to crimes they had not committed.
Some of them were forced to stand for as long as 60 hours in stifling heat above
a boiler's pump room. Forbidden lawyers and family visits, many of these prison-
ers slept on damp, cold, concrete floors. In Detroit, about 800 men were held in
a narrow corridor for several days, sharing the same toilet, after they had been
arrested at a local Communist Party office attending dances or eating meals. A
team of lawyers, led by Felix Frankfurter (who would become a U.S. Supreme
Court Justice) collected evidence such as this and concluded that Palmer had been
"the biggest violator of the law in the United States" (MacPherson, 2006, 58).

During times of war, Congress, following the popular path of least resistance,
has been quick to trade freedom for an illusion of security. During World War I,
for example, Congress passed three acts that provided the legal basis for the "red
scares" of the period: The Sedition Act of 1917 and the Espionage and Alien Acts
of 1918. The Espionage Act allowed fines of up to $10,000 and 20 years in prison
for all offenders "whosoever, when the United States is at war, shall willfully
utter, print, write, or publish any disloyal, profane, scurrilous, or abusive language
about the form of government of the United States, or the Constitution of the
United States, or the military or naval forces of the United states, or the flag . . . or
the uniform of the Army or Navy of the United States, or any language intended
to bring the form of government . . . or the Constitution . . . or the military or naval
forces . . . or the flag . . . into contempt" (Johnson, 2005, 104). At one point in its
drafting, this act allowed juries to impose the death penalty for these offenses.

The Espionage and Sedition Acts of 1917 and 1918 led to more than 1,000 convictions, but revealed few that were bona fide threats to national security. Most were union organizers and pacifists. About 100 members of the radical Industrial Workers of the World (IWW, or Wobblies) were convicted of being against U.S. participation in World War I. Eugene Debs, a socialist leader, was sentenced to 20 years in prison for favoring draft resistance; Victor Berger, a socialist and a Congressman, was sentenced to a similar term for advocating against capitalism in the *Milwaukee Leader* (Maharidge, 2005, 181–182). Anti-German xenophobia was so popular that sauerkraut was called "liberty cabbage," and dachshunds became "liberty pups," a direct analogue to anti-French feeling following that nation's expressed opposition to the U.S. invasion of Iraq, with its "freedom fries" and "freedom toast." For a time, the word "French" was even stricken from menus in the U.S. Capitol Building in retribution for that nation's less-than-enthusiastic support of the Iraq war (Maharidge, 182).

The third period of repression was instigated by Joseph McCarthy, junior senator from Wisconsin, during the early 1950s, partially as a reaction to the expansion of communist state doctrines into Eastern Europe and China after World War II. During the early and mid-1950s, awareness spread even among many Republicans that Joe McCarthy's tactics were profoundly un-American, to a point where the Army's top generals spoke out against him and major media figures, such as Henry Luce (owner of TIME, Inc.) and Edward R. Murrow (head of CBS News) denounced his damage to innocent people in public. Censured by a large majority of his Senate colleagues, McCarthy died in 1957 at age 48 of alcoholism so intense that it had destroyed two-thirds of his liver. At the end of his life, McCarthy was consuming a quart of hard liquor a day. Major political figures, even President Dwight Eisenhower, came to detest McCarthy. While Eisenhower said little in public (he did not want to cheapen the prestige of the presidency, he said, by joining McCarthy in the gutter) his private writings leave little doubt about how he felt:

> McCarthy is making the same plea of loyalty to him that Hitler made to the German people. Both tried to set up personal loyalty within the government while both were using the pretense of fighting communism. McCarthy is trying deliberately to subvert the people we have in government, people who are sworn to obey the law, the Constitution, and their superior officers. I think this is the most disloyal act we have ever had by anyone in the government of the United States. (Johnson, 2005, 402)

Add to these periods of national recrimination another undertow in U.S. politics, which is religious. From the torching of the first witches at Salem, the United States has been wracked by periods during which narrow definitions of godliness have been enforced by intolerant attitudes—good vs. evil, heaven vs. hell, saints vs. sinners. In our time, both the political and religious elements have been combined and reinforced by a "war on terror" waged by a president who believes he has been chosen by God to implant democracy in a Muslim world beset by Islamic terrorism. The September 11, 2001 attacks on the Pentagon and World Trade

Center very acutely presented us with a new set of hate-objects, which fit finely into a perceptual pattern shaped by witches, revolutionary Frenchmen, killer Indians, and Communists. Osama bin Laden shares some eclectic historical company.

My central thesis here is that restriction of free inquiry impoverishes everyone by restraining the search for knowledge. With neoconservatives (who do not suffer disagreement easily) in important positions of influence and power throughout the United States, this book presents case studies in the borderlands of free speech in a Jeffersonian cast—an intellectual framework assuming that open debate (especially of unpopular ideas) is essential to accurate perception of reality, and, thus, to sagacious decision-making. True liberty does not cherish acquiescence.

ACKNOWLEDGMENTS

Books are a little like icebergs—only parts of the work involved are easily visible. The references and bibliography outline much of the informational infrastructure, but what does not show is the work of many people who helped along the way: my mother, Hazel, brother, Drew, sister, Linda, wife Pat Keiffer, son Shannon, granddaughters Samantha and Madison (veteran critics already, at ages 13 and 8). University of Nebraska at Omaha School of Communication Director Jeremy H. Lipschultz and Dean of the College of Communication, Fine Arts, and Media Gail F. Baker helped create an atmosphere conducive to scholarly inquiry, as have all the usual suspects at the University of Nebraska at Omaha Library.

REFERENCES

"Churchill Inquiry Hits Another Wall." *Rocky Mountain News*, November 5, 2005, 14-C.

Churchill, Ward. Personal communication, December 10, 2006.

Clark, Elizabeth. "Committee Chosen for Inquiry; Five Profs Will Review Churchill Allegations." Boulder *Daily Camera*, November 2, 2005. http://www.dailycamera.com/bdc/buffzone_news/article/0,1713,BDC_2448_4205615,00.html.

Johansen, Bruce E., ed. *Enduring Legacies: Native American Treaties and Contemporary Controversies*. Westport, CT: Praeger, 2004.

Johansen, Bruce E. "Professor's Remarks Fall Under Free Speech." *Omaha World-Herald*, February 9, 2005, 7-B.

Johansen, Bruce E. "Parting Words from Member of Churchill Probe Panel." *Rocky Mountain News*, November 10, 2005. http://www.rockymountainnews.com/drmn/editorials/article/0,2777,DRMN_23964_4225837,00.html.

Johnson, Haynes. *The Age of Anxiety: McCarthyism to Terrorism*. Orlando, Florida: Harcourt/James H. Silberman, 2005.

MacPherson, Myra. *"All Governments Lie:" The Life and Times of Rebel Journalist I.F. Stone*. New York: Scribner, 2006.

Maharidge, Dale. *Homeland*. New York: Seven Stories Press, 2004.

Packer, George. "Keep Out." Talk of the Town. *The New Yorker,* October 16, 2006, 59–60.

Introduction

How often have we been told when going to war, that "freedom isn't free," the unstated assumption being that our armed forces are fighting and dying to safeguard our civil rights at home and abroad. Such is the official ideology. During recent years, however, freedom to inquire and debate without retribution has been under assault in the United States. This assault has been carried out under a distinctly Orwellian cast, under Newspeak titles such as the Patriot Act, parts of which might as well be honestly described as the Restriction of Freedom of Inquiry Act. Intelligent termites come to mind, carrying on their business under cover of the Society for the Integrity of Cellulite.

Thus, President George W. Bush in 2006 lobbied Congress for (and received) the Military Commissions Act, arguably to protect American lives, while eroding (at least until the courts review it) such fundamental guarantees as *habeas corpus*—destroying liberty in order to save it. The new law applied within the United States, and left to the government the definition of whom it applies to (as "unlawful enemy combatants"). *Habeas corpus*, Latin for "you have the body," is a fundamental principle of English and American law that requires government to provide a legal rationale for holding a prisoner.

Ever since witches were razed in Salem, Massachusetts, the hunt for enemies has been a constant in American history. From witches to Communists, the fearmongers always have dressed their assaults as socially and politically necessary and beneficial. Even Senator Joseph McCarthy told his audiences that he was safeguarding general liberty by cleansing the United States of Communist filth. Hitler was a vegetarian and loved dogs; when he looked in the mirror in the morning he didn't see a murderer of his own hate-objects (Jews, Gypsies, homosexuals et al.), but a savior of the Aryan race.

Enemies engender fear, and fear buys votes, or summons support for dicta-
tors. In our recent past, political capital has been shamelessly drilled from fear
of communism. During the late 1950s, the ultra-rightist activist Phyllis Schlafly
predicted, with serious certainty, "that Communism is advancing over the surface
of the globe with such rapidity that if it continues at the same rate for the next thirteen years that it has been advancing for the last thirteen years, America will be
Communist by 1970" (Kolbert, 2005, 136). One of the easiest ways to make a fool
of oneself is to predict history, where past often as not does not serve as precedent.
With the collapse of communism, new hate-objects arise. In our time, Osama bin
Laden has become the ideal hate-object. Unquestioning hatred directed at bin
Laden and his associates has become a central article of our civil religion. Violators of this canon risk skating outside the bounds that Noam Chomsky called the
limits of permissible debate.

This is a book about people whose ideological circumstances found them
on the opposite side of the powerful in our times—Arab scholars seeking visas
to the United States after 9–11, scholars advocating the Palestinian cause in a
very hostile climate, climate scientists defending themselves against defunding of
their laboratories by promulgators of near-religious defense of fossil-fuel interests
in high places, opponents of "creation science" under assault for teaching what
once was regarded as household-variety biology (a.k.a. Darwinism), or Marxists
in a country where mass political discourse has been distorted by neoconservative
assumptions, even in the absence of a credible international Communist threat.
Old habits seem to die hard.

We begin (in chapter 1, "Weather Wars: Hard Science and Hardball Politics"),
with arguably the most important debate of all, regarding the composition of the
atmosphere, as rising levels of carbon dioxide and methane take us back to levels
reminiscent of the notably toasty days of the dinosaurs. Toss into the mix a number of human-synthesized greenhouse gases that did not exist at that time, such as
chlorofluorocarbons (CFCs), and realize that the temperatures we feel today are
a result of greenhouse gases added to the atmosphere about 50 years ago, due to
feedback mechanisms. Ocean temperatures lag a century or two behind, providing scientists with unusual forecasting abilities if greenhouse-gas levels continue
to rise at business-as-usual rates. The feedbacks also produce a real problem for
people and politicians who react to problems only after their noses have been
rubbed in them. By the time our political nervous system catches on to just how
bad things are getting, they will be sure to become much worse.

Any debate with such stakes—the future of the Earth versus profits of fossil-
fuel industries, among the world's largest—is bound to get a bit testy at times, with
positions ranging from Chicken Little alarmism to outright denial that anything
is wrong, including occasional declarations that more carbon dioxide is *good* for
us. The main figure in chapter 1 is a climate scientist, James E. Hansen, director
of NASA's Goddard Institute for Space Studies in New York City. For a quarter
century, Hansen has been our Paul Revere of global warming, as three Republican
administrations have tried to shut him up. The level of heat on Hansen—no pun

intended—rises so high that he often prefaces his public remarks by saying that he speaks as a private citizen, leaving implied the fact that he is one of the best-informed private citizens on the planet regarding humankind's propensity for fouling the only atmospheric habitat we've got. Face it: with no sustainable habitat, we tell no stories.

Hansen, in his mid-60s by the sunset years of George W. Bush's second term, is a veteran of the "weather wars"—he fought defunding of his lab under Ronald Reagan back when Ollie North was telling us that the Nicaraguan Sandinistas would soon be wiping their boots in Texas—as well as a scientist of international renown. Hansen battles censorship as his laboratory reports steadily rising temperatures, collapsing ice shelves, and rising seas that could inundate many coastal cities around the world in a couple of centuries. Care to wager on when the toilets may back up on the first floor of the White House, which is 17 meters above high tide? If we keep pressing our gas pedals as usual until the end of this century, the year 2200 might be a good bet. That is, of course, beyond the life span of George W. Bush, who tells us that the future doesn't matter because we'll all be dead then.

Popular denial is popular in other "hard" sciences as well, one being biology, where the theory of evolution has come under challenge from advocates of "intelligent design," a belief that nature is too complex to have resulted from Darwinistic notions of natural selection. Chapter 2 ("Soft Science: How Intelligent Is This Design?") describes recent events around the United States debating whether intelligent design should be taught in public schools along with evolutionary theory. The major focus here is on the small town of Dover, Pennsylvania, because a debate in the schools on this issue there was accompanied by a landmark federal court case holding that "ID" is a gussied-up form of creationism, which the courts regard as an unconstitutional form of religion impinging upon public science education. Debates over the veracity of evolution take place against the background of an amazing irony: as scientific support for evolution grows, the proportion of people in the United States who object to it on religious grounds has not declined. Thus, the emphatic ruling from a federal judge in Dover is not likely to kill this debate.

Chapter 3 ("The Second Amendment Trumps the First") provides a cautionary tale for any historian who is planning to challenge the National Rifle Association's version of American history. Any such challenger is forewarned to bring to the debate a full data set, infinite patience, a strong stomach, and a good lawyer or two. Michael Bellesiles, as a history professor at Emory University, made a case in *Arming America* (2000) that the role of guns in our history had been over-emphasized by their advocates, who quickly laid down a rain of fire against his statistics and interpretations. Bellesiles had won the prestigious Bancroft Prize, which was withdrawn after problems with his research undermined the work. An investigatory committee at Emory largely supported the criticism of Bellesiles's research errors, provoking his resignation.

The academic career of Ward Churchill, professor of Ethnic Studies at the University of Colorado (Boulder), and chronicler of genocide against Native

Americans, encountered similar problems. His scathing histories with titles such as *A Little Matter of Genocide* had provoked debate over the years, but nothing like the reaction that followed attention by the *Wall Street Journal*, Bill O'Reilly, and other right-wing standard-bearers to his remark that some of the World Trade Center's victims resembled Adolf Eichmann, technician of the Jewish Holocaust. The firestorm of reaction is described in chapter 4 ("Gut-Based Discourse in the Age of the Internet"). This remark, posted on the Internet within days of the bombings, did not reach disapproving eyes for more than three years, at which point it raced through right-wing blogs with searing speed, drawing hundreds of death threats and many calls for Churchill's firing from the university.

University officials generally found Churchill's "Little Eichmanns" remark repugnant, but a matter of legally defensible free speech. In the meantime, however, a number of other complaints about Churchill's research caused the university to initiate an investigation that produced a 125-page report finding enough research misconduct to recommend that Churchill be suspended without pay or fired. The report was nothing if not through, at one point devoting more than 40 pages to analyzing two paragraphs of writing by Churchill in which he makes a case (falsely, according to the report) that the U.S. Army intentionally spread smallpox among the Mandan and other Native peoples in 1837. Churchill subsequently became the first University of Colorado tenured professor to face termination for cause, as he maintained strenuously that many others would suffer the same fate if the unpopularity of their political views provoked the same intensity of scrutiny to which he has subject. Unlike Bellesiles, who resigned quietly, Churchill plans to fight his dismissal in court.

Chapter 5, "Students and Faculty Rights (and Lefts)," describes the recent advocacy of "student bills of rights," meant to protect young minds against the assault of ideologically driven professors who use their classrooms as political soapboxes. This chapter also examines the careers of several right-wingers who have grown rich and famous (some of them *very* rich and *quite* famous) doing little except bringing the purported zaniness of the professoriate to large nonacademic audiences. Most of their names are household words—Rush Limbaugh, Bill O'Reilly, David Horowitz, Ann Coulter, et al. What would they do without loose-lipped liberals?

Other campus-related freedom of speech issues also are raised in this chapter. What, for example, about the military's "right" to recruit? Why has a gay "jack" (renegade) Mormon, whose histories debated official versions published by the church, been sacked? How about David Graeber, an anthropologist at Yale who joined protests against globalization as an outspoken anarchist, who was arrested, and then denied tenure? Can a high-school geography class be too relevant? Teacher Jay Bennish of Overland High School (near Denver) obliquely compared George W. Bush to Adolf Hitler and soon found himself pilloried as a Ward Churchill wannabe. Consider also the career of Kevin Barrett, at the University of Wisconsin, who maintained that Bush & Co. set up the 9–11 attacks—and that comparing Bush to Hitler is unfair, on basis of Intelligence Quotient, to the latter?

Following the September 11 attacks, scholars in Middle Eastern studies have felt a cold ideological wind that has chilled many who are known as advocates of Palestinian rights, or strident critics of the "war on terror." One can get into trouble for asserting that Osama bin Laden has political acumen, as well. Chapter 6 ("Terrorology 101") follows attempts in the U.S. Congress to regulate the field of Middle Eastern Studies to produce faculty research that is more user-friendly at the U.S. State Department.

This chapter also examines individual cases such as the controversy arising around Joseph Massad, who teaches at Columbia University, and who was targeted as anti-Zionist by some students; Nicholas de Genova, also at Columbia, who became the object of a media campaign after he opined off the cuff at an anti-war teach-in that U.S. soldiers should be "fragged." He wished for "a million Mogadishus," a reference to the killing of 18 U.S. troops in Somalia in an incident that became the basis for the movie *Blackhawk Down*. Very quickly, 78 New York State legislators signed a letter condemning his statements, as Governor George Pataki questioned de Genova's fitness to be a professor.

Sami al-Arian, a former Florida professor, a Palestinian-born academic in the United States on a permanent-resident visa who lost his job following federal indictment in 2003 on terrorism charges, was not convicted in the Tampa, Florida, federal court late in 2005 as the jury failed to return a guilty verdict on *any* of the 51 charges brought against him and three codefendants by federal prosecutors describing him as the ringleader of a North American front for Palestinian terrorists. The prosecution case alleged that Arias had helped finance and direct terrorist attacks in Israel, the Gaza Strip, and the West Bank, using his faculty position teaching computer engineering at the University of South Florida as cover. The case enabled use of the U.S. Patriot Act to present years of wiretaps on the defendants in a criminal context that earlier would not have been admissible in court. If this was a test, the Patriot Act failed miserably. While al-Arian was well known as a fiery advocate for Palestinian causes who also was known nationally for his acerbic criticism of Israel, his behavior was nearly totally an exercise of free speech.

Having investigated him for more than a decade (holding him in jail during the last three), having spent millions of tax dollars failing to make any of its charges stick, prosecutors hounded al-Arian into a plea-bargained guilty plea on *one* charge. A judge sentenced al-Arian to 19 more months in prison—*more* than the prosecution had requested—and then allowed the government to deport him. Welcome to the land of the free. Gulag gatekeepers take notes.

Mouthing off about killing Americans in the service of militant Islamism is obviously rather tactless in polite American company, but is it worth life in prison plus 70 years without parole? Ali al-Timimi, a biologist and Islamic scholar, in 2005, found out where a jury drew the line on free speech-even for a man, who, his defense maintained, never touched a weapon, much less carried out a bona fide terrorist act. According to the Justice Department, under cover of the U.S. Patriot Act, acting as a "spiritual advisor" to a group of would-be Virginia jihadis was terroristic enough. When play-acting jihad with a sharp tongue and real ammunition, the old adage that the First Amendment gives all of us the right to make fools of ourselves seems no longer to apply.

Chapter 6 ends with an examination of how restriction of visas post 9-11 has crimped access to scholars from outside the United States, and may hobble future technological development here. This is an instructive story of how a bumbling, over-zealous bureaucracy can ruin a nation's scientific reputation.

While some readers of this book may be asking by now whether any scholar who offends established interests can escape being trussed up in his or her own private Star Chamber, rest assured that some people draw large audiences, sell many books, and even receive grants testifying to their genius-all the while engaging in Marxist analysis in the era of George W. Bush. Mike Davis, for example, has written a number of very well-selling books criticizing the many dysfunctions of modern urban life, pulled no punches, and done very well. What kind of ideological Disneyland are we talking about here? Perhaps a country with a Constitution that protects freedom of expression? Maybe, even in the "era" of George W. Bush, there is hope for free expression in our venerable country.

REFERENCE

Kolbert, Elizabeth. "Firebrand: Phyllis Schlafly and the Conservative Revolution." *The New Yorker*, November 7, 2005, 134–138.

Chapter 1

Weather Wars: Hard Science and Hardball Politics

IF THE PRESIDENT's cabinet included a Secretary of Climate Security (imagine that!), James E. Hansen, who directs NASA's Goddard Institute for Space Sciences (GISS) in New York City (and teaches geological sciences at Columbia University) might be the best nominee. Hansen is too much of a scientist—and not enough of a politician—to accept the job. Regarding global warming, however, he may be our Paul Revere.

Hansen's long-term forecast: 10 more years of "business as usual" greenhouse gas emissions and we'll cross the "tipping point." At that point, humanity loses any chance of turning back accelerating feedbacks that lead to runaway heating of Earth's atmosphere. Mark your calendars; Jim Hansen has been forecasting global greenhouse weather for more than 25 years and his forecasting record is very good, even as he has run rear-guard actions to keep three Republican U.S. presidents backed by fossil-fuel partisans from defunding his laboratory and censoring his statements.

Michael Oppenheimer, chief scientist for the Environmental Defense Fund and an author of a major United Nations report on climate change, says of Hansen's work, "His science is impeccable, and his prescience is unparalleled" (Johansen, 2005, 52). In addition to being a renowned scientist, Hansen is often called upon to wage political "weather wars." Hansen speaks truth to power routinely—more than that, he speaks important, necessary truth to some of the largest aggregations of fossil-fueled power on planet Earth. He fought defunding of his lab under Ronald Reagan back when Ollie North was telling us that the Nicaraguan Sandinistas would soon be wiping their boots in Texas.

At 2880 Broadway in Manhattan, six floors above Tom's Restaurant, site of many *Seinfeld* sitcom episodes, Hansen leads a team of scientists assessing the climatic fate of the Earth. From these offices, Hansen warns by the end of this century the level of greenhouse gases in the atmosphere will be high enough to guarantee that within a few decades after that our planet will become as hot as it was during the days of the dinosaurs. The seas will be on their way to rising 25 meters, producing environmental refugees in the hundreds of millions as coastlines recede.

"CIRCUMSTANCES"

About 150 people work at GISS. Hansen occupies a spacious office framed with piles of scientific papers. For a man who has been so forthright about global warming for so many years—one who has stood up to three presidents—one might expect a more audacious personality. In *Field Notes from a Catastrophe*, Elizabeth Kolbert described him as "a spare man with a lean face and a fringe of brown hair. . . . In person, he is reticent almost to the point of shyness." When she asked Hansen how he had come to play such a prominent role in the debate over global warming, Kolbert wrote that he shrugged. "Circumstances," he said (Kolbert, 2006, 97–98).

Hansen finds himself an unlikely hero in a contest of titans that includes some of the most powerful established economic interests on Earth. The fifth of seven children (he has four older sisters), Hansen was born in a farmhouse in 1941 and raised in Denison, Iowa, where signs on highways to town proclaim that life is wonderful in this, the home of Donna Reed. Hansen's father, a tenant farmer, moved to Denison when Jim was four years of age, and took up work as a bartender; his mother worked as a waitress.

Hansen, who spent the first quarter century of his life in Iowa, was known for his intelligence as a child, even when he was not being overly studious. He also played second base in the Babe Ruth League. From an early age, before going to work on Manhattan Island, Hansen was a New York Yankees fan. With a scholarship and money saved from his Omaha *World-Herald* paper route, Hansen attended the University of Iowa, graduating summa cum laude in 1963, majoring in math and physics. At the same school, in physics, Hansen earned a master's degree in astronomy.

Iowa was an exciting place to study astronomy; the department had its own satellite, and its chairman was James Van Allen, who discovered the Earth-girdling radiation belts named after him. "I was so shy and unconfident that when I had an opportunity to take a course under Prof. Van Allen, I avoided it because I didn't want him to realize how ignorant I was," Hansen told an audience at his alma mater.

Remaining at Iowa, Hansen earned his doctorate in 1967 with a dissertation on the atmosphere of Venus. Hansen's research took place at a time when scientists were first describing the hellishly hot, carbon dioxide-rich atmosphere of Venus, product of a runaway greenhouse effect. His doctorate completed, Hansen began work at GISS. On leave for a year, 1969–1970, at the Leiden Observatory in the

Netherlands, Hansen met his wife-to-be, Anniek. In 1976, Hansen was working as principal investigator on the Pioneer Venus Orbiter when a Harvard postdoctoral researcher asked him to help calculate the greenhouse effect of human-generated emissions on Earth's atmosphere. Soon Hansen was "captivated" by the potential of global warming's effect on Earth. As he worked at GISS, the institute also was becoming more involved in Earth studies, a trend that accelerated after his appointment as director in 1981.

THE STAKES OF THE DEBATE

Scientific knowledge often develops amid political controversy—and very few fields of science are more controversial than global warming. On one level, global warming is a debate over the ecological future of the Earth. Thus, the geophysical stakes are obviously very high. On another level, it is a debate that will determine how the six-plus billion human beings who live on the Earth obtain, use, and profit from the energy that sustains our lives for the rest of the time that humankind will occupy the planet. This is, thus, a debate about the coming severe reformulation of an energy paradigm based on fossil fuels. The stakes being wagered by established industrial interests are enormous.

When scientists examined ice cores retrieved at the Vostok station in Antarctica containing evidence of carbon dioxide levels and indications of temperatures reaching 420,000 to 800,000 years into the past, they discovered "that both methane and carbon dioxide . . . are now at their highest levels in that span and that the carbon-dioxide curve is particularly alarming: since the start of the fossil-fuel era, it has spiked to a level nearly twice as high as any it has reached in almost half a million years" (Bowen, 2005, 288). Big news, no doubt, and deserving of a public-relations offensive wrought by an industry "with gross annual revenues on the order of two trillion dollars, operating facilities virtually everywhere on the planet, and a unified economic agenda that transcends all national boundaries and interests"—as well as, one may add, a hammerlock during the early twenty-first century on the federal government of the world's largest greenhouse gas producing nation (Bowen, 2005, 292).

The people of the United States of America have been the most profligate producers of greenhouse gases in the history of humankind. They have done this, in the main, without regard or regret for the future of the planet. Each U.S. citizen produces five times the world average per capita carbon dioxide load.

The fossil fuels we consume today come from the remains of plant growth in the past. In one year, however, human beings are returning as much plant matter to the atmosphere as grew in 400 years. Most of the carbon dioxide in the atmosphere (other than that generated by fossil-fuel use) has been injected by volcanoes. Most years, volcanoes produce 300 million to 1 billion tons of CO_2 a year. By the year 2000, human beings were pouring 20 billion tons into the air—20 to 90 times the emission rate of volcanoes (Bowen, 2005, 122).

GAG ORDERS BECOME MEGAPHONES

Confronted with politically motivated directives to tone down his public communications about global warming, Hansen repeatedly insisted that NASA's mission, to inform the public of scientific reality, was conflicting with a White House position that was mainly shaped by fossil-fuel executives' notions of spin control.

Bill McKibben, author of *The End of Nature* and eight other books on environmental topics, summarized the censorship controversy in the *Boston Globe*:

> Jim Hansen . . . is a dangerous man. Not a brash man or a rebel—I remember interviewing him many years ago, and when I asked him what he did to relax, he replied, "mow my lawn." Hansen has had to deliver unpopular news before, and he's always persisted—and this time, as usual, he managed to turn the gag order into a megaphone. What makes him so dangerous now, is that he's not just saying that the world is warming. He's not just saying we're the cause. He's saying: We have to stop it now. . . . You can argue with Hansen if you want. But you better bring a pretty big data set with you. He's been right so far. (McKibben, 2006, E-1)

In 1981, Hansen and his colleagues published a seminal article in *Science* that forecast continued climatic warming in the 1980s and beyond—with effects including enhanced droughts in Central North America and the interior of Asia, melting along the fringes of the West Antarctic Ice Sheet with worldwide rises in sea levels, and the opening of the once-fabled Northwest passage in the Arctic. The article forecast that the combined warming of carbon dioxide and trace gases should exceed natural temperature variability in the 1980s and cause the mean global temperature to rise above the maximum of the late 1930s (Hansen et al., 1981, 956).

President Ronald Reagan's Department of Energy responded to this seminal scientific article by canceling funding to GISS, which Hansen directed, because they didn't "like the results that we were getting" (Lacis, 2005). With changes of the ideological weather at the White House, Hansen's staff and their work was being targeted for termination. In *Thin Ice*, author Mark Bowen asked Hansen if Reagan had sent a "hatchet man." "Hansen nodded," he wrote. "It was too strong a word for him to use himself" (Bowen, 2005, 135). Other researchers were told their funding would be terminated if they used climate models developed by Hansen's lab, and some of his researchers were laid off, but the institute itself survived.

Even while under bureaucratic assault, Hansen never accused any of his opponents of pettiness. In the 30 years that he has been working on the global-warming issue, Hansen has been an object of endless scorn and personal attack, yet he has never responded in kind. He has always focused resolutely on the science and the facts and, "moreover, gone out of his way to point out the shortcomings in his own arguments" (Bowen, 2005, 159).

WHEN IS IT TIME TO CRY WOLF?

In 1988, Colorado Senator Timothy E. Wirth, whose hearings on global warming the previous winter had drawn little attention, played the weather card. He called another hearing, this time during the summer. As it happened, the hearing convened on a particularly hot, humid day in Washington, D.C., during which the temperature reached a record high 101°F.

At Wirth's hearing, Hansen testified that the unusually warm temperatures of the 1980s were an early portent of global warming caused by the burning of fossil fuels, not solely a result of natural variation. Hansen's remarks became front-page news nationwide within hours. At the same time, he also continued a running battle during the Reagan and first Bush administrations to raise the political salience of global warming. The Office of Management and Budget forced Hansen to censor the severity of his remarks several times. The pressure was so intense that Hansen sometimes asked to testify as a private citizen rather than as a federal employee (Hansen, 1989).

In the meantime, the scientific debate over global warming was intensifying. At the end of 1988, the United Nations General Assembly approved the creation of the Intergovernmental Panel on Climate Change (IPCC). A year later, Hansen said that it was "time to cry wolf":

> When is the proper time to cry wolf? Must we wait until the prey, in this case the world's environment, is mangled by the wolf's grip? The danger of crying too soon, which much of the scientific community fears, is that a few cool years may discredit the whole issue. But I believe that decision-makers and the man-in-the-street can be educated about natural climate variability. . . . A greater danger is to wait too long. The climate system has great inertia, so as yet we have realized only a part of the climate change [that] will be caused by gases we have already added to the atmosphere. Add to this the inertia of the world's energy, economic, and political systems, which will affect any plans to reduce greenhouse gas emissions. Although I am optimistic that we can still avoid the worst-case climate scenarios, the time to cry wolf is here. (Nance, 1991, 267–268)

Reflecting later, Hansen elaborated: "I said three things [in 1988]. The first was that I believed the Earth was getting warmer and I could say that with 99 per cent confidence. The second was that with a high degree of confidence we could associate the warming and the greenhouse effect. The third was that, in our climate model, by the late 1980s and early 1990s, there's already a noticeable increase in the frequency of drought" (Parsons, 1995, 7).

Between June 27 and 30, 1988, as the Earth's warmest summer on record (to that time) was beginning, more than 300 leaders in science, politics, law, and environmental studies gathered in Toronto at the invitation of Canada's government to address problems related to climate change, including prospects of global warming. A scientific consensus was forming around the idea that human activity already was altering the Earth's atmosphere at an unprecedented rate. A consensus statement issued by the Montreal climate conference asserted, "There can be a time lag of the order of decades between the emission of gases into the atmo sphere and their full manifestation in atmospheric and biological consequences. Past emissions have already committed planet Earth to a significant warming" (Ferguson, 1989, 48).

In 1989, a year after his headline-provoking testimony for Senator Wirth's hearings, Senator Al Gore of Tennessee invited Hansen to testify before the Senate Committee on Commerce, Science, and Transportation. George H. W. Bush was president, and the Office of Management and Budget directed Hansen, as a federal employee, to submit his testimony for review. Bureaucrats then rewrote his statement, changing his assertion that the greenhouse effect was changing climate to a bland, confusing mishmash, asserting that the cause of recently observed warming was unknown. Before the committee, Hansen calmly instigated an uproar by repudiating the rewritten testimony and submitting work by other authors asserting the seriousness of the issue. Senator Gore, in the meantime, described the editing at OMB and accused the Bush administration of "science fraud" (Bowen, 2005, 158–159). That evening, this conflict led the national evening news on television.

"A RECIPE FOR ENVIRONMENTAL DISASTER"

Among the clumsiest public-relations blunders during George W. Bush's administration was its ham-handed attempt to silence climate scientists whose findings did not follow the White House position on global warming. The Orwellian nature of the Bush administration's rhetoric extended to the physical sciences, most particularly to the atmospheric physics of global warming, which became an ever-more-obvious problem during the years that Bush held office. The Bush buzzword rubric here has been "sound science." Like "Patriot Act," or "Clean Air Act," the words connotatively mean the opposite of what the policy implies. In reality, the Bush White House's "sound science" on global warming came to resemble a mixture of right-wing political assumptions and oil-industry lobbying.

"You're talking about a president who says that the jury is out on evolution, so what possible evidence would you need to muster to prove the existence of global warming [to him]?" asked Robert F. Kennedy, Jr., author of *Crimes Against Nature* (2004). "We've got polar ice caps melting, glaciers disappearing all over the world, ocean levels rising, coral reefs dying. But these people are flat-Earthers" (Mieszkowski, 2004).

Hansen said that, on the subject of climate change, the Bush administration was "picking and choosing information according to the answer they want to get." "In my more than three decades in government, I have never seen anything approaching the degree to which information flow from scientists to the public has been screened and controlled as it is now" (Johansen, 2005, 52). "This process [censorship] is in direct opposition to the most fundamental precepts of science," Hansen said. "This, I believe, is a recipe for environmental disaster." Waiting another decade for a serious examination of climate change's effects, said Hansen, "is a colossal risk." When he made such remarks, Hansen often traveled at his own expense, as a government employee on leave (Hansen, October 26, 2004).

"SOUND SCIENCE" IN THE HALLS OF REPUBLICAN POWER

With the ascent of George W. Bush's administration in the year 2000, along with Republican majorities in the U.S. Congress, global warming came to be regarded by some important powerful political figures as something of a bothersome joke. Witness, for example, Senator James Inhofe, Republican of Oklahoma, and former chair of the Senate Environment and Public Works Committee. From the Senate floor July 28, 2003, Inhofe called global warming "a hoax" that is "predicated on fear rather than science," perpetuated by "environmental extremists." Inhofe reserved special spite for Hans Blix, as a "ridiculous alarmist" (Inhofe Calls, 2003). Blix, the United Nations' chief weapons inspector in Iraq, had said that global warming poses a greater threat to humankind than terrorism.

To Inhofe, by contrast, a warmer climate is a friend of humankind: "Numerous studies," he told the Senate, "have shown that global warming can actually be beneficial to mankind" (Inhofe Calls, 2003). One might invite the senator to tell this to the polar bears, but polar bears don't vote in Oklahoma. Inhofe embraced the Republican climate change mantra du jour, "natural variability," (e.g., we can't do anything about warming, so gas up that SUV, grin, and bear it).

Inhofe's ideological calculus was borrowed from the George W. Bush White House. In June 2003, Bush took a detailed report on global warming from the U.S. Environmental Protection Agency and reduced it to one noncommittal paragraph. Thus, an administration larded with fossil-fuel interests once more dismissed global warming as a nonissue. Satirist Molly Ivins wrote at the time: "Think of the possibilities presented by this ingenious solution. Let's edit out AIDS and all problems with drugs, both legal and illegal. . . . We can do away with unemployment, the [medically] uninsured, heart disease, obesity, and the coming Social Security crunch. We could try editing out death and taxes . . ." (Ivins, 2003, 4-A). As the Bush administration was editing global warming off its cognitive map, Britain's Office of Science and Technology was warning that English coastal residents would face a 30-fold increase in flood damage by the end of the century, due to rising seas and increasingly violent winter storms aggravated, in part, by global warming.

Inhofe's "sound science" was drawn principally from an article published in the June 2003 edition of a small scientific journal, *Climate Research*, by Willie Soon and Sallie Baliunas, two well-known climate-change contrarians. Their research, which was partially funded by the American Petroleum Institute, asserted that the period from 1900 to 2000 was not unusually warm compared to earlier centuries, notably the Medieval Warm Period. The paper's methodology drew "stinging rebukes" from many climate scientists as it became an article of faith in the Bush White House (Regalado, 2003, A-3). In late July, following copious attention, three editors of *Climate Research* (including its editor-in-chief, Hans von Storch) resigned in protest over the journal's handling of the review process that had allowed the article into print. They said, "It was flawed and should not have been published" (Regalado, 2003, A-3).

President Bush has read very little climate science, but he did read and endorse Michael Crichton's novel, *State of Fear*, which debunks global warming. According to one account, Bush was "so excited by the story, which pictures global warming as a hoax perpetuated by power-mad environmentalists, that he invited the author to the Oval Office. They talked for an hour and emerged in— surprise!—near-total agreement." Thus, wrote David Remnick in *The New Yorker*, "President Bush has made fantasy a guide to policy" (Remnick, 2006, 48).

Crichton also was invited to testify before Inhofe's Senate Committee on Energy and Environment, as was an expert witness—such was the state of "sound science" on Republican Capitol Hill until the 2006 election. Inhofe henceforth also repeated his belief that global warming is "a hoax" that is "predicated on fear rather than science," perpetuated by "environmental extremists" (Inhofe Calls, 2003). "This is fairyland!" exclaimed Michael Meacher, a member of the British Parliament who served as Prime Minister Tony Blair's environmental minister from 1997 to 2003. "You have a science-fiction writer testifying before the United States Senate on global-warming policy. . . . It's just ludicrous" (Hertsgaard, 2006, 241).

Thus, with a Republican hammerlock on the federal legislative process, the very real threat of global warming was reduced to comic-book material, as Hansen and his colleagues reported rising temperatures year by year. At the same time, scientists reported that methane and carbon dioxide were being added to the atmosphere by the melting of permafrost in the Arctic at higher rates than expected, precursors of natural feedbacks that could accelerate human-initiated contributions out of control.

Fossil-fuel interests responded by doing their best to create confusion and doubt. In a memo from a 1998 meeting at the American Petroleum Institute, Exxon management described a strategy of providing "logistical and moral support" to climate-change dissenters, "thereby raising questions about and undercutting the 'prevailing scientific wisdom.' And that's just what Exxon Mobil has done: lavish grants have supported a sort of alternative intellectual universe of global warming skeptics" (Krugman, 2006).

Commented *New York Times* columnist Paul Krugman:

> The people and institutions Exxon Mobil supports aren't actually engaged in climate research. They're the real-world equivalents of the Academy of Tobacco Studies in the movie *Thank You for Smoking*, whose purpose is to fail to find evidence of harmful effects. But the fake research works for its sponsors, partly because it gets picked up by right-wing pundits, but mainly because it plays perfectly into the he-said-she-said conventions of "balanced" journalism. A 2003 study, by Maxwell Boykoff and Jules

Boykoff, of reporting on global warming in major newspapers, found that a majority of reports gave the skeptics—a few dozen people, many if not most receiving direct or indirect financial support from Exxon Mobil—roughly the same amount of attention as the scientific consensus, supported by thousands of independent researchers. (Krugman, 2006)

THE HUMAN RACE NOW CONTROLS CLIMATE

By 1996, Hansen was writing that "The continued increase of fossil-fuel use would lead to about 2.5 degrees C. [4.5°F] global warming by the end of the twenty-first century, making the Earth warmer than it has been in millions of years—in fact, approaching the warmth of the Mesozoic, the age of the dinosaurs" (Hansen 1996, 173–190). Humankind's influence on climate is so strong, in Hansen's estimation, that the Earth will not experience another ice age unless the human race goes extinct—and even then it would take several thousand years to restore natural equilibrium to natural cycles that have been disrupted by the burning of fossil fuels. The human race now controls climate, said Hansen, for better or for worse.

Humankind's influence on climate today is so emphatic that "acts of nature" are partially man-made, or "anthropogenic." We may still colloquially refer to "acts of God," wrote Donald Kennedy, editor of *Science*, but humankind's hand is writ in "natural" disasters. Referring to hurricanes in the Atlantic Basin, Kennedy wrote:

> We know with confidence what has made the Gulf [of Mexico] and other oceans warmer than they had been before: the emission of carbon dioxide and other greenhouse gases from human industrial activity, to which the United States has been a major contributor. That's a worldwide event, affecting all oceans. When Katrina hit the shore at an upgraded intensity, it encountered a wetland whose abuse had reduced its capacity to buffer the storm, and some defective levees gave way. Not only is the New Orleans damage not an act of God; it shouldn't even be called a "natural" disaster. These terms are excuses we use to let ourselves off the hook. (Kennedy, January 20, 2006, 303)

Every month, the GISS takes the Earth's temperature, monitoring 10,000 temperature gauges around the planet. Year by year, the average temperature rises. The year 2006, as of this writing, was the warmest yet, a fact that Hansen's superiors at one point told him not to release. The political pressure had become so intense that Hansen was being told to withhold factual data. He released the information anyway.

Hansen's eyes are always on the public policy debate, as well as on the science of global warming. He has warned that reducing carbon dioxide emissions will be difficult "because fossil fuels are central to our energy systems, and hence the economy. However, we have slowed the growth rate from the 4 percent per year that existed to the mid-1970s to 2 percent [now]. If we could slow that further, to 0 percent, keeping fossil fuels at today's rate, we could keep the climate change small" (Johansen, 2005, 53).

Global average surface temperature has risen about 0.75°C since a worldwide temperature network became established in the late 1800s, with most of the increase, about 0.5°C, after 1950. About 70 percent of the increase in human-generated greenhouse gases occurred after 1950. The Earth already has absorbed 0.4 to 0.7°C worth of warming that is not yet reflected in the atmosphere because of delayed feedback, mainly a lag in ocean warming. Hansen warned that while generally moderate warming thus far "leave[s] the impression that we are not close to dangerous anthropogenic interference, I will argue that we are much closer than is generally realized, and thus the emphasis should be on mitigating the changes rather than just adapting to them" (Johansen, 2005, 53).

HANSEN ASSESSES THE PACE OF WARMING

During a presentation at the American Geophysical Union's annual meeting in San Francisco on December 6, 2005, Hansen addressed a fundamental question in climate science: how much "wiggle room" do the Earth and its inhabitants have before global warming becomes a truly unavoidable disaster? The Earth's temperature, with rapid global warming during the past 30 years, said Hansen, is now passing through the peak level of the Holocene, a period of relatively stable climate that has existed for more than 10,000 years. Further warming of more than 1°C "will make the Earth warmer than it has been in a million years. 'Business-as-usual' scenarios, with fossil fuel CO_2 emissions continuing to increase at about 2 percent a year as in the past decade, yield additional warming of 2 or 3°C this century and imply changes that constitute practically a different planet" (Hansen, December 6, 2005).

Stop for a moment and ponder the words, "practically a different planet," delivered in the measured tones of a veteran scientist—a very real probability by the end of the twenty-first century. Hansen is not the type of person who engages in hyperbole for the fun of it. Hansen continued: "I present multiple lines of evidence indicating that the Earth's climate is nearing, but has not passed, a tipping point, beyond which it will be impossible to avoid climate change with far-ranging undesirable consequences" (Hansen, December 6, 2005). Coming to cases, Hansen described changes that will include

> not only loss of the Arctic as we know it, with all that implies for wildlife and indigenous peoples, but losses on a much vaster scale due to worldwide rising seas. Sea level will increase slowly at first, as losses at the fringes of Greenland and Antarctica due to accelerating ice streams are nearly balanced by increased snowfall and ice sheet thickening in the ice sheet interiors. But as Greenland and West Antarctic ice is softened and lubricated by melt-water and as buttressing ice shelves disappear due to a warming ocean, the balance will tip toward ice loss, thus bringing multiple positive

feedbacks into play and causing rapid ice sheet disintegration. The Earth's history suggests that with warming of 2 to 3 degrees C. the new equilibrium sea level will include not only most of the ice from Greenland and West Antarctica, but a portion of East Antarctica, raising sea level of the order of 25 meters (80 feet). (Hansen, December 6, 2005)

To be judicious—we don't want to ruin our case with overstatement—one might allow perhaps a century or two for a temperature rise in the atmosphere to express itself as sea-level rise from melting ice feeding rising seas. Contrary to lethargic ice sheet models, Hansen suggests, real-world data suggest substantial ice sheet and sea-level change in centuries, not millennia. Now take a look at a map of the world and pay attention to the coastal urban areas. Is anyone worried yet?

Hansen said he hoped that "the grim 'business-as-usual' climate change" could be avoided by slowing the growth of greenhouse gas emissions during the first quarter of the present century, requiring "strong policy leadership and international cooperation" (Hansen, December 6, 2005). However, he noted (venturing into the realm of politics), that "special interests have been a roadblock wielding undue influence over policymakers. The special interests seek to maintain short-term profits with little regard to either the long-term impact on the planet that will be inherited by our children and grandchildren or the long-term economic well-being of our country" (Hansen, December 6, 2005). Hansen left to the audience the task of putting names and faces to the special interests who, along with the rest of us, are attending this crucial juncture in the history of the planet and its inhabitants.

WHITE HOUSE CENSORSHIP

In the meantime, the Bush White House was listening. Hansen was assigned his own personal White House "minder" after his AGU talk. Subsequently, on January 29, 2006, the front page of the Sunday *New York Times* was topped by a large headline reading, "Climate Expert Says NASA Tried To Silence Him" (Revkin, January 29, 2006, A-1). Hansen said that officials at NASA headquarters had ordered the public affairs staff to review his coming lectures, papers, postings on the GISS Web site, and requests for interviews from journalists. Hansen said emphatically that he would ignore the restrictions. "They feel their job is to be [a] censor of information going out to the public," he said (Revkin, January 29, 2006, A-1).

Dean Acosta, deputy assistant administrator for public affairs at NASA, replied to Hansen's allegation: "That's not the way we operate here at NASA. We promote openness and we speak with the facts" (Revkin, January 29, 2006, A-1). However, Acosta said, according to the *Times* account, restrictions imposed on Hansen applied to all NASA employees. He added that government scientists were free to discuss scientific findings, but that "policy statements should be left to policy makers and appointed spokesmen" (Revkin, January 29, 2006, A-1). Acosta then justified all the restrictions Hansen had alleged. Requiring press officers to review interview requests was justified, for example, to create an orderly flow of information from a sprawling agency and to avoid surprises. "This is not about any individual or any issue like global warming," he said. "It's about coordination" (Revkin, January 29, 2006, A-1).

Hansen said that the policies, in Revkin's words, "Had already prevented the public from fully grasping recent findings about climate change that point to risks ahead. . . . Communicating with the public seems to be essential," he said, "because public concern is probably the only thing capable of overcoming the special interests that have obfuscated the topic" (Revkin, January 29, 2006, A-1). Hansen said it would be irresponsible not to speak out, particularly because NASA's mission statement includes the phrase "to understand and protect our home planet." Attempts to silence him had come through telephone conversations and not through formal channels, leaving no significant trails of documents, Hansen said (Revkin, January 29, 2006, A-1).

Hansen's "minder," George Deutsch, rejected a request from a producer at National Public Radio (NPR) to interview Hansen, said Leslie McCarthy, a public affairs officer at GISS. Citing handwritten notes taken during the conversation, McCarthy said that Deutsch called NPR "the most liberal" media outlet in the country. She said that Deutsch said his job was "to make the president look good" and that "as a White House appointee that might be Mr. Deutsch's priority" (Revkin, January 29, 2006, A-1).

Deutsch was a 24-year-old presidential appointee in the press office at NASA headquarters whose résumé said he was an intern in the "war room" of the 2004 Bush-Cheney reelection campaign and a 2003 journalism graduate of Texas A&M. Deutsch sought more control not only over Hansen's public statements, but he also gave the "big bang" theory a religious spin at NASA. In October 2005, wrote Andrew Revkin in the *New York Times*, Deutsch told a Web designer working for NASA to add the word "theory" after every mention of the big bang. According to Deutsch, "The Big Bang is not proven fact; it is opinion. . . . This is more than a science issue, it is a religious issue. And I would hate to think that young people would only be getting one-half of this debate from NASA. That would mean we had failed to properly educate the very people who rely on us for factual information the most" (Revkin, February 4, 2006).

Mary L. Cleave, deputy associate administrator for NASA's Office of Earth Science, was quoted as saying that the agency insisted on monitoring interviews with scientists to ensure they are not misquoted. "People could see it as a constraint," Cleave said. "As a manager, I might see it as protection" (Eilperin, January 29, 2006, A-1). This kind of attention was clearly not regarded as "protection" to Hansen. Having dealt with the media for more years than Deutsch had been alive, he was able to speak for himself.

Within a week of Hansen's allegations, a number of other NASA scientists voiced similar accounts of bureaucratic interference with their public communications in which political appointees had tried to influence scientific information, even as the agency's administrator, Michael D. Griffin, issued an emphatic statement calling for "scientific openness." "It is not the job of public-affairs offi-cers," Griffin wrote in an e-mail message to the agency's 19,000 employees, "to alter, filter or adjust engineering or scientific material produced by NASA's tech-nical staff." Griffin contended that "NASA has always been, is and will continue to be committed to open scientific and technical inquiry and dialogue with the public" (Revkin, February 4, 2006).

Following publicity regarding his attempts to censor Hansen and other NASA scientists, the résumé that Deutsch had used to apply for his job was checked, and he was found to have fabricated the claimed 2003 journalism degree from Texas A&M. Deutsch then resigned (Censoring Truth, 2006). Hansen characterized him as a "bit player" in the Bush administration's efforts to politicize many areas of science, from global warming to birth control to environmental regulation, includ-ing forest-cutting policy and air pollution (Censoring Truth, 2006). Hansen's dis-closures about Deutsch occurred the same week that Bush touted an emphasis on science in his 2006 State of the Union address.

After he resigned, Deutsch maintained that Hansen was promulgating a "culture war." "There is no pressure or mandate, from the Bush administration or elsewhere, to alter or water down scientific data at NASA, period," Deutsch said, adding that after being tasked to work with Hansen,

> I quickly learned one thing: Dr. Hansen and his supporters have a very partisan agenda and ties reaching to the top of the Democratic Party. Anyone perceived to be a Republican, a Bush supporter or a Christian is singled out and labeled a threat to their views. I encourage anyone interested in this story to consider the other side, to consider Dr. Hansen's true motivations and to consider the dangerous implications of only hearing out one side of the global warming debate. (Eilperin, February 7, 2006, A-11)

Donald Kennedy, the editor of *Science*, wrote that

> for at least two reasons, the treatment of Hansen may establish a new high-water mark for bureaucratic stupidity. First, Hansen's views on this general subject have long been widely available; he thinks climate change is due to anthropogenic sources, and he's discouraged that we're not doing more about it. For NASA to lock the stable door when this horse has been out on the range for years is just silly. Second, Hansen's history shows that he just won't be intimidated, and he has predictably told the *Times* that he will ignore the restrictions. The efforts by Acosta and Deutsch are reminiscent of the slapstick antics of Curley and Moe: a couple of guys stumbling off to gag someone who the audience knows will rip the gag right off. (Kennedy, February 17, 2006, 917)

According to Kennedy, these two incidents are part of a troublesome pattern for which the Bush administration had become well known: Ignore evidence if it doesn't favor the preferred policy outcome. Above all, don't let the public get an idea that scientists inside government disagree with the White House party line.

The new gag rules supported the new Bush mantra, an interesting inversion of Secretary of Defense Donald Rumsfeld's view on war: "You don't make policy with the science you have. You make policy with the science you WANT." But the late-breaking good news is that NASA Administrator Griffin has said that there will be no more of this nonsense, and Deutsch, the 24-year-old Bush appointee sent to muzzle Hansen, has left the agency abruptly after his résumé turned out to be falsified. A change of heart? Stay tuned. (Kennedy, February 17, 2006, 917).

In the meantime, Hansen said that officials at the National Oceanic and Atmospheric Administration (NOAA) were muzzling researchers who study global warming. Speaking in a panel discussion about science and the environment before a full house at the New School, in New York City, Hansen said that NOAA insists on having "a minder" monitor its scientists when they discuss their findings with journalists. "It seems more like Nazi Germany or the Soviet Union than the United States," prompting applause from the audience. He added that while NOAA officials said they maintain the policy for their scientists' protection, "if you buy that one please see me at the break, because there's a bridge down the street I'd like to sell you" (Eilperin, February 7, 2006, A-11).

PUBLIC RELATIONS AND ICE DYNAMICS

An important issue in global warming relates to the question of how quickly ice sheets may disintegrate, raising worldwide sea levels and inundating coastlines. In the real world, wrote Hansen, ice-sheet disintegration is driven by highly nonlinear processes and feedbacks. For example, higher sea levels can cause marine ice shelves to decline and break up accelerating movement of land-based ice toward the seas. In addition, melting glacier water flows downward through holes in the ice to the bottom of an ice mass, where it serves as a lubricant that further accelerates the disintegration of the land ice and its flow into the sea.

As Hansen was evading his "minder" at NASA, he was receiving word that reports were being prepared in the journal *Science* that melting of the Greenland ice cap had been accelerating markedly. New studies were indicating that the flow of several large glaciers draining the Greenland ice sheet was speeding up and that this change, combined with increased melting, suggested that existing estimates of future sea-level rise were too low (Dowdeswell, 2006, 963–964).

Using satellite radar interferometry (remote-sensing) observations of Greenland, Eric Rignot and Pannir Kanagaratnam detected widespread glacier acceleration below 66 degrees north latitude between 1996 and 2000, which rapidly expanded to 70 degrees north by 2005. "Accelerated ice discharge in the west and particularly in the east doubled the ice sheet mass deficit in the last decade from 90 to 220 cubic kilometers per year. As more glaciers accelerate farther north, the contribution of Greenland to sea-level rise will continue to increase," they wrote (Rignot and Kanagaratnam, 2006, 986). The melting speed of some of these glaciers into the sea doubled in roughly five years to 12 kilometers a year. These glaciers play a crucial role in the mass balance of the Greenland ice sheet, which doubled between 1996 and 2005 (Rignot and Kanagaratnam, 2006, 988).

Rignot and Kanagaratnam concluded that present models used to estimate the Greenland ice melt's contribution to world sea-level rise do not include ice-sheet dynamics that tend to accelerate. Melting ice tends to increase in speed as it flows toward the sea. "As such," they wrote, "They only provide lower limits to the potential contribution of Greenland to sea-level rise. If more glaciers accelerate father north, especially along the west coast, the mass loss from Greenland will continue to increase well above predictions" (Rignot and Kanagaratnam, 2006, 990).

Although buildup of glaciers is gradual, Hansen said, "Once an ice sheet begins to collapse, its demise can be spectacularly rapid." The darkening of ice by black-carbon aerosols (soot), pollution associated with the burning of fossil fuels, also accelerates melting. "While the timing of melting is uncertain," wrote Hansen, "global warming beyond some limit will make a large sea-level change inevitable for future generations." Hansen estimated that such a limit could be crossed with about 1°C of additional worldwide warming, half of which was already in the pipeline by 2004.

After Deutsch tried and failed to "handle" him, Hansen wrote a piece in the London *Independent*, which published it on the front page February 26, 2006. Hansen said that a satellite survey of the Greenland ice cap indicates it is melting more quickly than scientists had thought. The amount of Greenland ice melting into the sea has increased roughly 100 percent in five years. He recounted how NASA's public-relations office, "staffed by political appointees from the Bush administration," had tried to muzzle his distribution of this information. "I ignored the restrictions," Hansen wrote. "The first line of NASA's mission is to understand and protect the planet" (Hansen, February 26, 2006, 1).

Hansen described the satellite data as "a remarkable advance," illustrating for the first time how rapidly ice is draining from Greenland into the sea at a rate of 200 or more cubic kilometers a year. Two years earlier, most scientists had thought the Greenland ice sheet was in balance. While this may sound like a lot of ice, wrote Hansen, it is "just the beginning. Once a sheet starts to disintegrate, it can reach a tipping point beyond which break-up is explosively rapid. The issue is how close we are getting to that tipping point. The summer of 2005 broke all records for melting in Greenland. So we may be on the edge" (Hansen, February 26, 2006, 1).

How quickly can sea levels rise? Hansen asked. Roughly 14,000 years ago, sea levels rose by 20 meters in 400 years—five meters per century. Temperatures were not warming as quickly as today. "That is what we can look forward to if we don't act soon" (Hansen, February 26, 2006, 1). Sea-level rise of this magnitude could imperil hundreds of millions of people who live in urban areas at or near sea level throughout the world.

FEBRUARY RAIN ON BAFFIN ISLAND

As Hansen was engaged in this debate with the White House, on February 26, 2006, rain fell on Baffin Island. Sheila Watt-Cloutier, who at the time was president of the Inuit Circumpolar Conference, e-mailed me February 27 from Iqaluit, on Baffin Island, describing a heretofore unheard-of event there: rain, lightning, thunder, and mud in February. The temperature had risen to 6–8°C, the average temperature in Iqaluit for June, winds had reached 55 miles an hour, and the town was paralyzed in a sea of dirty slush. "Much of the snow has melted on the back of my house and all the roads are already slushy and messy. All planes coming up from the south were cancelled because the runways were icy from the rain," she wrote. "Unfortunately the predictions of the Arctic Climate Impact Assessment are unfolding before my very eyes" (Watt-Cloutier, February 27, 2006). Iqaluit hunters expressed concern for the caribou, which would go hungry once freezing temperatures returned and encased the lichen, their food source, in a crust of ice. Instead of waiting until spring, the usual hunting season, Inuit were taking caribou in early March, believing that they would be too skinny later to be useful as food.

Watt-Cloutier watched the rain with a sense of horror, because it was so out of line with the usual weather patterns in her homeland. For the time in anyone's memory, local ice was melting in *winter*. I passed Watt-Cloutier's message on to Hansen, who thanked me, because, he said, his presentations had been strong on theory but lacking the impact of present and impending climatic changes on people and the natural world.

Hansen's contretemps with the White House and Watt-Cloutier's report from Iqaluit occurred days before the annual meeting of the American Association for the Advancement of Science (AAAS) in St. Louis. An editorial in *Nature* described a panel at that meeting on the Bush administration's repression of science as "the highlight of the annual meeting." "A packed and emotional hall" debated the issue, according to the editorial, including AAAS's incoming president David Baltimore, a Nobel laureate (Science Under Attack, 2006, 891).

Hansen maintains an e-mail list of colleagues to whom he sends drafts of his papers as they are being refined (I am honored to be on this list). On March 13, 2006, Hansen sent a letter to his correspondents observing that the ideological weather improved at NASA after he went public. At the Environmental Protection Agency, however, "where double-speak ('sound science,' 'clear skies') has achieved a level that would make George Orwell envious, [the situation] is much bleaker, based on the impression that I receive from limited discussion with colleagues there," Hansen wrote. "The situation in NASA regarding free speech . . . is promising. There is no doubt that Administrator Griffin recognized the problem, fully supports openness and free speech, and intends to have supportive rules and procedures. If implementation by Public Affairs differs from that spirit, you will hear about it," Hansen wrote (Hansen, March 13, 2006).

"Unless some new event demands it"—and precedent indicates that this battle never ends—Hansen said he would like to avoid whistle-blowing activities in favor of full-time science, "quantifying options for dealing with global warming" (Hansen, March 13, 2006).

Following Hansen's letter to his colleagues, the agency's administrator, Michael D. Griffin, released new rules regarding employees' relations with the media and public. The new policy, written by an internal team of scientists, lawyers, public affairs specialists, and managers, said that NASA scientists were free to talk to members of the media about their scientific findings, and to interpret them. Scientists were no longer required to have a public affairs officer with them when they spoke with members of the media, but Griffin advised it. "If you're not a media professional, then to go into an interview without a media professional is courting trouble," he said. "But you can do as you like" (Weiss, 2006, A-10).

A DECADE OF DENIAL

Hansen blamed a sluggish federal response to curb U.S. greenhouse gas emissions on the influence of "special interest groups." "One way you can judge this is by looking at the situation in other countries, especially in Europe, where there has not been as strong a disinformation campaign," he said at a briefing sponsored by the National Environmental Trust. "They have accepted the need to take action to deal with the problem, while we haven't." The price tag for dealing with global warming's economic, social, and environmental impacts could "conservatively" reach $10 trillion, Hansen said, calling the current national debt "chicken feed" in comparison (Morello, 2006).

"We've lost a decade due to denial, but we cannot afford to lose another decade," he said, predicting catastrophic economic and social impacts if greenhouse gas emissions are not addressed. "When the sea rises, when coastlines and cities are inundated, when island nations must abandon their islands and seek refuge. . . large parts of Florida, Bangladesh, China, various places around the world will be affected," he said. "If you stop to think about who's going to pay, well, it's not going to be the politicians and it can't be the oil companies either, because of the magnitude of the damages." U.S. interests would be best served by taking the same approach to climate change that the government took in addressing depletion of the ozone layer in the 1980s, he said: "In that case we prevented what could have been a tragedy because we acted and we did not listen to the special interests" (Morello, 2006).

As he fought political battles, Hansen was compiling the scientific "tale of the tape" in support. Filing an expert report in support of automobile efficiency standards in California (which were being challenged there in court), Hansen estimated the number of people around the world who could be displaced by various levels of sea-level rise. Hansen's exhibits contained topographic maps of the United States, Europe, India, and China shaded according to levels of land loss for a 6, 25, 35, and 75 meter sea-level rise. The Washington, D.C., area included one spot pointedly labeled "White House" (17 meters above high tide), over a light-blue hue signifying that it would go under at between 6 and 25 meters, well within the range of sea-level rise that Hansen expected to be "in the pipeline" by the end of the twenty-first century at business-as-usual rates of greenhouse gas rise (Hansen, May 5, 2006).

By Hansen's estimate, 235 million people would be displaced in these areas at 6 meters, 703 million at 25 meters, 881 million at 35 meters, and 1.4 billion at 75 meters, using population estimates for the year 2000 (Hansen, May 5, 2006). The 75-meter figure would equal melting of about 80 percent of all permanent pack ice on Earth.

Hansen's campaign to raise the salience of the science has taken him to some unusual venues. *Vanity Fair*'s "green issue" (May 2006) amid the glitz, the well-oiled young skin, and vacuous features about the beautiful people, included a full-length portrait of *Vanity Fair*'s "Hall of Fame" nominee of the month, Jim Hansen, wearing a strained smile and an old suit, going, perhaps, where no serious climate scientist has ever gone before (Hall of Fame, 2006, 106). Hansen was standing in front of a world map, doing what was necessary to get information out to the public.

MASSAGING NASA'S MISSION STATEMENT

The Bush White House's denial of global warming as a serious issue reached beyond its attempts to silence Hansen and other scientists. Unknown to scientists at NASA (who were not consulted), in late January or early February of 2006—just as articles describing how Hansen was resisting White House pressure hit the front pages of the *New York Times* and *Washington Post*—the Bush administration's annual budget reached Congress with an altered version of the agency's mission statement. Gone—down the memory hole in Orwellian fashion—was the statement that had been used since 2002: "to understand and protect our home planet; to explore the universe and search for life, to inspire the next generation of explorers . . . as only NASA can." The phrase "to understand and protect our home planet," which Hansen had used time and again to support his resistance to White House censorship of scientific data on global warming, had vanished. The 2002 statement, an extension of NASA's original statement of purpose ("the expansion of human knowledge of the Earth and of phenomena in the atmosphere and space") had been adopted with advice from NASA's 19,000 employees. The new, sans Earth mission was written by fiat. NASA employees did not learn of their new mission statement until summer (Revkin, July 22, 2006, A-1, A-10).

Without explicitly saying so, the change seemed aimed squarely at the parts of NASA, such as GISS, that had shifted their focus to earth sciences over the years. Hansen said that the change might reflect White House eagerness to shift federal resources away from the study of global warming. "They're making it clear that they have the authority to make this change, that the president sets the objectives for NASA, and that they prefer that NASA work on something that's not causing them a problem," Hansen told Andrew Revkin of the *New York Times* (July 22, 2006, A-10).

A *New York Times* editorial noted that:

> The agency has canceled a deep space observatory to monitor solar radiation, water vapor, clouds, aerosols and other things important to climate change. It has delayed a mission with Japan to measure global precipitation, decided not to pay for a mission to measure soil moisture around the world, and reduced the money available to analyze data. Under Congressional pressure, the agency has reinstated a mission to study aerosols and solar radiation from orbit. But it has little money to do much else in coming years. A National Academy of Sciences panel warned that the nation's system of environmental satellites was "at risk of collapse." . . . This is happening right at a time when NASA data are yielding spectacular and startling results. A pair of small satellites that measure the Earth's gravitational field with remarkable precision found that the mass of Greenland decreased by the equivalent of 50 cubic miles of ice in 2005. The area on Greenland with summer melting has increased 50 per cent, the major ice streams on Greenland (portions of the ice sheet moving most rapidly toward the ocean and discharging icebergs) have doubled in speed, and the area in the Arctic Ocean with summer sea ice has decreased 20 per cent in the last 25 years. (What About Us?, 2006)

Hansen mused that the White House had found yet another way to avoid bad news about climate change: "Stop the measurements! Only hitch: the first line of the NASA mission is 'to understand and protect our home planet.' Maybe that can be changed to "protect special interests' backsides" (Hansen, July 26, 2006).

REFERENCES

Bowen, Mark. *Thin Ice: Unlocking the Secrets of Climate in the World's Highest Mountains.* New York: Henry Holt, 2005.

"Censoring Truth." [editorial] *New York Times*, February 9, 2006, http://www.nytimes. com/2006/02/09opinion/09thu2.html.

Dowdeswell, Julian A. "The Greenland Ice Sheet and Global Sea-Level Rise." *Science* 311 (February 17, 2006):963–964.

Eilperin, Juliet. "Censorship Is Alleged at NOAA; Scientists Afraid to Speak Out, NASA Climate Expert Reports." *Washington Post*, February 7, 2006, A-11.

Eilperin, Juliet. "Debate on Climate Shifts to Issue of Irreparable Change." *Washington Post*, January 29, 2006, A-1.

Ferguson, H. L. "The Changing Atmosphere: Implications for Global Security." In *The Challenge of Global Warming*, edited by Dean Edwin Abrahamson, 48–62. Washington, D.C.: Island Press, 1989.

"Hall of Fame: *Vanity Fair* Nominates: Dr. James Hansen." *Vanity Fair*, May 2006, 106.

Hansen, James E. "The Case for Action by the State of California to Mitigate Climate Change." Expert Report, Submitted to United States District Court of California— Fresno, in Regard to Case No: 1:04-CV-06663 REC LJO. *Central Valley Chrysler-Jeep, Inc. v. Catherine E. Witherspoon; Automobile Manufacturers v. California Air*

Resources Board. May 5, 2006. Graphic exhibits: ftp://ftp.giss.nasa.gov/outgoing/
    california/california_figs_2may06.pdf.

Hansen, James E. "Climatic Changes: Understanding the Global Warming." In *The Health
    and Survival of the Human Species in the 21st Century*, edited by Robert Lanza, 173–190.
    Santa Fe, N.M.: Health Press, 1996.

Hansen, James E. "Dangerous Anthropogenic Interference: A Discussion of Humanity's
    Faustian Climate Bargain and the Payments Coming Due." Presentation on October
    26, 2004, in the Distinguished Public Lecture Series at the Department of Physics and
    Astronomy, University of Iowa, Iowa City.

Hansen, James E. "The Greenhouse, the White House, and Our House." Typescript of a
    speech at the International Platform Association, Washington, D.C., August 3, 1989.

Hansen, James E. "Is There Still Time to Avoid 'Dangerous Anthropogenic Interference'
    with Global Climate? A Tribute to Charles David Keeling." A paper delivered to
    the American Geophysical Union, San Francisco, December 6, 2005. http://www.
    columbia.edu/~jeh1/keeling_talk_and_slides.pdf.

Hansen, James E. "On the Edge: Greenland Ice Cap Melting at Twice the Rate It Was
    Five Years ago, Says Scientist Bush Tried to Gag." *London Independent.* February
    26, 2006, 1.

Hansen, James E. Personal correspondence, March 13, 2006.

Hansen, James E. "Swift Boating, Stealth Budgeting, and the Theory of the Unitary Execu-
    tive." Unpaginated draft supplied to the author by Hansen, July 26, 2006.

Hansen, James, D. Johnson, A. Lacis, S. Lebedeff, P. Lee, D. Rind, and G. Russell. "Cli-
    mate Impact of Increasing Atmospheric Carbon Dioxide." *Science* 213(August 28,
    1981):957–966.

Hertsgaard, Mark. "While Washington Slept." *Vanity Fair*, May, 2006, 200–207, 238–243.

"Inhofe Calls Global Warming Warnings a Hoax." Associated Press, Oklahoma State and
    Local Wire, July 29, 2003, http://www.lexis-nexis.com.

Ivins, Molly. "Ignoring Problem Works—For a While." Charleston (West Virginia) *Gazette*,
    June 28, 2003, 4-A.

Johansen, Bruce E. "A Man With A Mission: James Hansen." *Omaha Magazine*, October/
    November 2005, 51–53.

Kennedy, Donald. "Acts of God?" *Science* 311(January 20, 2006):303.

Kennedy, Donald. "The New Gag Rules." Editorial. *Science* 311 (February 17, 2006): 917.

Kolbert, Elizabeth. *Field Notes from a Catastrophe: Man, Nature, and Climate Change.*
    New York: Bloomsbury, 2006.

Krugman, Paul. "Enemy of the Planet." *New York Times*, April 17, 2006.

Lacis, Andrew. Personal communication, February 10, 2005.

Mieszkowski, Katharine. "Bush: Global Warming Is Just Hot Air." Salon.com, September
    10, 2004, http://www.lexis-nexis.com.

McKibben, Bill. "Too Hot to Handle; Recent Efforts to Censor Jim Hansen, NASA's Top
    Climate Scientist, Are Only the Latest. As His Message Grows More Urgent, We
    Ignore Him at Our Peril." *Boston Globe*, February 5, 2006, E-1.

Morello, Lauren. "Warming's Toll Could Exceed $10 Trillion, NASA's Hansen Warns."
    Greenwire Spotlight 10(9), April 14, 2006, http://www.lexis-nexis.com.

Nance, John J. *What Goes Up: The Global Assault on Our Atmosphere.* New York: William
    Morrow, 1991.

Parsons, Michael L. *Global Warming: The Truth Behind the Myth.* New York: Plenum
    Press/Insight, 1995.

Regalado, Antonio. "Skeptics on Warming are Criticized." *Wall Street Journal*, July 31, 2003, A-3, A-4.

Remnick, David. "Ozone Man" [Talk of the Town]. *The New Yorker*, April 24, 2006, 47–48.

Revkin, Andrew. "Climate Expert Says NASA Tried to Silence Him." *New York Times*, January 29, 2006, A-1.

Revkin, Andrew. "NASA Chief Backs Agency Openness." *New York Times*, February 4, 2006, http://www.nytimes.com/2006/02/04/science/04climate.html.

Revkin, Andrew C. "NASA's Goals Delete Mention of Home Planet." *New York Times*, July 22, 2006, A-1, A-10.

Rignot, Eric, and Pannir Kanagaratnam. "Changes in the Velocity Structure of the Greenland Ice Sheet." *Science* 311 (February 17, 2006): 986–990.

"Science Under Attack." (Editorial) *Nature* 439 (February 23, 2006): 891.

Watt-Cloutier, Sheila. Personal communication, February 27, 2006.

Weiss, Rick. "NASA Sets New Rules On Media: Employees May Discuss Findings, Agency Says." *Washington Post*, March 31, 2006, A-10.

"What About Us?" (Editorial) *New York Times*, July 28, 2006, http://www.nytimes.com/2006/07/28/opinion/28fri2.html.

Chapter 2

Soft Science: How Intelligent Is This Design?

A CENTURY AFTER Albert Einstein published his first major article on relativity, in 1905, the world of science remained truly another country (and maybe even another planet) for many citizens of the United States of America. Various polls indicated that only about 40 percent of U.S. citizens subscribed to the theory of evolution, about 20 percent insisted that the sun revolved around the Earth, one-half believed that human beings coexisted with the dinosaurs, and only 13 percent could correctly define the word "molecule" (Kristof, 2005, 7–B). In 1993, an international study ranked U.S. students dead last, behind Bulgaria and Slovenia, in knowledge of evolution's basic facts (Phillips, 2006, 248).

In such an atmosphere, some science teachers have been required to give equal time to creationism (dressed up as "intelligent design"). Resistance to evolution is an old story in the United States, of course. Recently, creationism has been revived, along with a general upsurge in religious fundamentalism. Today, most card-carrying creationists have stretched the biblical six days of godly labor and one day of rest to 6,000 to 10,000 years—still a far cry from the 4.5 billion years many scientists now accept as the age of the Earth, and the 13.7 billion years since the "big bang" that gave birth to the universe.

Acceptance of intelligent design as "science" has been part of a general retreat from rationality in large sections of U.S. culture. Bill Moyers, himself an ordained Baptist minister, told an audience at the Harvard Medical School that "one of the biggest changes in politics in my lifetime is that the delusional is no longer marginal. It has come in from the fringe, to sit in the seat of power in the Oval Office and in the Congress. For the first time in our history, ideology and theology hold a monopoly of power in Washington [D.C.]" (Phillips, 2006, xv).

Delusion enjoys a considerable constituency. By 2005, the *Left Behind* series of "Rapture" books by Tim LaHaye, which anticipate the end of the world at the hands of an angry, fundamentalist Christian god who condemns nonbelievers to hell on Earth, had sold more than 62 million copies, many to members of the religious right wing, who constituted President George W. Bush's "base." These books "posit the ultimate Left Behind message: God so loved the world that he sent World War III" (Rossing, *The Rapture Exposed*, 2004, 4, 42, cited in Phillips, 2006, 254). According to a poll taken by *Time* magazine, 59 percent in the United States believe that John's prophecies of the world's violent end and the eradication of nonbelievers in fundamentalist Christianity will come to pass (Berman, 2006, 4). It is estimated that one in eight U.S. citizens has read a "Rapture" book, in which the Book of Revelation is "pretty much the road map," in which Jews, Muslims, Hindus, Catholics, and those who profess other "aberrant religions" are consigned to an everlasting hell on Earth as seas turn to blood and waves of locusts torment nonbelievers (Berman, 2006, 4).

As debates over evolution raged in Texas, the cotton industry there was being threatened by a moth that had evolved resistance to pesticides. A frustrated entomologist said: "It's amazing that cotton growers are having to deal with these pests in the very states whose legislatures are so hostile to the theory of evolution—because it is evolution they are struggling against in their fields every season. These people are trying to ban the teaching of evolution while their own cotton crops are failing because of evolution" (Phillips, 2006, 247–248).

Intolerance to basic science and freedom of inquiry rides shotgun with political power in a modern-day America that Benjamin Franklin and Thomas Jefferson might be hard-pressed to recognize. In the "State of the First Amendment Survey," conducted in 2003, 34 percent of the sample said that the First Amendment "goes too far," 46 percent said there is too much freedom of the press, 28 percent advocated prior approval by government of newspaper content, and 31 percent expressed a belief that in a time of war, anti-war public protest should be illegal. Given such attitudes, remarked author Morris Berman in *Dark Ages America*, "We may be only one more terrorist attack away from a police state" (Berman, 2006, 5).

This is not to say that traditional physical sciences draw no support in the United States. Scientists even occasionally needle religious myths, even in the land of mass-merchandised Rapture. Those scientific spoilsports! In 2006, a team of Israeli and U.S. scientists speculated that Jesus walked on water because it was solid. The Sea of Galilee has never frozen in modern times, but the scientists said temperatures were colder 2,000 years ago. Doron Nof, who teaches oceanography at Florida State University, (and describes himself as an "equal opportunity miracle buster") has advanced this theory. In 1992, he also proposed that a freak Red Sea windstorm parted the Red Sea for Moses (Cooperman, 2006, A-3).

INTELLIGENT, BY DESIGN

Reduced to basics, intelligent design—"ID" in headline-writer's shorthand—is a belief that life, especially human life, is too complex to have been a natural accident, or, as Charles Darwin's theories propound, an evolutionary adaptation to environmental conditions over many births and deaths. A concept of intelligent design implies a purposeful designer, driven by a conscious purpose. Attempting to sound scientific, the inventors of this line of theoretical reasoning sometimes go to great lengths to avoid using religious-sounding nomenclature (such as "God") to designate the character of the intelligent designer. Such vagueness is sometimes deemed necessary when arguing that "ID" should be taught in public schools as "theory" alongside the "theory" of evolution, thus avoiding arguments that it is nothing more than lipstick on the pig of creationism, which has been deemed ideologically out of bounds as public-school subject matter by the federal courts for two decades.

Not to rain on anyone's religious parade, but if design is so intelligent, why is biology so inconsistent? Why do women have hot flashes? Which node of the intelligent designer's brain gave us crotch rot? Why are so many foods that taste so good so bad for our health—why did the designer give us ice cream? Why does bacon, that invitation to nutritional suicide, taste so good? Why do otherwise good people sometimes die cruel, slow deaths?

Creationism is hardly a novel idea in the United States. Almost 75 years after the peak of Charles Darwin's career (he published *The Origin of Species* in 1858), John Scopes, a high-school teacher, was brought to trial in Tennessee and convicted on charges of violating a state law against teaching that humankind was descended "from a lower order of animal" (Talbot, 2005, 66). Darwin has had a rocky time in the United States ever since. He does better in England, his home, where Christian evangelism gets little traction. To this day, he rides quite comfortably in British pockets on the flipside of the 10-pound note, opposite Queen Elizabeth.

During the famous "Monkey Trial," the judge refused to consider the merits of evolution *vis a vis* creationism. The court also refused to permit testimony by evolutionists as requested by defense attorney Charles Darrow. The argument regarding the merits of evolution as scientific theory was deemed beyond the court's jurisdiction; the issue was restricted to what Scopes had taught, and whether it violated the state's existing law. The teaching of creationism was Tennessee state law in 1925.

As late as 1968, in *Epperson v. Arkansas*, a biology teacher (Susan Epperson) successfully overturned an Arkansas state law, passed in 1928, banning the teaching of evolution. More than a century after Darwin promulgated his theory, as late as 1961, John C. Whitcomb, a theologian, and Henry Morris, an engineering professor at Virginia Tech, published *The Genesis Flood*, arguing that geology proves the Earth is only a few thousand years old, and that most of the Earth's strata were laid down at the time of the Great Flood and Noah's Ark.

Not until 1987 did the U.S. Supreme Court (in *Edwards v. Aguillard*) strike down a Louisiana state law requiring that creationism and evolution be taught side-by-side in public high schools' science courses. Unlike the Scopes trial, the 1987 case in Louisiana, *Edwards v. Aguillard*, provided ample running room for scientific definitions and discussion of evolution. Seventy-two Nobel laureates, 17 state academies of science, and 7 other scientific organizations submitted an *amicus curiae* brief to the U.S. Supreme Court supporting the appellees' challenge to Louisiana's Balanced Treatment for Creation Science and Evolution Science Act (Shermer, 2006, 96). The U.S. Supreme Court voted seven-to-two to overturn the act, using the verbal template that Judge John E. Jones III would follow in Dover, Pennsylvania, almost two decades later: the Louisiana law violated the Establishment Clause of the First Amendment because it endorsed religion by advancing a belief that a supernatural being created the human race.

Thus, in 2004, when the Kansas State Board of Education voted to include challenges to Darwinist theory in state-school standards (a requirement that later was withdrawn when the board's composition changed), the only news was that the religious undertow in public-school science had never really completely subsided. The difference in our time is that religious fundamentalists now approach public schools from the outside, legally, as they try to insert creation-based ideas into curricula of science.

While the terms of debate may not have changed much since the days of the Scopes "Monkey" trial, the rules under which the legal game is played have been fundamentally altered. In Dover, Pennsylvania, an attempt to insert intelligent design was carried out during 2005 and 2006 in the face of Pennsylvania Academic Standards that require instruction of Darwin's theory of evolution. In its decision, the Kansas school board did not require specific mention of intelligent design. "The heart of science should be looking at the gaps in theory and trying to figure out what that's about," said Steve Abrams, a Kansas school board member. "This decision will perhaps have an effect on other states, but we don't talk about intelligent design" (Powell, December 22, 2005, A-3).

SHOWDOWN IN DOVER

Conflict regarding whether intelligent design should be taught in the public schools arrived at an important political and legal juncture during 2005 in Dover, Pennsylvania, a town of 19,000 people in York County. The local school board enacted a four-paragraph statement that cast doubt on the validity of Darwinist theory, "touting intelligent design as an alternative" (Talbot, 2005, 66).

The statement that was debated in Dover observed that the state's academic standards require students to learn about the theory of evolution and to take a standardized test that covers it. The statement then asserted that "because Darwin's theory is a theory it is still being tested. . . . Gaps in the theory exist for which there is no evidence" (Shermer, 2006, 101). The statement went on to say that intelligent design is an alternative explanation that is discussed in the book *Of Pandas and People*, by Percival Davis and Dean H. Kenyon. Biology teachers at Dover Senior High School refused to read the statement, which had been composed by the school board. It was read to students by administrators. Eight of nine school-board members were subsequently voted out of office during November 2005. Only Heather Geesey, who was not required to run for reelection that year, was not turned out of office.

The election was held four days after the conclusion of a trial in *Kitzmiller v. Dover Area School District*, the first case to test the constitutional basis of public-school classes that present an argument regarding intelligent design. The case, argued in Harrisburg federal district court before Judge John E. Jones III, ended during the first week of November; Jones, a Republican who had been appointed by President George W. Bush, rendered his verdict during the first week of January, just before ninth-grade students at Dover Senior High School were scheduled to begin a unit on evolution. He was charged with deciding whether "ID" was valid science or an endorsement of religion in violation of the constitutional separation of Church and State.

Matthew Chapman, an Englishman and a great-great grandson of Darwin, wrote about the "Dover monkey trial" in *Harpers*, expressing consternation at American fundamentalist eccentricities, including such things as a "creationist theme park" near Pensacola, Florida run by Kent Hovind, an ex-science teacher, a.k.a. "Dr. Dino." Chapman marveled at the American propensity for holding Darwin and the concept of evolution responsible for all manner of sin and wickedness:

> By this time, it was public knowledge that I was an offspring of Darwin. . . . It became apparent to me, really for the first time, how hated the poor old codger is. People . . . believe that Darwin marks a point in history from which materialism sprang, bringing with it Hitler, Stalin, Pol Pot, pot, sex, prostitution, abortion, homosexuality, and everything else nasty in the world. (Chapman, 2006, 58)

Once his presence at the trial became known to the fundamentalists, Chapman and his remarks were being videotaped by fundamentalists very nearly as a proxy for Satan's, as an example for various congregations of personal beliefs and behaviors that might land a person in hell.

A CBS News survey released during October 2005 indicated that 51 percent of Americans believe God created humans in their present form, a 10 percent increase in roughly a decade (Chapman, 2006, 58). A poll released the previous summer by the Pew Forum on Religion and Public Life and the Pew Research Center for the People and the Press found that 42 percent expressed strict creationist views and nearly two-thirds were willing to have creationism taught in schools along with evolutionary theory. The percentage of teachers advocating equal time for creationism ranged as high, on a statewide basis, as 69 percent in a study of 330 Texas high school biology teachers published in the journal *Science Education* in 1993.

The trial in Harrisburg included three days of testimony from Michael Behe, a Lehigh University biochemist widely regarded as a leading supporter of intelligent design. The idea has at least one textbook devoted to it (*Of Pandas and People*) but no scientific peer-reviewed literature, even after 15 years of discussion. Most scientists dismiss intellectual design because it is argument by inference. No observers were present at the moment of design. Science seeks explanations that can be observed, tested, and replicated. Intelligent design invokes a nonnatural cause that cannot be observed or tested.

Kenneth Miller, a Brown University biology professor and author of several popular high-school and college textbooks that some opponents of evolution at Dover complained were "laced with Darwinism," said during the trial in Jones's court that 99.9 percent of the organisms that ever have lived on Earth are now extinct. "An intelligent designer who designed things, 99.9 per cent of which didn't last, certainly wouldn't be very intelligent," he said (Talbot, 2005, 70).

The day after the trial ended, a local drama company, Theatre Harrisburg, opened a performance of *Inherit the Wind*, which is based on the Scopes "Monkey" trial, on a stage one block from the courthouse. At about the same time, Bryan Rehm, a high-school physics teacher who was among the plaintiffs who sued the school board, received dozens of angry e-mails from supporters of intelligent design, at the same time that atheists satirized Christians on local cable television. The school board that was voted into office in November 2005 considered a compromise: A comparative religion class that would include discussion of intelligent design as well as evolution, as philosophy, rather than science.

Judge Jones ruled December 20, 2005 that intelligent design is religion disguised as science and that Dover High School biology teachers were under no legal obligation to discuss it in classes. Jones's ruling was emphatic. A report in the *New Scientist* said that Judge Jones "systematically dismantled the arguments of the proponents of intelligent design. Jones said that the history of intelligent design shows that it is essentially creationism with explicit references to God and the *Bible* removed." At the Dover trial, one observer called I.D. "creationism in a cheap tuxedo" (Shermer, 2006, 102).

As such, "ID" is primarily a religious theory, not a scientific one, and cannot be taught in U.S. public schools, which are prevented from promoting religion ("Judge Rules," 2005). Jones ruled that teaching intelligent design as science in public school violates the "Establishment Clause" of the Constitution's First Amendment, which prohibits public officials from imposing or establishing a particular religion, "a particular version of Christianity." Media reports characterized his ruling as a "broad, stinging rebuke to its advocates and a boost to scientists who have fought to bar intelligent design from the science curriculum" (Goodstein, 2005).

Jones criticized as misleading the school board's statement characterizing evolution as a theory, saying that the statement confuses the scientific and colloquial meaning of "theory." The judge asserted, "singling out evolution from all other scientific theories . . . suggests that there is some special doubt about the truth of evolution" ("Judge Rules," 2005). Jones's ruling stated that that intelligent design could not be considered science because it calls upon the supernatural in a way that violates the basic ground rules of science as they have been used since the emergence of scientific method in the sixteenth century. He also said that intelligent design relies on a "false dualism": that if evolution can be disproved, then intelligent design has been proven. Their arguments were characterized by Jones as examples of "breathtaking inanity" that had dragged the community into "this legal maelstrom with its resulting utter waste of monetary and personal resources" (Goodstein, 2005).

Jones excoriated members of the Dover school board who he said had lied to cover their religious motives. Jones said that two of the most outspoken proponents of intelligent design on the school board, William Buckingham and Alan Bonsell, had lied in their depositions about how they raised money in a church to buy *Of Pandas and People* for public-school libraries. Both men, according to the testimony, had repeatedly said at school board meetings that they objected to evolution for religious reasons, and wanted to see creationism taught as its equal. Judge Jones wrote, "It is ironic that several of these individuals, who so staunchly and proudly touted their religious convictions in public, would time and again lie to cover their tracks and disguise the real purpose behind the ID Policy" (Goodstein, 2005).

Jones described intelligent design as a form of Christian fundamentalism, supporting testimony by Barbara Forrest, a science historian, that the authors of *Of Pandas and People* had removed 150 references to "creationism" from an earlier edition and substituted "intelligent design" after the Supreme Court's ruling in 1987 that prohibited the teaching of creationism in public schools. That was, wrote Jones, "compelling evidence" that intelligent design is little but "creationism re-labeled" (Lawrence, 2005, 3-A). "We conclude that the religious nature of intelligent design would be readily apparent to an objective observer, adult or child," he said. "The writings of leading ID proponents reveal that the designer postulated by their argument is the God of Christianity" (Goodstein, 2005).

"To be sure, Darwin's theory of evolution is imperfect," Judge Jones wrote. "However, the fact that a scientific theory cannot yet render an explanation on every point should not be used as a pretext to thrust an untestable alternative hypothesis grounded in religion into the science classroom or to misrepresent well-established scientific propositions" (Goodstein, 2005).

REACTION TO JONES'S RULING

Jones's decision was legally binding only for school districts in the middle district of Pennsylvania, but its role as a practical precedent reached across the United States. The six-week trial soon was being compared to the Scopes case.

Some creationists remarked that Jones's ruling bespoke an "activist" judiciary, a charge that the ruling anticipated: "Those who disagree with our holding will likely mark it as the product of an activist judge. This is manifestly not an activist court. Rather, this case came to us as the result of the activism of an ill-informed faction on a school board. . . . The breath-taking inanity of the [school board's] decision is evident when considered against the factual backdrop revealed through this trial" (Lawrence, 2005, 3-A).

Before the start of a celebratory news conference in Harrisburg, Tammy Kitzmiller, a parent of two daughters in the Dover district and a named plaintiff in the case, *Kitzmiller et al. v. Dover*, joked with other plaintiffs that she had an idea for a new bumper sticker: "Judge Jones for President." Christy Rehm, another plaintiff, said to the others, "We've done something amazing here, not only with this decision, but with the election" of a new school board—a surprising outcome in which Dover voters ousted eight board members who had backed the intelligent design policy. The winners ran on a Democratic ticket, while Dover usually votes majority Republican (Goodstein, 2005).

John West, a senior fellow at the Discovery Institute's Center for Science and Culture, a leading intelligent-design think tank based in Seattle, said that Judge Jones had displayed a "grandiosity" and "egregious" judicial activism. He agreed that the decision had dealt a heavy blow, however. "There's no doubt that people will trumpet this and that now they can say a federal judge agrees and that doesn't help," West said. "His angry tone was not helpful" (Powell, 2005, A-1).

While Jones's 139-page decision raised the legal bar for intelligent design, even those who agreed with him doubted that his ruling had closed the case completely, as some polls still indicated that 40 to 55 percent of U.S. citizens favored a strict biblical creationist view of evolution. "We thought we had put a stake through the heart of creation science 25 years ago and it evolved and here we are again," said Michael Ruse, a philosopher of science at Florida State University, who frequently debates intelligent-design advocates (Powell, 2005, A-1). "Jones saw it for the shoddy theory it is, but its advocates are intelligent and savvy men and women and they'll be back" (Powell, 2005, A-1). Indicating the enduring nature of the issue, one of the school board members who were defeated in November, William Buckingham, told the press: "I'm still waiting for a judge or anyone to show me anywhere in the Constitution where there's a separation of church and state" (Lawrence, 2005, 3-A). Thompson indicated that challenges to evolution based on intelligent design were going forward in more than 20 other states, and that he was considering representation of several teachers and parents there (Lawrence, 2005, 3-A).

"This decision is a poster child for a half-century secularist reign of terror that's coming to a rapid end with [U.S. Supreme Court] Justice Roberts and soon-to-be Justice Alito," said Richard Land, who is president of the Southern Baptist Convention's Ethics & Religious Liberty Commission and is a political ally of White House adviser Karl Rove. "This was an extremely injudicious judge who went way, way beyond his boundaries—if he had any eyes on advancing up the judicial ladder, he just sawed off the bottom rung" (Powell, 2005, A-3). Still, few advocates of intelligent design tried to hide their dismay with the judge's decision. The Discovery Institute declared that the judge has a "pernicious understanding of what intellectual and religious freedom in America means" (Powell, 2005, A-3). William A. Dembski, a philosopher and math professor at Southern Seminary in Louisville, wrote in his Web log that the loss in Pennsylvania means thousands more young people "would continue to be indoctrinated into a neo-Darwinian view of biological origins" (Powell, 2005, A-3).

The battle over teaching of evolution didn't die with Judge Jones's decision. During 2006, for example, right-wing religious interests played a role in the House of Representatives' passage of the Public Expression of Religion Act—HR 2679—which prohibits attorneys who successfully challenge violations of the First Amendment's Establishment Clause from recovering attorneys' fees. The bill thus discourages suits that challenge unconstitutional government actions advancing religion, such as teaching of intelligent design. This bill, if passed by the Senate and signed by the president, would effectively negate a federal statute, 42 United States Code Section 1988, which allows attorneys to recover compensation from defendants for their fees after successful representation of plaintiffs asserting violation of constitutional or civil rights.

THE VATICAN VIEWS DOVER DECISION AS CORRECT

The official Vatican newspaper published an article early in January 2006 calling Judge Jones's decision correct. "If the model proposed by Darwin is not considered sufficient, one should search for another," Fiorenzo Facchini, a professor of evolutionary biology at the University of Bologna, wrote in the January 16–17 edition of the paper, *L'Osservatore Romano* (Fisher and Dean, 2006).

"It is not correct . . . to stray from the field of science while pretending to do science," Facchini wrote, calling intelligent design unscientific. "It only creates confusion between the scientific plane and those that are philosophical or religious" (Fisher and Dean, 2006). Facchini wrote that scientists could not rule out a divine "superior design" to creation and the history of mankind. But he said Catholic thought did not preclude a design fashioned through an evolutionary process. "God's project of creation can be carried out through secondary causes in the natural course of events, without having to think of miraculous interventions that point in this or that direction," he wrote (Fisher and Dean, 2006).

The article was not an official edict of the Catholic Church, but some observers took it as indicative of Pope Benedict XVI's thinking. Others dismissed it. Robert L. Crowther, spokesman for the Center for Science and Culture at the Discovery Institute dismissed the article as little more than trying "to put words in the Vatican's mouth" (Fisher and Dean, 2006). Advocates of intelligent design pointed out that Pope Benedict has indicated that human beings "are not some casual and meaningless product of evolution." In November, he called the creation of the universe an "intelligent project," wording welcomed by supporters of intelligent design.

"Physical scientists have it easy. Astronomers don't feel obligated to argue with those who think the moon is made of green cheese, nor geographers with those who think the world is flat," wrote John Southin in Ontario's *Brockville Recorder and Times*. "Suggestions that such 'controversies' be taught in science classes are brushed aside without apology or public outcry. Crackpot notions like creationism and intelligent design deserve the same fate, but biologists have become burdened with the Sisyphean task of endlessly defending both the fact and the theory of evolution. If evolution were just a peripheral issue in biology, no one would bother. Unfortunately, evolution underlies and unifies the whole of biological science, and almost none of biology would make any sense without that fundamental understanding" (Southin, 2005, A-6). "Although religious delusion accounts for most of the so-called controversy, part has to do with the common misunderstanding of what the term 'theory' means in science. In everyday parlance, a theory is a hunch, a speculation, an imperfect fact. In science, however, a theory is something quite different: it's a model that organizes and explains all the relevant data in a consistent manner," wrote Southin (2005, A-6.).

The controversy reached Australia as well. Peter Goers wrote in the South Australia *Sunday Mail*:

> Thus is a heartfelt apology. Call me ignorant. Recently I criticised Intelligent Design as "born-again creationism." How dare I. Now I've seen the error of my ways I realize I have no right to my opinion. I had a record number of letters and emails from born-again Christians and I thank them for their intolerant self-righteousness. They told me I was "stupid," "ignorant," "a man who believes the garbage of science." My heinous mistakes include reading books other than the *Bible* or texts they sanction. "Unless you see the foolishness of evolution there is no hope for you," wrote one fine, wise Christian. Now . . . I am part of the inquisition against science and reason. . . . I'm sorry I wrote sarcastically that God created the fossils to confuse us. He didn't. All the fossils came from Noah's flood when Noah, his wife Joan of Arc and his sons Shemp, Curly and Moe were saving every species on Earth. I now realise I was not fit to be called a Christian and that I was really a part of the "atheistic conspiracy" which, as one correspondent kindly indicated, includes scientists, astronomers, judges, lawyers, magistrates, solicitors, barristers, doctors, dentists and politicians. They are all going to hell. (Goers, 2005, 42)

INTELLIGENT DESIGN CONTESTED IN CALIFORNIA

As scientists toasted new understandings of evolution, and shortly after Judge Jones's ruling in Pennsylvania, a group of parents sued a rural California school district, complaining that its four-week high-school elective course on intelligent design, creationism, and evolution, offered as philosophy, was biased in favor of religion. Eleven parents sought a temporary restraining order to stop the course, which had been scheduled to end February 3, 2006. The class had started January 3 with 15 students. The high school in the Tehachapi Mountains about 75 miles north of Los Angeles enrolls about 500 students from several small communities.

Sharon Lemburg, a social studies teacher and soccer coach, had proposed the course at Frazier Mountain High School in Lebec, north of Los Angeles, during December 2005. The course was approved by the board of trustees on a three-to-two vote, despite testimony from science and math teachers that it would undermine the science curriculum (Goodstein, 2006). Lemburg, wife of the local Assemblies of God's minister, amended her syllabus and the course title, from "Philosophy of

Intelligent Design" to "Philosophy of Design" after parents complained. Lemburg defended the course in a letter to the weekly *Mountain Enterprise*. "I believe this is the class that the Lord wanted me to teach," she wrote (Barbassa, 2006).

The parents, represented by lawyers associated with Americans United for Separation of Church and State, contended that Lemburg was advocating intelligent design and "young earth creationism" and was not examining those ideas in a neutral way *vis a vis* evolution. The parents asserted that the initial course syllabus listed 24 videos, 23 of which were, they said, "produced or distributed by religious organizations and assume a pro-creationist, anti-evolution stance." A course description distributed to students and parents said, "This class will take a close look at evolution as a theory and will discuss the scientific, biological and biblical aspects that suggest why Darwin's philosophy is not rock-solid" (Goodstein, 2006).

The suit also contended that the syllabus listed two evolution experts who would speak to the class. One was a local parent and scientist who said he had already declined the speaking invitation and was now suing the district; the other was Francis H. C. Crick, the codiscoverer of the structure of DNA, who died in 2004. "This sends a strong signal to school districts across the country that they cannot promote creationism or intelligent design as an alternative to evolution, whether they do so in a science class or a humanities class," said Ayesha N. Khan, legal director for Americans United for Separation of Church and State (Barbassa, 2006). A settlement of the suit was reached just before a federal judge was scheduled to hold a hearing on it. All five of the cash-strapped district's trustees voted to settle the potentially expensive case, according to Pete Carton, the district's attorney, even as Superintendent John Wight said, he thought the subject was proper for a philosophy class (Barbassa, 2006).

The Discovery Institute, which prefers to "teach the controversy" about evolution, not to out-and-out deny its relevance, said it had opposed the overt nature of this particular class. "We oppose mandating the teaching of ID [intelligent design]," said John West of the Discovery Institute. "We opposed that class," which was laden with young-Earth creationism as well as ID. The institute also opposed the Dover, Pennsylvania policy that was removed by Judge Johnson's ruling in 2005. The Discovery Institute has produced a video, "How to Teach the Controversy Legally" that does not mention intelligent design (Culotta, 2006, 770).

CHRISTIAN SCHOOLS VERSUS THE UNIVERSITY OF CALIFORNIA

At about the same time, also in California, an evangelical day school sued the University of California system alleging bias against conservative Christian viewpoints. The suit was provoked after the university refused to accept for-credit courses taken by applicants at Calvary Chapel Christian School in Murrieta, Calif., which endorse the Bible's absolute authority and challenges the theory of evolution. Federal district Judge S. James Otero in Los Angeles disallowed a motion by the university's lawyers to throw the lawsuit out of court. This may have been the first lawsuit of its type. "This is potentially a very serious lawsuit," said University of Akron political scientist John C. Green, with "important implications for the broader set of relations between religious groups and universities" (Locke, 2006, 3-E). The important question is whether a public university system will accept students from conservative Christian schools.

Calvary's suit asserts that Christian schools are being forced to avoid references to scripture in their curricula in favor of secular points of view, which is "pure discrimination against a particular viewpoint," according to Ken Smitherman, president of the Colorado Springs-based Christian schools association, with 800 member campuses in California alone. The lawsuit asserts that the University of California system disallows classes from conservative Christian academies as it approves other courses with particular viewpoints such as "Introduction to Buddhism" and "Issues in African History." University of California officials respond that those courses are taught from an academic standpoint, not for personal religious growth (Locke, 2006, 3-E).

Officials at the University of California replied that their objections are academic, and that they have a right to set standards for the qualifications of applicants. Courses like "Christianity and Morality in American Literature" and "Christianity's Influence on American History" do not meet those standards as now written (Locke, 2006, 3-E). Textbooks that University of California questions come from Beka Books of Pensacola, Fla., and Bob Jones University Press of Greenville, SC. "Biology for Christian Schools" appears to settle the evolution debate in an introduction that says the Bible trumps any contradictory information students might encounter.

The suit, filed on behalf of six college-bound students at Calvary, alleges that they face unusual difficulty getting into University of California's ten campuses because the university will not certify certain courses at their school. Robert Tyler, an attorney representing the school, said that the students score above average on standardized tests, indicating that they receive a solid education regardless of the courses' advocacy of Christianity. Tyler said that Calvary students are getting the information they need. "They're going to be well-prepared entering college because they're not hearing just a creationist viewpoint or just an evolutionist viewpoint. They're learning all the viewpoints" (Locke, 2006, 3-E).

A SCHOOL BOARD SWITCH IN OHIO

The Ohio State Board of Education unanimously adopted a statement during December 2002 requiring that tenth graders be able to "describe how scientists continue to investigate and critically analyze aspects of evolutionary theory," with a parenthetical note that "this benchmark does not mandate the teaching or testing of intelligent design." The proposed lesson plan was optional and did not use the words "intelligent design," but its explanation of basic concepts related to the fossil record and other matters paralleled those in the texts *Icons of Evolution* and *Of Pandas and People*, written by proponents of intelligent design (Rudoren, 2006). The Discovery Institute supported Ohio's "critical analysis" approach as a model for the nation, and ardently defended the lesson plan.

After that, New Mexico, Minnesota, and Kansas adopted similar standards, and Pennsylvania listed evolution among half a dozen theories to be critically analyzed (before Judge Jones's decision). Only Ohio had a model lesson plan, however, which was adopted by a divided board in 2004, which provided teachers a practical how-to guide. It is unclear how frequently it is used (Rudoren, 2006). Supporters of evolution asserted that the standard was borrowed from intelligent design and creationist literature. "It's the same stuff that went to trial in Dover and was found not to be science," said Patricia Princehouse, a biology professor at Case Western University (Lawrence, 2005, 3-A).

Following the Dover decision, however, the Ohio Board of Education, which had been the first in the United States to single out evolution for special scrutiny, voted 11 to 4 February 14, 2006 to eliminate the guideline that tenth-grade biology classes include critical analysis of evolution and a model lesson plan. Opponents of the Ohio intelligent-design statement also had threatened to sue along the lines of the Dover case. The president of the National Academy of Sciences also urged the board to change the lesson and the underlying curriculum guidelines to "conform to established scientific standards" (Rudoren, 2006).

The switch was based more on the Dover case than public opinion in Ohio. The Discovery Institute released a Zogby International poll it had commissioned indicating that 69 percent of Ohio voters believe scientific evidence against evolution should be included in public-school curricula, and 76 percent agreed that "students should also be able to learn about scientific evidence that points to an intelligent design of life" (Rudoren, 2006).

Even after the school board ditched it, supporters of the proposed-then-scuttled evolution critique believed that the curriculum was constitutional. "If I had the money, I'd pay for the lawsuit," said David Zanotti, president of the conservative American Policy Roundtable in Strongsville, Ohio. "They should sue or shut up" (Rudoren, 2006).

EVOLUTION CHALLENGE DEFEATED IN UTAH

The Utah House of Representatives on February 27, 2006 defeated 46–28 a bill meant to challenge the theory of evolution in high-school science classes, dealing a blow to critics of evolution in a conservative state with a legislature dominated by Republican members of the Church of Jesus Christ of Latter-day Saints (Mormon). The defeat came as the majority whip, Stephen H. Urquhart, a Mormon, said he thought God did not have an argument with science. The Origins of Life Bill, in its initial form, would have required teachers to issue a disclaimer to students saying that not all scientists agree about evolution, *vis a vis* the origin of species. It did not mention any alternative theory to Darwinism (Johnson, 2006).

CONFLICT IN COBB COUNTY, GEORGIA

A child's fascination with dinosaurs sparked a dispute over evolution in Marietta, Georgia, a fast-growing, affluent suburb of more than 600,000 people northwest of Atlanta. One of Marjorie Rogers's two sons told her that old textbooks described the dinosaurs' great antiquity. Like others who adhere to a literal reading of the Book of Genesis, Rogers, a lawyer, believes that Earth is several thousand years old, while most scientists who base their estimates on the radioactive decay of rock samples, place Earth's age at about 4 billion years. Rogers challenged the books' description of evolution, drawing support from other residents in Marietta, a complex of upscale homes, high-tech office parks, and shopping malls.

This dispute provoked the Cobb County school board to affix warning labels on biology textbooks saying that evolution "is a theory, not a fact" (Whoriskey, 2005). The labels made Cobb County one more fissure of conflict in the national debate over evolution, as they became grounds for a federal-court lawsuit by parents who believe that such study is an illegal intrusion of religious doctrine into public education. A trial in the case began during December 2005, about the same time as the case before Judge Jones in Dover, Pennsylvania.

Rogers was described by Peter Whoriskey in the Washington *Post* as "a BMW-driving graduate of the University of Georgia who plays tennis twice a week and says her life is wrapped around caring for her two sons." Jeffrey Selman, the lead plaintiff in the case to remove the stickers, was a technical worker who belonged to the same tennis group and lives with his wife and son in a Colonial-style subdivision on a lake. Selman and Rogers had moved to Cobb County from elsewhere: Rogers is a self-described "Navy brat," Selman was born in the Bronx (Whoriskey, 2005).

As Cobb County was considering purchase of new biology textbooks during late 2001, Rogers began a petition drive among friends and church groups that acquired 2,300 signatures. The school board then held a meeting that was brisk with debate, and voted to paste the stickers on several science textbooks, which said: "This textbook contains material on evolution. Evolution is a theory, not a fact, regarding the origin of living things. This material should be approached with an open mind, studied carefully, and critically considered" (Whoriskey, 2005). The wording was described by board members as a compromise that took into consideration the beliefs of students and parents who objected to the theory of evolution while continuing to teach it.

After considering Selman's suit during January 2005, presented by lawyers supported by the American Civil Liberties Union, U.S. District Judge Clarence Cooper ordered the stickers removed. An "informed, reasonable observer would interpret the sticker to convey a message of endorsement of religion," he wrote.

The sticker "sends a message to those who believe in evolution that they are political outsiders," wrote Cooper (Whoriskey, 2005). The school board then appealed.

On May 25, 2006, a federal appeals court vacated the district court's ruling that had ordered removal of stickers from 35,000 textbooks telling students evolution is "a theory not a fact." Judge Ed Carnes of the circuit court wrote that the record did not indicate that the school board acted with religious intent (which would have been unconstitutional), but with "rampant confusion." The appeals court asked the district court to "flesh out" the record or conduct a new trial (Holden, 2006, 1292).

THE ULTIMATE IN RELATIVITY, KANSAS STYLE

How many versions of reality do we share? During the early 1990s, the Czech playwright and former president Vaclav Havel and the French philosopher Bruno Latour held that the age of a singular truth had ended. According to this view, "the end of objectivity" has arrived, recognizing that the "laws" of science are socially constructed, not "discovered," as just one more angle on the intellectual fire. Everyone has a view, and all were equally valid.

Havel may not have had the Kansas State Board of Education in mind went he served up this version of relativity. Provoked by popular opposition to Darwin's theory of evolution, the board revised the state's science standards to include criticism of evolution, and in so doing, according to at least one observer, "promulgated a new definition of science itself" (Overbye, 2005). The Kansas State Board of Education has had a record of meddling with big scientific issues. It tried to abolish the teaching of evolution and the Big Bang in schools during 1999, but retreated in 2001.

The changes in the official state definition of scientific inquiry for the purposes of public education in Kansas were legalistic, involving, for the most part, removal of two words: "natural explanations." This action erased a previously ironclad distinction between the natural and the supernatural that has been fundamental to the physical sciences since the time of Galileo. Moves were being undertaken late in 2005 by some state legislators in Michigan and Indiana to revise science-education standards to challenge evolutionary theory in some ways similar to the decision made by the Kansas state school board. Late in 2005 and early in 2006, bills seeking to teach intelligent design in public schools failed to pass in Indiana, Mississippi, and Utah.

The former definition in Kansas had read: "Science is the human activity of seeking natural explanations for what we observe in the world around us." The new definition called science "a systematic method of continuing investigation that uses observation, hypothesis testing, measurement, experimentation, logical argument and theory building to lead to more adequate explanations of natural phenomena" (Overbye, 2005).

Adrian Melott, a physics professor at the University of Kansas who opposed the change, said, "The only reason to take out 'natural explanations' is if you want to open the door to supernatural explanations." Gerald Holton, a professor of the history of science at Harvard, said removing those two words means "anything goes" (Overbye, 2005).

Proponents of the school board's revised definition of scientific method argued that an assumption that the methods of science can explain all natural phenomena promotes materialism, secular humanism, and atheism, leading to a doctrine that life is accidental. Indeed, they said in material online at kansasscience2005.com, it might even be unconstitutional to promulgate that attitude in a classroom because it is not ideologically "neutral" (Overbye, 2005).

Most scientists' daily work is usually more prosaic than a search for the laws of human motivation, however. The scientist's job description, said Steven Weinberg, a physicist and Nobel laureate at the University of Texas, provokes a search for natural explanations, just as a mechanic looks for mechanical reasons why a car won't run. "This doesn't mean that they commit themselves to the view that this is all there is," Weinberg wrote. "Many scientists (including me) think that this is the case, but other scientists are religious, and believe that what is observed in nature is at least in part a result of God's will." Many scientists define their work according to the notion of falsifiability as elucidated by the philosopher Karl Popper. A scientific statement, he said, is one that can be proved wrong, like "the sun always rises in the east" or "light in a vacuum travels 186,000 miles a second" (Overbye, 2005). According to Popper's definition, a scientific theory cannot be "proved"; but only disproved. A scientific theory may be used as a basis for a prediction to be tested and possibly proved incorrect. Scientists generally agree however, that requiring a theory to be testable excludes supernatural explanations. The supernatural, by definition, includes elements of faith that cannot be tested by ordinary observation.

INTELLIGENT DESIGN A FADING MOVEMENT?

By the summer of 2006, intelligent design seemed to be fading as an intellectual movement. Even in Kansas, where criticism of Darwinism had been popular for several years, primary elections for school board positions in August indicated voters' growing preference for traditional biological sciences. Newspapers in the Midwest that are not noted for their liberalism also came out in support of Darwin. The consistently Republican Omaha *World-Herald*, for example, concluded an editorial on the subject by quoting John G. West of the Discovery Institute: "The debate over Darwin's theory will be won or lost over the science." "Please," remarked the newspaper, "Let him be correct" ("Let Science Win," 2006, 6-B).

In Kansas, fundamentalist Republicans who had approved new classroom standards that called evolution into question (urging students to seek "more adequate explanations of natural phenomena") lost control of the State Board of Education.

Janet Waugh, a Kansas City Democrat who opposed the new standards, defeated a more conservative Democrat who favored the anti-evolution language with 65 percent of the vote. A victory by pro-evolution Republican candidate Jana Shaver over conservative Republican Brad Patzer, who supported the standards treating evolution as a flawed theory, meant conservatives would probably be reduced to four seats of ten. "In a state where a fierce fight over how much students should be taught about the criticism of evolution has gone back and forth since 1999," commented the *New York Times*, "the election results were seen as a significant defeat for the movement of intelligent design" (Davey and Blumenthal, 2006).

Five seats were contested, all held by fundamentalists, two of whom lost. Because voter turnout in the primary was only 18 percent, the representative nature of this change was open to question. The Kansas standards, which were to take effect in classrooms in 2007, do not specifically require or prohibit discussion of intelligent design. They call for students to learn about "the best evidence for modern evolutionary theory, but also to learn about areas where scientists are raising scientific criticisms of the theory" (Davey and Blumenthal, 2006). The standards called for students to learn about "the best evidence for modern evolutionary theory, but also to learn about areas where scientists are raising scientific criticisms of the theory." In one of many "additional specificities" that the board added to the standards, it stated, "Biological evolution postulates an unguided natural process that has no discernable direction or goal" (Blumenthal, 2006).

The chairman of the board, Dr. Steve E. Abrams, a veterinarian and the leader of the former fundamentalist majority, said his belief that God created the universe 6,500 years ago had nothing to do with the board's consideration of science standards. "In my personal faith, yes, I am a creationist," he said. "But that doesn't have anything to do with science. I can separate them." Abrams said he agreed "my personal views of Scripture have no room in the science classroom" (Blumenthal, 2006).

NO JOKE AT COLLEGE LEVEL IN KANSAS

Paul Mirecki, professor and chair of Religious Studies at the University of Kansas, has a talent for ironic humor and self-mockery. When Mirecki got to joshing about creationism in Kansas, he was told that some things are not funny. He might as well have been cracking jokes about mullahs having phone sex in Tehran. Mirecki's intellectual pursuits soon led to a severe roadside beating.

On November 19, 2005, Mirecki sent an e-mail to a Yahoo listserv discussion board moderated by the University of Kansas' Society of Open-Minded Atheists and Agnostics (SOMA), for which Mirecki served as faculty adviser. Among other activities, SOMA holds a "soul auction" during which members auction off their souls for charity. It also hosts guest speakers on Darwin Day, February 14. In the e-mail message, Mirecki referred to religious conservatives as "fundies." He also said that a course depicting intelligent design as mythology would be a "nice slap in their big fat face" (Milburn, December 1, 2005). Mirecki addressed the message to "my fellow damned" and signed off with: "Doing my part to [tick] off the religious right, Evil Dr. P" ("Professor Apologizes," 2005).

Mirecki's course, "Special Topics in Religion: Intelligent Design, Creationism and Other Religious Mythologies," had enrolled 25 students for the spring 2006 semester by the end of November 2005, when the "fundies" came a' calling. The class quickly went down in flames as the university scrambled to limit potential damage to its state appropriation. Mirecki canceled the class November 30, 2005. Thus, by 2005, religious fundamentalists in Kansas were shaping some state-university curricula.

Mirecki's class had been a reaction to the Kansas Board of Education's decision to include more criticism of evolution in its science standards for public-school students. Mirecki, who holds a doctorate in theology from Harvard University, by 2005 had taught biblical studies and other religious-studies courses at University of Kansas for 16 years and enjoyed an international reputation for his research. He specializes in ancient Mediterranean cultures' languages and religions, as well as ancient Greek and Coptic manuscripts.

Mirecki apologized, saying:

> My concern is that students with a serious interest in this important subject matter would not be well served by the learning environment my e-mails and the public distribution of them have created. It would not be fair to the students. It was not my intent when I wrote the e-mails, but I understand now that these words have offended many on this campus and beyond, and for that I take full responsibility. I made a mistake in not leading by example, in this student organization e-mail forum, the importance of discussing differing viewpoints in a civil and respectful manner. ("Religious Studies," 2005)

The faculty of Mirecki's department had approved the course but dropped the reference to mythology. The course, originally called "Special Topics in Religion: Intelligent Design, Creationism and other Religious Mythologies," was then called "Intelligent Design and Creationism." Following the furor, Mirecki said he would teach the class "as a serious academic subject and in a manner that respects all points of view" ("Professor Apologizes," 2005).

Mirecki's intention to critique creationism and intelligent design was taken as "vile" and "hateful" by several responsible people in Kansas. University of Kansas Chancellor Robert Hemenway wasted no words condemning Mirecki. He was quoted by the Associated Press as saying that Mirecki's comments were "repugnant and vile" (Milburn, December 1, 2005). "It misrepresents everything the university is to stand for," Hemenway was reported to have said. State Senator Kay O'Connor said that the university did the right thing. "I'm glad they decided to listen to the public. The public response was so negative because of what seemed to be so hateful coming from the K.U. professor," said O'Connor, a Republican. "I am critical of his hatefulness toward Christians" (Milburn, December 1, 2005).

Despite the chancellor's off-the-cuff remark, the university officially defended the class. "Given the current national debate, it is especially appropriate that intelligent design and creationism be treated as academic subjects in a university-level religious studies class," Provost David Shulenburger said ("Professor Apologizes," 2005).

Talk swirled among state legislators regarding withholding funding from the university. "If you read his e-mail, it's not a short e-mail. It's not a little blurb. It's venomous," said Rep. Brenda Landwehr, vice chairwoman of the House Appropriations Committee. "He's not sorry he wrote it. He's sorry it became public," said Landwehr, a Republican from Wichita. Steve Abrams, chairman of the Kansas State Board of Education and chief architect of the board's new science standards, said Mirecki's e-mail shows he "doesn't have much respect for other viewpoints" ("Professor Apologizes," 2005).

Mirecki was not left alone after he apologized. On December 5, he reported being beaten with a metal object by two men. Mirecki told Douglas County, Kansas, police that he was on his way to breakfast at about 6:40 a.m. along a rural road south of Lawrence when he noticed two white men between 30 and 40 years of age in a large pickup truck tailgating his vehicle. When Mirecki stopped and confronted them, Mirecki was beaten as the men condemned his contempt for religious fundamentalists. Mirecki was treated for a broken tooth, bruises, and abrasions at Lawrence Memorial Hospital (Klepper, 2005, n.p.).

Even after the beating, pressure rose on Mirecki to resign his position as chair of the University of Kansas' Department of Religious Studies. On December 7, Mirecki resigned, but remained a tenured professor. Late in December 2005, Mirecki's position as chair was filled by Timothy Miller, a scholar of alternative religions in the United States, a University of Kansas faculty member since 1973, who had been department chair between 1997 and 2002.

Mirecki later said he had been forced to give up his department chairmanship, and faulted the university for caving in to pressure that denied his First Amendment rights ("Religion Professor," 2005). The University has a duty, as a protector of intellectual honesty and debate, to support its teachers, Mirecki said, adding that he felt let down by the administration and colleagues who sought his resignation. "Creationism is mythology," Mirecki told the Lawrence *Journal-World*. "Intelligent design is mythology. It's not science. They try to make it sound like science. It clearly is not. At this point, I just want this to be over. . . . The university penalized me and denied me my Constitutionally protected right to speak and express my mind," he wrote in a statement. "I've become radioactive and the university's administrators won't support me" ("Religion Professor," 2005).

University spokeswoman Lynn Bretz replied that Mirecki had stepped down from his chairmanship on the recommendation of faculty members and that he decided to cancel his intelligent design course on his own. Bretz said the university believes the course should be taught in the future. "The university stands unequivocally in support of his First Amendment rights and his rights to academic freedom," Bretz said. Chancellor Robert Hemenway said the university has supported Mirecki. "Professor Mirecki still has a job at the University of Kansas," Hemenway said. "That would appear to be support for his rights to his tenured position and his rights to free speech. . . . The university deplores the fact that he was apparently attacked. We've said so" ("Religion Professor," 2005).

Ironically, as controversy exploded over Mirecki's class, a religious college in Kansas set up a class with similar subject matter with very little fanfare. The difference, perhaps, was that the faculty members who taught the class had not circulated any jokes about "fundies" on the Internet. Ottawa University of Kansas offered its class during the spring semester of 2006, titled: "Intelligent Design: Neither Science Nor Theology." The course was taught by Richard Menninger, a religion professor, and Henry Tillinghast, a biology professor. Ottawa University, with about 500 students, is affiliated with the American Baptist Churches U.S.A. According to an Associated Press report, "The two professors teaching the class side with the science community in saying intelligent design shouldn't be considered science. Menninger said he also was not willing to relegate the course to religion or theology classes, where some scientists said it belonged. "We're not convinced it falls into either category," he told *The Topeka Capital-Journal* ("Ottawa University," 2005).

"CLOSET CREATIONISM" IN SCIENCE CLASSROOMS?

A majority of science teachers accept and teach evolutionary theory, but a national survey in 2005 indicated that one-third of the teachers said that they have faced pressure, mainly from parents and students, to marginalize evolution as subject matter. Many often do so to avoid conflicts. Additionally, "There's a consistent, a significant number of biology teachers in public schools who are creationists," asserted Randy Moore, a professor of biology at the University of Minnesota who has written extensively on what might be called "closet creationism" in public schools. "Despite decades of science education reform, these numbers have remained pretty consistent" (Hirsch, 2005, 1-A).

About ten studies have been published since 1999 that attempt to assay science teachers' attitudes toward intelligent design and creationism. In six of them, public school biology teachers endorsed teaching creationism in some form alongside evolutionary theory in numbers ranging from nearly 20 percent in Minnesota to nearly half in some Kansas schools and more than two-thirds in Kentucky (Hirsch, 2005, 1-A).

According to Arthur Hirsch, writing in the Baltimore *Sun*:

> In two states, 40 percent of biology teachers say they allow little or no class time for evolutionary theory. . . . In five states, nearly one in five teachers do not accept the scientific validity of evolutionary theory. In Texas, Louisiana, and Minnesota, more than

one in five teachers say they accept the scientific validity of creationism—rejecting common ancestry of living things and accepting the involvement of a supernatural force in the development of life on Earth. (Hirsch, 2005, 1-A)

According to a survey of nearly 800 Indiana biology teachers published in 2002, 19 percent rejected evolutionary theory and 14 percent said they were "undecided" about it. More than 40 percent described their classroom approach to evolutionary theory as "avoidance," or "briefly mentioned." Wayne W. Carley, executive director of the National Association of Biology Teachers, said, "It disturbs me greatly when I see those numbers," reflecting teachers who "don't understand the difference between science and religion" (Hirsch, 2005, 1-A).

"I'm a creationist and I plan my schedule so that I run out of time and don't have to cover evolution," one teacher said. Another said, "I present evolution and creationism and let students make up their minds." Another said, "I talk a lot about the holes in evolution; students need to know this information more than [that] they came from monkeys." A public school teacher in Faribault, Minn., Rodney LeVake, was transferred from teaching biology during 1998 when he refused to follow the curriculum on evolution. LeVake later sued the school district; ultimately the U.S. Supreme Court declined to hear the case (Hirsch, 2005, 1-A).

Barbara Reger, head of the science department in an Indianapolis middle school, said that she believes God created the Earth, animals, plants, women, and men. She tells children that some scientists insist nature shows the mark of a higher power's design. "In her eighth-grade science class at Creston Middle School," reported Hirsch, "Reger says she highlights the strengths and what she believes are flaws in the evidence for evolution, presenting the intelligent design argument as a competing scientific concept. She does not accept the notion that natural causes alone could account for the variety and complexity of life" (Hirsch, 2005, 1-A). "I point out people who believe that a higher power created all this," Reger said. "Other people believe we evolved from earlier life forms" (Hirsch, 2005, 1-A).

Doug Cowan, a science teacher at Curtis Senior High School in University Place, Washington, published articles in *The Christian Science Monitor* and other newspapers during 2005, which describe his approach as "teaching the controversy," which is advocated by the Discovery Institute. To encourage student engagement in critical thinking, Cowan presents his students with the evidence for evolutionary theory and its weaknesses, offering intelligent design as a competing argument (Hirsch, 2005, 1-A).

On the other hand, Colin Dovichin said that his contract to teach in a northwestern Minnesota rural school district was not renewed in 2001 because he taught evolutionary theory. Dovichin said that the parents and the superintendent spoke with him, and objected to his teaching of the subject. The school board said the decision not to renew the contract was not related to his teaching of evolution (Hirsch, 2005, 1-A).

AN ANTI-DARWINIST "INSURGENCY"

Caroline Crocker, teaching at Northern Virginia Community College, has said that she wants to "establish a small beachhead for an insurgency that ultimately aims to topple Darwin's view that humans and apes are distant cousins." As a nontenured instructor, Crocker, an advocate of intelligent design, had little institutional protection, but as a biologist, she wanted to tell students she believes that the scientific establishment is perpetrating fraud, then hunting down critics of evolution to ruin them, disguising an atheistic view of life as science (Vedantam, 2006).

Crocker lectures that Nazi Germany adopted Darwin's ideas about natural selection, the credo that only the fittest survive, and followed them to extreme conclusions—anti-Semitism, eugenics, and death camps. "What happened in Germany in World War II was based on science, that some genes and some people should be killed," Crocker said quietly. "My grandfather had a genetic problem and was put in the hospital and killed" (Vedantam, 2006). "Right now, in our society, we have an underlying philosophy of naturalism, that there is a material explanation for everything," Crocker replied. "Evolution came with that philosophy" (Vedantam, 2006).

Crocker asserted that she lost a job at George Mason University for teaching about problems with evolution, a charge that the university denies. George Mason University spokesman Daniel Walsch denied that the school had fired Crocker. She was a part-time faculty member, he said, and was let go at the end of her contract period for reasons unrelated to her views on intelligent design. "We wholeheartedly support academic freedom," he said. But teachers also have a responsibility to stick to subjects they were hired to teach, he added, and intelligent design belonged in a religion class, not biology. Does academic freedom "literally give you the right to talk about anything, whether it has anything to do with the subject matter or not? The answer is no" (Vedantam, 2006).

Those who argue that Darwin was, himself, a believer in "social Darwinism" have a point. In *The Descent of Man*, Darwin noted that it was "highly injurious to the race of man" that civilized nations care for and keep alive "the imbecile, the maimed and the sick." And while natural selection ascribes no particular value to any trait or race—fitness is merely how well an organism adapts to its environment—Darwin reflected Anglo-centric prejudices of his time, in nineteenth-century colonial Britain, when he quoted others who worried that the "careless, squalid, unaspiring Irishman" and the "inferior" Celt usually multiply faster than the "frugal, foreseeing, self-respecting, ambitious" Scot and the Saxon. Darwin believed society would be aided by "the weak in body and mind refraining from marriage" (Vedantam, 2006). Darwin also spoke out strongly against slavery.

Darwin was a complex individual and (as when studying the Bible) an exploration of his life can take a reader to more than one ideological destination. Darwin, for example, had planned to become an Anglican clergyman before an opportunity allowed him to become a naturalist aboard the HMS Beagle. On his travels, Darwin expected "to see God's magnificence manifested in nature," said Russell Moore, dean of the theology school at Southern Baptist Theological Seminary in Louisville, Kentucky. Throughout the voyage, Darwin held closely to his faith. He was even teased for being such a devout believer, said Thomas Dixon, a historian at Lancaster University in England. That faith endured as Darwin was writing *The Origin of Species*, and it was eventually shaken less by his scientific findings than by a personal tragedy that caused Darwin to reject the existence of a Christian God who was loving and good. At one point in Darwin's voyage to South America, Moore told Vedantam, it was in Brazil, where, "His blood ran cold to see slaves in manacles being tortured by Catholic traders. Darwin was enraged as a Christian, but also as a scientist, because he recognized that the slave trade relied on the false notion that slaves were a different, inferior and exploitable species" (Vedantam, 2006).

EVOLVING HUMOR

Replying to intelligent design and creationism, scientists have developed a number of deprecating jokes and jest-filled songs. "The scientific community just isn't touching John Q. Public," said Donald U. Wise, an emeritus professor of geology at the University of Massachusetts. "We just have to find a way of breaking through. The only way we will do that is with humor" (Dean, 2005). Wise's first foray into evolution humor was a parody song about intelligent design called "Marching Song of the Incompetents," which was sung "lustily and completely off key" by about 300 of geologists at an otherwise conventional meeting of the Geological Society of America during October 2005 (Ohpurleese, 2005).

The song, to the tune of "Battle Hymn of the Republic," describes the author's bones as proclaiming "a story of incompetent design," in that "My back still hurts, my sinus clogs, my teeth just won't align . . . If I had drawn the blueprint I would certainly resign . . . Design is but a mere illusion. Writing in the *New York Times*, Cornelia Dean described the song as describing "some of the ills to which the human body is prey, all of which result from the way evolution produced *Homo Sapiens* from our hairier hominid ancestors." The spine, for example, was well adapted to four-footed locomotion or even knuckle-dragging, but it has "doomed primates to ruptured disks and lower back pain ever since they began walking on two feet. And people suffering from crooked teeth or sinus trouble can thank the way the large human brain evolved and expanded to crowd the mammalian skull (Dean, 2005).

Diane Kelly, an adjunct professor of biology at the University of Massachusetts, founded Zygote Games, which produced "Bone Wars: The Game of Ruthless Paleontology," in which players compete to reconstruct dinosaurs, using scientific methods. In 2005, the company offered the game at a 20 percent discount to residents of Kansas, due to its school board's evolution-related decisions, which have since been reversed (Dean, 2005). If our design was so intelligent, one might ask how the grand designer came up with a species that makes decisions by committee.

In a Doonesbury comic strip, a doctor and a patient confer over how to treat tuberculosis. "If the patient is a creationist," the doctor says, "he might want drugs used decades ago against the disease. If he believes in evolution, though, he might want newer drugs, 'intelligently designed,'" the doctor notes, "to match the TB microbe's evolving resistance to the earlier drug" (Dean, 2005).

WHERE DOES THE CONSENSUS LIE?

Writing in the *Washington Post Sunday Magazine*, Shankar Vedantam said that evolution's advocates and critics are mostly talking about different things. While the controversy over intelligent design is superficially about scientific facts, the real debate is more emotional, he wrote. "Evolution cuts to the heart of the belief that humans have a special place in creation. If all things in the living world exist solely because of evolutionary competition and natural selection, what room is left for the idea that humans are made in God's image or for any morality beyond the naked requirements of survival?" Beneath all the complex arguments of intelligent design advocates, Georgetown theologian John Haught agreed, "there lies a deeply human and passionately religious concern about whether the universe resides in the bosom of a loving, caring God or is instead perched over an abyss of ultimate meaninglessness" (Vedantam, 2006).

In *Why Darwin Matters*, author Michael Shermer said:

> Belief in God depends on religious faith. Acceptance of evolution depends on empirical evidence. This is the fundamental difference between religion and science. . . . Intelligent-design creationism reduces God to an artifice, a mere watchmaker piecing together life out of available parts in a cosmic warehouse. (Shermer, 2006, 123, 130)

With most federal courts rejecting intelligent design and other suggestions of religious doctrine in public-school science classes, where does the legal consensus lie regarding the study of religion (notably Christianity) in public schools? Bruce Feiler, author of *Where God Was Born: A Journey by Land to the Roots of Religion*, argued that the debate over religion has been characterized as a struggle between two groups that Noah Feldman calls "values evangelicals," such as Roy Moore, who placed the Ten Commandments in the Alabama Supreme Court, and "legal secularists," such as Michael Newdow, who attacked the use of "under God" in the Pledge of Allegiance. Such a polarized debate does not represent reality, he said (Feiler, 2005).

Feiler's solution is:

> Put the teaching of the Bible back where it belongs in our schools: not in the science laboratory, but in its proper historical and literary context. An elective, nonsectarian high school Bible class would allow students to explore one of the most influential books of all time and would do so in a manner that clearly falls within Supreme Court rulings. (Feiler, 2005)

In its landmark 1963 Abington case (which, like the Dover suit, also involved Pennsylvania public schools), the U.S. Supreme Court outlawed reading the Bible as part of morning prayers but clearly permitted study of the Bible. Writing for the 8–1 majority, Justice Thomas Clark stated that the Bible is "worthy of study for its literary and historic qualities," and added, "Nothing we have said here indicates that such study of the Bible or of religion, when presented objectively as part of a secular program of education, may not be effected consistent with the First Amendment" (Feiler, 2005).

By helping to design an academic course on the Bible, moderates can show that it is not composed entirely of talking points for the religious right. Feiler wrote,

> In fact, on a wide range of topics, including respecting the value of other faiths, shielding religion from politics, serving the poor and protecting the environment, the Bible offers powerful arguments in support of moderate and liberal causes. In the Book of Jonah, God offers a message of forgiveness and tolerance when he denounces his own prophet and spares his former enemies, the Ninevehites, when they repent and turn toward him. (Feiler, 2005)

Feiler cites surveys indicating that U.S. society is not religiously polarized as other statistics and some news reports suggest. For example, The Fourth National Survey of Religion and Politics, completed in 2004 by the University of Akron, shows that only 12.6 percent of Americans consider themselves "traditionalist evangelical Protestants," which the survey equates with the term "religious right." A mere 10.7 percent of Americans define themselves as "secular" or "atheist, agnostic." The vast majority of Americans are what the survey-takers called centrist or modernist in their religious views (Feiler, 2005). Responses to such polls may depend a great deal on the wording of questions. David Masci, a senior fellow at the Pew Forum on Religion & Public Life, helped conduct a recent poll that found that only about one in four Americans believes that humans came about through evolution alone (Vedantam, 2006).

Darwin himself struggled with similar questions. His religious worldview was shaken after a daughter died during 1851, and he was unable to reconcile the death to God's will. Realizing that natural selection would be controversial, Darwin also sought to fuse the belief with Christianity as evidence of an orderly, Christian God's workings. His findings ran counter to literal interpretations of the Bible and the special place it assigns human beings in the creation, but Darwin believed that he was showing something even grander—"that God's hand was present in all living things" (Vedantam, 2006).

"EVOLUTION SUNDAYS"

Some religious people have attempted to fuse the traditions in the face of turmoil. On Darwin's one-hundred-and-ninety-seventh birthday, ministers at several hundred churches around the United States preached February 12, 2006 against efforts to undermine the theory of evolution, opposing what they believe is a false dichotomy between science and faith.

"Evolution Sunday," celebrated on or near the birthday of Darwin (February 12) is an outgrowth of the Clergy Letter Project, started by academics and ministers in Wisconsin early in 2005 as a response to efforts discrediting teaching of evolutionary theory in public schools. "There was a growing need to demonstrate that the loud, shrill voices of fundamentalists claiming that Christians had to choose between modern science and religion were presenting a false dichotomy," said Michael Zimmerman, dean of the College of Letters and Sciences at the University of Wisconsin, Oshkosh and the major organizer of the letter project (Bannerjee and Berryman, 2006). Mr. Zimmerman said more than 10,000 ministers had signed the letter, which states, in part, that the theory of evolution is "a foundational scientific truth." To reject it, the letter continues, "is to deliberately embrace scientific ignorance and transmit such ignorance to our children." The Clergy Letter Project by 2006 included Evolution Sunday observances by 441 congregations in 48 states and the District of Columbia (Bannerjee and Berryman, 2006).

Reacting to polls indicating that half or more Americans believe that God created human beings within the last 10,000 years, academics, notably in the conservative southern United States, have initiated lectures and institutes that promote the role of evolution in life sciences. At the University of Georgia, evolutionary geneticist Wyatt Anderson, ecologist Patty Gowaty, and others started the Center for the Study of Evolution, which brings in speakers, maintains a certificate program, and does outreach to public schools. At the University of Alabama, faculty members have organized Alabama Lectures on Life's Evolution (ALLE). The University of Tennessee started its Darwin Day in 1997; the College of Charlestown started a Darwin Day in 2000; the University of Alabama started a similar celebration in 2006 (Holden, 2006, 771).

EVOLUTION AS "BREAKTHROUGH OF THE YEAR"

As debate over evolution continues in general society, scientists have been refining the theory. Within days of Judge Jones's ruling in Harrisburg, for example, the journal *Science* announced its "breakthroughs of the year," advances in the study of evolution: "Equipped with genome data and field observations of organisms from microbes to mammals," *Science*'s editors said, "In 2005, biologists made huge strides toward understanding the mechanisms by which living creatures evolve" (Culotta and Pennisi, 2005, 1878–1879).

Donald Kennedy, editor of *Science*, commented that during 2005 concrete genome data had allowed researchers to describe the molecular modifications that drive evolutionary change in organisms from viruses to primates. Many scientists also recorded painstaking field observations that shed new light on how populations diverge to form new species. He continued:

I hear you cry, hasn't it been a trying year for evolution, considering the debates about teaching evolutionary theory in science classes in the United States and the headlines about intelligent design? On the contrary, in the research community, it's been a great year for understanding how evolution works, through both experiment and theory. No single discovery makes the case by itself; after all, the challenge of understanding evolution makes multiple demands: How can we integrate genetics with patterns of inherited change? How do new species arise in nature? What can the new science of comparative genomics tell us about change over time? We have to put the pieces together, and it could not be a more important challenge: As the evolutionary geneticist Theodosius Dobzhansky once said, "Nothing in biology makes sense except in the light of evolution." (Kennedy, 2005, 1869)

FINDING THE "MISSING LINKS"

Among scientists, the case for evolution all but closed early in April 2006, when an evolutionary "missing link" was found between fish and land animals—bones as long as 9 feet from an ancient, river-dwelling predator with scales, fins, and gills, as well as arm joints in its fins, an alligator-like head and ribs heavy enough to support its body on dry land. The animal dragged itself on land like a seal, and may have had an ability to stand on shallow water bottoms (Gugliotta, 2006, A-3). Researchers led by paleontologist Neil H. Shubin of the University of Chicago and Edward B. Daeschler of Philadelphia's Academy of Natural Sciences found the fossils in red siltstone on Canada's Ellesmere Island, about 600 miles from the North Pole.

The scientists named the newly discovered creature *Tiktaalik roseae*, after "tiktaalik" an Inuktitut word for "large, shallow water fish," and "roseae," one of the project's patrons, who wishes to remain anonymous. This discovery supports the theory that fish emerged from the oceans and rivers perhaps 370 million years ago, then evolved into vertebrates, the first being amphibians and reptiles, then, much later, mammals. "This is extremely significant, because while we have been amassing evidence for years on the link between fish and tetrapods [four-legged animals], there was still a gap," said Hans Sues, associate director of research and collections at the Smithsonian National Museum of Natural History. "This link is one we would have predicted, but it's nice to see that it really exists" (Gugliotta, 2006, A-3).

REFERENCES

Banerjee, Neela and Anne Berryman. "At Churches Nationwide, Good Words for Evolution." *New York Times*, February 13, 2006. http://www.nytimes.com/2006/02/13/national/13evolution.htm.

Barbassa, Juliana. "Philosophy of Design Class Cancelled." Associated Press, January 17, 2006 (in LEXIS).

Berman, Morris. *Dark Ages America: The Final Phases of Empire*. New York: W. W. Norton & Co, 2006.

Blumenthal, Ralph. "Evolution's Backers in Kansas Start Counterattack." *New York Times*, August 1, 2006. http://www.nytimes.com/2006/08/01/us/01evolution.html.

Chapman, Matthew. "God or Gorilla: A Darwin Descendant at the Dover Monkey Trial." *Harpers*, February, 2006, 54–63.

Cooperman, Alan. "Floating Ice May Explain How Jesus Walked on Water, Researchers Say." Washington *Post*, April 6, 2006, A-3.

Culotta, Elizabeth. "Is ID [Intelligent Design] on the Way Out?" *Science* 311(February 10, 2006):770.

Culotta, Elizabeth and Elizabeth Pennisi. "Breakthrough of the Year: Evolution in Action." *Science* 310(December 23, 2005):1878–1879.

Dean, Cornelia. "Helping Out Darwin's Cause With a Little Pointed Humor." *New York Times*, December 27, 2005. http://www.nytimes.com/2005/12/27/science/27evol.html.

Davey, Monica and Ralph Blumenthal. "Evolution Fight Shifts Direction in Kansas Vote." *New York Times*, August 3, 2006. http://www.nytimes.com/2006/08/03/us/03evolution.htm.

Feiler, Bruce. "Teach, Don't Preach, *The Bible*." *New York Times*, December 21, 2005. http://www.nytimes.com/2005/12/21/opinion/21feiler.htm.

Fisher, Ian and Cornelia Dean. "In 'Design' vs. Darwinism, Darwin Wins Point in Rome." *New York Times*, January 19, 2006. http://www.nytimes.com/2006/01/19/science/sciencespecial2/19evolution.html.

Goers, Peter. "I'm a Heathen; I Won't Repent." *Sunday Mail* (South Australia), November 27, 2005, 42.

Goodstein, Laurie. "Judge Bars 'Intelligent Design' From Pa. [Pennsylvania] Classes." *New York Times*, December 20, 2005. http://www.nytimes.com/2005/ 12/20/education/20cnd-evolution.html.

Goodstein, Laurie. "California Parents File Suit Over Origins of Life Course." *New York Times,* January 11, 2006. http://www.nytimes.com/2006/01/11/national/11design.html.

Gugliotta, Guy. "'Link' Between Fish and Land Animals Found; Discovery Called Key Evidence Of Vertebrates' Ocean Origins." Washington *Post*, April 6, 2006, A03.

Hirsch, Arthur. "Science, Faith Clash in Class; Some Biology Teachers are Among Evolution's Challengers." Baltimore *Sun*, November 27, 2005, 1-A.

Holden, Constance. "Darwin's Place on Campus is Secure—but Not Supreme." *Science* 311(February 10, 2006):769–771.

Holden, Constance. "Court Revives Georgia Sticker Case." *Science* 312(June 2, 2006):1292.

Johnson, Kirk. "Anti-Darwin Bill Fails in Utah." *New York Times*, February 28, 2006. http://www.nytimes.com/2006/02/28/national/28utah.html.

"Judge Rules Against 'Intelligent Design' in Class." *New Scientist*, December 20, 2005. http://www.newscientist.com/article.ns?id=dn8493.

Kennedy, Donald. [Editorial] *Science* 310(December 23, 2005):1869.

Klepper, David. "Professor Resigns Chairmanship After Religion Course Controversy." Kansas City *Star*, December 8, 2005 (in LEXIS).

Kristof, Nicholas D. "Hubris of the Humanities Fuels Shortcomings in Science, Math." *New York Times* in Omaha *World-Herald*, December 27, 2005, 7-B.

Lawrence, Jill. "Intelligent Design is Religion, Judge Says." *USA Today*, December 21, 2005, 1-A, 3-A.

"Let Science Win." Editorial, Omaha *World-Herald*, August 9, 2006, 6-B.

Locke, Michelle. "Christians Throw the Book at University." Associated Press in Omaha *World-Herald*, January 7, 2006, 3-E.

Milburn, John. "University Cancels Class on Creationism after Professor's Comments." Associated Press, December 1, 2005 (in Lexis).

Ohpurleese Magazine. Accessed December 27, 2005. http://www.ohpurleese.com/month_ archive_24.htm.

"Ottawa University Planning Class on Intelligent Design." Associated Press, December 23, 2005 (in LEXIS).

Overbye, Dennis. "Philosophers Notwithstanding, Kansas School Board Redefines." *New York Times*, November 15, 2005. http://www.nytimes.com/2005/11/15/science/ sciencespecial2/15evol.html.

Phillips, Kevin. *American Theocracy: The Peril and Politics of Radical Religion, Oil, and Borrowed Money in the 21st Century*. New York: Viking, 2006.

Powell, Michael. "Judge Rules Against 'Intelligent Design': Dover, Pa., District Can't Teach Evolution Alternative." Washington *Post*, December 21, 2005, A-1.

Powell, Michael. "Advocates of 'Intelligent Design' Vow to Continue Despite Ruling." Washington *Post,* December 22, 2005, A-3. http://www.washingtonpost.com/wp-dyn/ content/article/2005/12/21/AR2005122101959_pf.html.

"Professor Apologizes for E-mail about New Class," Associated Press, November 29, 2005 (in LEXIS).

"Religion Professor Says University Hasn't Supported Him." Associated Press, December 10, 2005 (in LEXIS).

"Religious Studies Professor Withdraws Intelligent Design Class, Cites Controversy." University of Kansas Press Release, December 1, 2005. http://www.news.ku.edu/2005/ December/Dec1/course.shtml.

Rossing, Barbara R. *The Rapture Exposed: The Message of Hope in the Book of Revelation*. Boulder, CO: Westview Press, 2004.

Rudoren, Jodi. "Ohio Expected to Rein In Class Linked to Intelligent Design." *New York Times*, February 14, 2006. http://www.nytimes.com/2006/02/14/education/14evolution.html.

Shermer, Michael. *Why Darwin Matters: The Case Against Intelligent Design*. New York: Times Books/Henry Holt, 2006.

Southin, John. "Creationism, Intelligent Design Aren't Scientific Theories." [Letter to the Editor] *Brockville Recorder and Times* (Ontario), November 30, 2005, A-6.

Talbot, Margaret. "Darwin in the Dock: Intelligent Design has its Day in Court." *The New Yorker*, December 5, 2005, 66–77.

Vedantam, Shankar. "Eden and Evolution: Religious Critics of Evolution are Wrong about Its Flaws; But are They Right that It Threatens Belief in a Loving God?" *Washington Post Sunday Magazine*, February 5, 2006, W-8. http://www.washingtonpost.com/wp-dyn/content/article/2006/02/03/AR2006020300822_pf.html.

Whoriskey, Peter. "Warning Label on Darwin Sows Division in Suburbia; Parents in Cobb County, Ga., Clash Over Sticker in Textbooks." Washington *Post*, December 11, 2005. http://www.washpost.com.

Chapter 3

The Second Amendment Trumps the First

AMERICAN ENGLISH BRIMS with metaphors of armament, many of which were applied to Michael Bellesiles, historian formerly of Emory University, as he shot it out with supporters of the right to bear arms, contending that their version of American history was a flint-loaded myth. Armed with massive indignation and fact-checking furor, independent scholars and the armaments-industrial complex shot back. With critics locked and loaded, Bellesiles's book *Arming America: The Origins of a National Gun Culture* (Bellesiles, 2000) was picked apart, as his critics laid down a rain of fire contending that, factually, he couldn't shoot straight. Worse than that, they asserted that Bellesiles was shooting blanks. By stretching statistics to fit his predetermined conclusions, the critics charged, Bellesiles had fired from the hip and thereby shot himself in the foot—both feet, in fact. Friendly fire, this was not.

Following a university inquiry that largely agreed with the critics, Bellesiles resigned his academic position at Emory, which earlier had sponsored his Institute on the Study of Violence in America. Bellesiles was also stripped of Columbia University's prestigious Bancroft Prize, as one of his publishers canceled a contract. Quickly, proud gun owners, asserting that Bellesiles had been righteously cut off at the knees (or cut off at the pass), took aim at public-library holdings of *Arming America*, sniping it off shelves, suggesting, in their kinder moods, that the book should be moved to the fiction stacks. Bellesiles supporters, or people sporting merely a soft spot in their hearts for wide-open debate, contended that Bellesiles had been shot in the back, a victim of critics armed and dangerous, in a case of the Second Amendment trumping the First.

Guns are serious business in the United States. The Second Amendment, originally enacted to prevent recolonization of the United States by the British during the years after the American Revolution (or so we have been taught, at any rate), protects their ownership in a way unknown in any other modern industrial polity. Devotees of the right to bear arms go to great lengths to protect it against all enemies, real and imaginary, foreign and domestic. In *Arming America*, Bellesiles asserted that "The nation's past has been meticulously reconstructed to promote the necessity of a heavily armed American public" (Bellesiles, 2000, 4). Why, then, did the Bill of Rights include a right to bear arms? As a sop to states'-rights advocates, Bellesiles asserted, and as a device by which the federal government could avoid paying for a standing army and properly stocked citizen militias, Bellesiles contended.

This is a story of trenchant devotion to gun culture–but also an instructive tale about the perils of sailing into a perfect storm of well-organized special interests while relying on flimsy memory, as Bellesiles admitted, while incompletely and erroneously reconstructing complex historical records. Like Ward Churchill, Bellesiles made just enough errors to supply passionate opponents enough rope with which to hang him. Bellesiles thus quickly learned the perils of national notoriety among enemies on an incendiary subject.

Anyone consenting to an intellectual gun battle with the National Rifle Association (NRA) is advised to enter the fray with plentiful factual ammunition. America's gun aficionados are not known for their sense of forgiveness following a shoot-out.

RETHINKING GUN CULTURE

Once he became infamous at the NRA, Bellesiles was described in some media reports as a new-left radical historian. He told Jon Wiener of *The Nation*, however, that he had been a registered Republican and John McCain supporter until he reregistered as a Democrat during the debates over *Arming America*. Bellesiles described himself as a "Burkean conservative" who believes in "tradition and authority," as well as a long-time gun owner who gave up skeet shooting only after the armaments-industrial complex took aim at him. The nastiness of the debate over his work forced Bellesiles to rethink "what it means to be a Christian and own guns" (Wiener, 2002).

In *Arming America*, Bellesiles summarizes his thesis in one sentence: "[T]he vast majority of those living in British North American colonies had no use for firearms, which were costly, difficult to locate and maintain, and expensive to use" (Bellesiles, 2000, 110). *Arming America* contends that gun industry supporters' assertions that America was settled by men with firearms were a myth. "Instead," the book makes a case that "gun culture is a relatively recent development in American history"–that for two centuries before the Civil War, few Americans owned guns; that the guns they had were unreliable; that few people hunted with guns, instead relying on trapping and animal husbandry; that even in the Revolutionary War, swords, axes, and fire were more deadly than guns. Not until the Civil

War put guns in the hands of millions of men did gun culture flourish, Bellesiles argued.

The political implications of such an argument resonated with the NRA and other gun advocates. The Second Amendment, Bellesiles suggests, was not adopted to protect the widespread ownership or popularity of guns. It was instead intended to address the inadequacy of the weapons in the hands of local militias, on which the early United States relied in the absence of a standing army.

Initially, *Arming America* also was lavishly praised in some important review venues. "Bellesiles has dispersed the darkness that covered the gun's early history in America. He provides overwhelming evidence that our view of the gun is as deep a superstition as any that affected Native Americans in the 17th century," wrote Garry Wills in the *New York Times Book Review* (Wills, 2000, 1). Edmund Morgan, an eminent historian at Yale, wrote in the *New York Review of Books*, "No one else has put [the facts] together in so compelling a refutation of the mythology of the gun or in so revealing a reconstruction of the role the gun has actually played in American history" (Morgan, 2000, 30; Wiener, 2002).

As his fame spread, Bellesiles found himself shadowed at speaking engagements by avid supporters of the Second Amendment. Speaking at the University of California, Irvine, members of the audience "were greeted at the door of the Humanities Lecture Hall by four unusually large men passing out a brochure titled 'The Lies of Michael Bellesiles.' One wore a flak jacket, one had a shaved head; they did not look like faculty members or even history grad students" (Wiener, 2002).

The *Federal Lawyer* was the first periodical to repudiate a previous favorable review of *Arming America*, in its January 2001 edition. In the October edition of the journal, the reviewer, Michael Coblenz wrote that the common-sense premises of the book had misled him ("How the Bellesiles," 2002).

During April 2001, having been asked by a colleague at Northwestern University what he presently thought of *Arming America*, Wills was quoted as replying: "I was took. The book is a fraud" ("How the Bellesiles," 2002). Additionally, during May of 2002, the National Endowment for the Humanities removed its name from a $30,000 fellowship Bellesiles was completing at Chicago's Newberry Library.

Bellesiles fielded hate mail and death threats as pressure built on Emory University to fire him. Shooters.com said "Everything Bellesiles wrote is false, bogus, a big lie"; KeepAndBearArms.com posted a Web page headlined "Michael A. Bellesiles: Mega Anti-Gun-Nut-Part XVI" (Wiener, 2002). The *Wall Street Journal*, *The New Criterion*, *The Weekly Standard*, and the *National Review* (among others) raked the book for errors. Historians who had reviewed the book favorably were e-mailed and advised to reverse their opinions.

STATISTICAL ERRORS

Attacks against Bellesiles started well before *Arming America*'s publication in 2000. The book followed many other writings with similar themes. Bellesiles won the Binkley-Stephenson Award from the Organization of American Historians in 1996 for an essay on the origins of U.S. gun culture, which was cited as the best piece published that year in the *Journal of American History* (Bellesiles, 1996, 425–455). After reading a summary of Bellesiles's research in *The Economist*, NRA president Charlton Heston wrote in the December 1999 issue of *Guns & Ammo* that "Bellesiles clearly has too much time on his hands." By the time *Arming America* came out, complete with a fiery introduction that mentioned the gun lobby, Heston told the *New York Times* that Bellesiles's work was "ludicrous" (Wiener, 2002).

Even before *Arming America* was published, readers with an interest in demographic history were finding problems in Bellesiles's work. Peter Charles Hoffer, in *Past Imperfect* (2004), described in detail holes in the statistical tables that accompanied Bellesiles's prize-winning article in the *Journal of American History*, which formed the basis for problems with his statistical tables in *Arming America*. Bellesiles, for example, did not provide the total number of records he had studied in the original version of his work, and later, when he did, it kept changing. He didn't list the locations at which he had found probate and other records, and sometimes his regional totals for gun ownership did not average anywhere near his national average, absent huge (unprovided) differences in sample sizes (Hoffer, 2004, 145–151). These problems somehow had eluded the *Journal of American History*'s editors, its peer reviewers, and the judges who awarded the prize.

A leading critic of Bellesiles's probate record data was James Lindgren, Stanford Clinton Sr. Professor of Law and Director of the Demography of Diversity Project at the Northwestern University School of Law. Writing with Justin Lee Heather, Lindgren published a critique of the probate data in the *William & Mary Law Review* (Lindgren, 2002, 1777–1842). Their article dissecting Bellesiles's one-page table of probate records was nothing if not exhaustive, totaling 66 pages, with 173 references. The two authors asserted that more people listed guns in early wills than swords or bibles. They reported finding more guns, in good condition, than Bellesiles, leading to a conclusion that Bellesiles had substantially misrecorded the seventeenth- and eighteenth-century data on numbers of gun owners. Lindgren also published another attack on Bellesiles in *The Yale Law Journal*, 54 pages, with 247 footnotes. He agreed with another Bellesiles critic, Randolph Roth, in a *William and Mary Quarterly* "Forum," that Bellesiles had "a 10 per cent error rate in finding homicide cases in the Plymouth (Colony) records."

Bellesiles critic Clayton Cramer asserted:

> Wiener . . . makes the claim that the probate records are only a small part of *Arming America*. Very true. But Wiener, for some odd reason, neglects the much larger set of problems with Bellesiles's pack of lies: the altered quotes, the altered dates, and the misrepresentation of sources. ("How the Bellesiles," 2002)

For example, wrote Cramer, Bellesiles asserted that an absence of gunsmiths in the United States prior to the Civil War strongly indicated that the country lacked a "gun culture" at that time. Cramer said he was building a database that listed 2,273 gunsmiths and gun makers in America before 1840 (Cramer, 2000, 2001).

While Bellesiles's review of probate records before 1850 found that 14.7 percent of households had owned guns and that half of these were in poor condition, Lindgren asserted that 63 percent owned guns and that 9 percent were poorly maintained or broken (Robin, 2004, 8, 69). Lindgren also contended that some of the wills Bellesiles said he had examined did not exist.

Historians checked Bellesiles's footnotes in the archives where he did his research, and found problems with his use of probate records. Lindgren and others criticized one of his basic premises: that probate records were a reliable indicator of gun ownership. "Bellesiles is virtually alone among historians who work with probate records in thinking that they are more or less complete" (2002), wrote Lindgren, who also attacked what he said was Bellesiles's spotty use of the records; at one point he asserted that *Arming America* had cited from roughly 300 estate records from an area that should have had 5,000 to 8,000 (Lindgren, 2002).

"The data fit together almost too neatly," wrote Lindgren.

> In particular, if anyone had looked closely at the probate data, they would have seen that it did not look right. The regional differences were suspiciously slight; the increases over time were extremely regular; the study did not indicate which counties were in which categories; and in most unconventional fashion, the probate data were published with no sample or cell sizes. The results were directly contrary to the existing literature counting guns in probate records. (Lindgren, 2002)

The prestigious *William and Mary Quarterly* devoted a forum to the issue (Rakove, 2002, 205; Main, 2002, 212–216; Gruber, 2002, 217–222; Roth, 2002, 223–240; Bellesiles, 2002, 241–268). Critics of Bellesiles in this forum zeroed in on data that he had used to compare murder rates. Although Randolph Roth found Bellesiles's data lacking, specifically in the Plymouth Colony case, Mary Beth Norton, a historian of early America who has worked in those records, checked records herself, then concluded that Bellesiles's interpretation of the documents was "just as plausible" as that of his critics, "if not more so." She did find Bellesiles's use of probate records "slapdash and sloppy," but contended that other criticisms of *Arming America* "strike me as the usual sorts of disagreements historians always have about how to interpret documentary evidence, although those criticisms have been expressed more vehemently than is usual in the scholarly literature" (Wiener, 2002).

In the *William and Mary Quarterly* "Forum," Gloria Main, an expert on quantitative sources in U.S. history, said that Bellesiles had overemphasized the completeness of probate records, an assertion that she said undermined his entire case. She argued that because wills were recorded for a per-page fee, many of them avoided listing anything except the largest items, such as parcels of land. She said that while many wills did not list horses and cows (with values at least that of guns), no one has insisted that farmers owned no livestock (Robin, 2004, 73;

Main, 2002, 212). Indeed, where "[Bellesiles] found only 7 percent in Maryland with guns [,] my own work in the probate records of six Maryland counties from the years 1650 to 1720, ignored by Bellesiles, shows an average of 76 percent of young fathers owning arms of some sort" (Cockburn, 2002).

AFTER THE FLOOD

Bellesiles admitted that his use of probate data contained problems, induced by the fact that a flood in April 2000 at the Bowden Hall, the history office building at Emory, had destroyed his notes. The flood also seriously damaged several other offices; the university said that the damage totaled almost $1 million. An article in the Manchester *Guardian* quoted Bellesiles as asserting that the flooding of his Emory University office lasted six hours. Emory's official report on the flood (May 8, 2000) said that on the evening of Sunday, April 2, a connector on a sprinkler main broke on the building's third floor, where contractors were working on the plumbing. When the water was finally cut off about 25 minutes later, it left standing water 2 inches deep in some places, and practically no part of Bowden Hall escaped completely dry.

Bellesiles's book manuscript was safe, but his probate notes were on yellow legal pads on a chair, and were turned, according to his account, into unreadable pulp. After the flood, he went to work trying to recreate the notes, and when his book was published a few months later, he posted notices on several history Web sites warning that his original notes on the probate records had been destroyed (Wiener, 2002). Critics of Bellesiles argued, however, that after the office flood, Bellesiles had reported no damage.

The ruined notes were important because charges of research sloppiness against Bellesiles that were later raised by Lindgren and several other critics focused on a footnote to a table in the appendix of *Arming America*, listing 40 U.S. counties as sources of probate records. The list included San Francisco, an improbable citation because the city's archives had been destroyed in an earthquake and fire during 1906. According to an account by Jon Wiener in *The Nation*, Bellesiles recreated from memory the list of the counties where he researched probate records, after the flood in his office destroyed his notes. Bellesiles said that he returned to the San Francisco Bay area and found the documents in question across the bay, in the Contra Costa County archives. He photocopied and distributed the documents in question and posted examples on his Web site www.emory. edu/HISTORY/BELLESILES/index.html. The records were labeled "City and County of San Francisco." Contra Costa archivists confirmed that the documents are real–and that they came from the Contra Costa County archives, not San Francisco. In the opinion of Wiener, "That's error, not fraud" (Wiener, 2002).

The director of the Contra Costa County Historical Center told inquiring reporters that Bellesiles had never been to that archive, because his name didn't appear on the sign-in sheet. New charges of fraud ricocheted around the gun Web sites, the history listservs, and the media. Bellesiles explained that he simply had neglected to sign in. In the meantime, Lindgren asserted that records Bellesiles said he had examined at a national archives center in East Point, Georgia, did not exist.

In their rush to condemn Bellesiles, few critics seemed to have noticed the conclusion that he drew from the "San Francisco" documents: "probate records from the late 1850s reinforce the portrait of increased gun use in America." Wiener pointed out that those 15 words are the only reference to "San Francisco probate records in his 600-page book–and none of the critics appeared to disagree with those fifteen words" (Wiener, 2002).

THE LIMITS OF CRITICISM

Lindgren was a very energetic critic of Bellesiles's work–so energetic, according to some defenders of Bellesiles, that he exceeded the bounds of scholarly decency. Wiener wrote that in addition to reviewing *Arming America* in great detail himself, Lindgren also contacted historians who had written previous, positive reviews of *Arming America* and (according to *Chronicle of Higher Education*, cited by Wiener), "urged them to reconsider their positions–in print." Matthew Warshauer, who had reviewed *Arming America* approvingly in *Connecticut History*, told Jon Wiener that Lindgren asked him to publish a retraction. "He added something like he would hate to have this affect my career. I viewed that as a veiled threat," said Warshauer, an untenured associate professor at Central Connecticut State University (Wiener, 2002).

"This is pretty much unheard of in academia," wrote Wiener (Wiener, 2002). Lindgren, for his part, criticized Wiener's "false charge that I have urged people to retract their reviews of *Arming America*. If I had done so, that would indeed have been unusual, though not improper" ("How the Bellesiles," 2002). Lindgren said that he "urged" two authors to correct or retract one statement in each of their separate reviews. Lindgren said that the statements were retracted. Lindgren also denied having said what Matthew Warshauer took to be a veiled threat.

Despite his passion in pursuit of Bellesiles's errors, Lindgren asserted that he was no friend of the gun lobby. In a review of *Arming America*, Lindgren wrote:

> Let me state my biases up front: I dislike guns; I have never owned a gun; I have not touched one since the age of nine. Yet I don't understand the passion that people bring to the issue of their regulation. My own prior writing on guns has been on the pro-gun-control side of the dispute. (Lindgren, 2002)

Wiener concluded that even after dozens of researchers had devoted months to checking every line in *Arming America*'s 125 pages of endnotes, they produced some factual errors but "no proof of intentional deception, no proof of invented documents, no proof of fraud." The campaign against Bellesiles demonstrated one indisputable fact, according to Wiener: "Historians whose work challenges powerful political interests like the N.R.A. better make sure all their footnotes are correct before they go to press" (Wiener, 2002).

INVESTIGATION AND RESIGNATION

Emory University appointed a panel of three distinguished scholars from other universities to review charges against Bellesiles: Stanley Katz, a professor of public and international affairs at Princeton University; Hanna H. Gray, of the University of Chicago; and Laurel Thatcher Ulrich, of Harvard University. The group issued its report October 25, 2002, finding "evidence of falsification" and "serious failures of and carelessness in the gathering and presentation of archival records and the use of quantitative analysis" ("The Bancroft," 2002). The committee reached its conclusions July 10, 2002, but the university withheld the report until late in October, during an appeal by Bellesiles.

The Emory Committee's report concluded that Bellesiles was "guilty of both substandard research methodology and of willfully misrepresenting specific evidence in *Arming America*" (Merced, 2002, 1). The committee investigated five questions related to probate records in Vermont, Rhode Island, and San Francisco, as well as the book's much-criticized table of probate records. Finally, the committee was asked if Bellesiles committed "other serious deviations 'from accepted practices in carrying out or reporting results from research'" (Merced, 2002, 1).

The committee found that Bellesiles's "Table One" arranged data in such a way that it is almost impossible to determine where he got his information. Thus, Bellesiles's numbers (and therefore conclusions based upon them) were "mathematically improbable or impossible." In addition to his "casual method of recording data," Bellesiles, according to the committee's report, confused wills and inventories, thereby creating even more statistical confusion. The committee said that failure to identify sources on Table One, which listed his probate records, "moved into the realm" of falsification, in violation of Emory's policies and procedures. The report also criticized the *Journal of American History* for failing to edit Bellesiles's original report on guns, which was published in 1996, asking why "did no editor or referees ever ask that he supply" the basic information needed to understand his tables? Furthermore, the report found that "no one has been able to replicate Professor Bellesiles' results [of low percentage of guns] for the places or dates he lists" ("Summary," 2002).

The committee was not convinced that Bellesiles had used San Francisco records in Contra Costa County, especially after its members learned that some of the records he claimed to have read at the Contra Costa History Center in 1993 were not transferred there until 1998. This was not the only problem with the documents. Some critical Massachusetts records Bellesiles said that he had used did not exist. The investigators also said that while they "do not see evidence of outright deception in his use of materials related to militias . . . we do see abundant evidence of superficial and thesis-driven research." Summarizing, the

Emory Committee concluded that "Bellesiles's scholarly integrity is seriously in question" ("Summary," 2002).

Bellesiles replied:

> I have never fabricated evidence of any kind nor knowingly evaded my responsibilities as a scholar. I have been open to evidence that contradicts my hypothesis. I have never consciously misrepresented any data or evidence. I have spent twenty years conducting research in archives scattered throughout this country and in Europe. I have corrected every error possible and continue to work to replace the lost probate data. ("Summary," 2002)

Bellesiles said that while he welcomed scholarly criticism, he was being held to a higher standard than other scholars: "Many scholars have admitted and corrected errors in their own research, enriching our knowledge in the process. I believe that if we begin investigating every scholar who challenges received truth, it will not be long before no challenging scholarly books are published." Bellesiles also said that he has been unfairly tried and convicted: "The report casts aspersion on my integrity as a scholar based on three paragraphs and a table in a six hundred-page book. It seems to me that raising uncertainties that question the credibility of an entire book without considering the book as a whole is just plain unfair." Bellesiles said that a new edition of *Arming America* would correct mistakes and add new material. *Arming America*, he said, "has been subjected to the most thorough scrutiny of any work of history." Yet, apart from the probate records, "only a single misquote has been found, and only the most minor errors discovered" ("Summary," 2002).

His defense notwithstanding, Bellesiles announced his resignation from Emory late in October 2002. In a statement quoted by the *Emory Wheel*, the student newspaper, Bellesiles said that "he could not continue his teaching commitments given the controversy surrounding him and his book. 'I will continue to research and report on the probate materials while also working on my next book, but cannot continue to teach in what I feel is a hostile environment'" (Merced, 2002, 1).

Following release of the Emory report, Wiener countered: "The point is that historians have to deal with the messy confusion of things, and they offer interpretations of it. Historical knowledge advances by the testing of interpretations, not by stifling interpreters . . ." ("How the Bellesiles," 2002). Wiener argued that the Emory report's authors had "abdicated their intellectual responsibility" by letting the pro-gun crowd—which has tried to discredit the book by "focusing attention on errors in a tiny portion of the documentation"—set the terms of the debate. As a result, argued Wiener, the Emory report "has ominous implications for other historians dealing with controversial issues ("How the Bellesiles," 2002).

On November 20, 2002, the Chicago *Tribune* reported that Bellesiles had resigned believing that Emory planned to demote him and "that would have been an affront to my honor." Regarding the Emory report, Bellesiles told the paper: "I was absolutely shocked! Obviously, they were very angry at me." Bellesiles indicated to the newspaper that he had been victimized by an "intellectual lynching." He continued to insist that he made few mistakes, noting that the Emory Commit tee found errors in just five of the 1,347 footnotes. "Look, I've never been good at math," he explained when asked about the errors in counting guns ("How the Bellesiles," 2002). Bellesiles said that he would be teaching on visiting professorships in England for the next academic year (2002–2003).

On January 8, 2003, the Associated Press reported that Knopf had decided to stop selling *Arming America* and would terminate its contractual relationship with Bellesiles, who reportedly had offered to revise the book; the revisions, once submitted, were considered inadequate by editors at Knopf. Jane Garrett, Bellesiles's editor, told the Associated Press: "I still do not believe in any shape or form he fabricated anything. He's just a sloppy researcher." Knopf told the wire service that *Arming America* had sold 8,000 in hardback and 16,000 in paperback ("How the Bellesiles," 2002).

During mid-February 2003, however, Soft Skull Press announced that it would publish a revised edition of *Arming America*. "It is imperative that we stand up to the N.R.A. smear machine," the press said in a press release ("How the Bellesiles," 2002). The new book, published late in 2003, was promoted as containing several clarifications of research, including a new table of probate data.

The debate continued regarding how severe academic misconduct should be to cost a historian his job. "Wiener sees [Bellesiles's downfall] as the result of a campaign by a powerful pressure group," said one observer. "If he had published research showing that there were fewer books in early America than previously believed rather than fewer guns, he might be wrong, but he'd still be teaching at Emory" (Schrecker, 2005). "Obviously, Bellesiles should have been more conscientious in the archives, but as Wiener explains, he is hardly the only historian whose research methods have proved less than impeccable. But, because he offended a powerful right-wing interest group, his lapses cost him his career" (Schrecker, 2005).

BANCROFT PRIZE REVOKED

Meeting December 7, 2002, Columbia University's Board of Trustees voted to rescind the Bancroft Prize that had been awarded to Bellesiles during 2001 for *Arming America*–the first such action in the history of the prize, since 1948. The board also asked Bellesiles to return the $4,000 prize money. The decision, announced a week later, followed the review of an investigation confirming charges of scholarly misconduct against Bellesiles by Emory University, as well as Bellesiles's resignation. The Bancroft Prize is awarded for works in American history of "distinguished merit and distinction." The selection criteria for the Prize specify that it "should honor only books of enduring worth and impeccable scholarship that make a major contribution to our understanding of the American past" ("The Bancroft," 2002).

In addition, on May 2, 2002, the Atlanta *Journal-Constitution* reported that the Newberry Library had provided answers to the National Endowment for the Humanities' (NEH) questions about a $30,000 fellowship awarded to Bellesiles to study the history of American gun laws. "The NEH request is unprecedented," said the Newberry's James Grossman, vice president for research and education: "They're asking questions that they're entitled to ask, and we're answering them as best we can" ("How the Bellesiles," 2002).

Bellesiles responded to the NEH action in an e-mail sent to the *Chronicle of Higher Education* (May 23, 2002): "They simply made a political decision that should send chills through academics everywhere. The spirit of Joe McCarthy stalks the halls of the NEH." He said the NEH's action was "completely gratuitous." He added: "I regret that my name has been associated with an agency that values so little the principles of the First Amendment, due process, and academic freedom" ("How the Bellesiles," 2002).

GUN-FRIENDLY THESIS-DRIVEN RESEARCH

While many of Bellesiles's critics pilloried him for thesis-driven research (defining a conclusion first and making the data fit), gun-friendly author John Lott was doing much the same thing on the other side of the issue, and suffering little more than the usual slings and arrows of political debate. Despite indications that his findings were based on nonexistent research, Lott's career fared well. While Bellesiles was forced to resign under fire for sloppy research, Lott was, by 2005, a resident scholar at the American Enterprise Institute, and the author of *More Guns, Less Crime* (Lott, 1998). Numerous critics charged that Lott built statistical bias into his work, trying to use "objective" numbers to embellish his biases. In addition, Lott was accused of advocating his own work on various Internet Web sites by using various pseudonyms known as "sock puppets" ("Mary Rosh" in Lott's case) to create an impression that he is being supported by third parties. An alert Internet blogger noticed that Mary Rosh's Internet provider was the same as Lott's.

Donald Kennedy, editor of the journal *Science*, concluded, "What [Lott] did was to construct a false identity for a scholar, whom he then deployed in repeated support of his positions and in repeated attacks on his opponents. In most circles, this goes down as fraud" ("John Lott," 2005). Lott's methodology also has raised a host of questions. The purported survey produced no paper records. While Bellesiles had a flood to blame, Lott maintained that electronic records had been lost in a computer crash. The work was supposedly done by students who were paid in cash, leaving no recruitment or payroll records.

Nevertheless, *More Guns, Less Crime* was trumpeted a "bible" of the gun industry, selling 100,000 copies (Wiener, 2004, 136), and becoming an important political and legal exhibit in the debates over concealed-carry laws in 35 states by 2003. Lott's *curriculum vitae* sounds spectacular—Texas A & M, UCLA's School of Management, University of Chicago Business School, Yale Law School, but most of these were visiting appointments. Something of an academic gypsy, Lott never achieved tenure.

Despite a drumbeat of incisive criticism, Lott never lost his job, nor was his book withdrawn from circulation *a la* Bellesiles. In fact, a search for "John Lott" in LEXIS early in 2006 indicated that he was still exercising his dubious expertise liberally (in frequency, not political inclination) in venues as diverse as National Public Radio and the *Investors' Business Daily*.

Lott's studies indicating that concealed weapons led to less crime were still being used during a debate on the issue in Omaha during 2006, despite the fact that a National Academy of Sciences report in 2004 indicated that "flaws in methodologies, difficulties with data collection, and conflicting findings rendered [them] inconclusive." The NAS study found "no credible evidence that the passage of right-to-carry laws decreases or increases violent crime" (Grace, 2006, A-2).

Meanwhile, in 2004, the American Library Association listed *Arming America* as the third most-often challenged book in libraries—that is, the book was third most likely to spark a demand of removal from a library collection. The first most-often challenged was Robert Cormier's *The Chocolate War*, cited for sexual content, violence, and language. Number two was Walter Myers' *Fallen Angels*, a young-adult novel set in Harlem and Vietnam, which was criticized for racism, language, and violence.

For roughly five years, Bellesiles largely disappeared from public life (he did write a few book reviews in scholarly journals), while his case was dissected from various viewpoints in several books (Hoffer, 2004; Robin, 2004; Wiener, 2005). In 2006, however, Bellesiles published a new book, with Christopher Waldrep, *Documenting American Violence: A Sourcebook*, an anthology that surveys violence as a theme in U.S. history, from the revolutionary overthrow of British rule, to the struggle for civil rights, to the present-day debates over the death penalty (Waldrep and Bellesiles, 2006). This book collects excerpts from a range of primary sources to document the incidences of violence. Some include Benjamin Franklin's account of the Conestoga massacre, during which a village of American Indians was killed by the Paxton Boys, a group of frontier settlers; militant abolitionist John Brown's attack on Harper's Ferry; Ida B. Wells's condemnation of lynchings in the South; Cheyenne war chief Two Moon's account of the Battle of the Little Bighorn (1876), curiously described as a "massacre" by the Indians, although Custer initiated the battle with an attack.

REFERENCES

"The Bancroft and Bellesiles." History News Network. December 14, 2002. http://hnn.us/articles/1157.html

Bellesiles, Michael A. *"The Origins of Gun Culture in the United States, 1760–1865."* *Journal of American History* 83 (1996):425–455.

Bellesiles, Michael A. *Arming America: The Origins of a National Gun Culture.* New York: Knopf, 2000, 110.

Bellesiles, Michael. "Exploring America's Gun Culture." *William and Mary Quarterly* 59(2002):241–268.

Cockburn, Alexander. "The Year of the Yellow Notepad." *The Nation*, April 8, 2002. http://www.thenation.com/doc/20020408/Cockburn.

Cramer, Clayton E. "Firearms Ownership and Manufacturing in Early America." April 4, 2001. http://www.claytoncramer.com.

Cramer, Clayton E. and Dave Kopel. "Disarming Errors." *National Review*, October 9, 2000, 54–55.

Grace, Erin. "Concealed-carry Absolutes are a Moving Target." *Omaha World-Herald*, July 16, 2006, A-1, A-2.

Gruber, Ira D. "Of Arms and Men: Arming America and Military History." *William and Mary Quarterly* 59(2002):217–222.

Hoffer, Peter. *Past Imperfect: Facts, Fiction and Fraud, American History from Bancroft and Parkman to Ambrose, Bellesiles, Ellis and Goodwin*. New York: PublicAffairs, 2004.

"How the Bellesiles Story Developed." History News Network, October 25, 2002. http://hnn.us/articles/691.html.

"John Lott." Source Watch: A Project of the Center for Media & Democracy. July 29, 2005. http://www.sourcewatch.org/wiki.phtml?title=John_Lott.

Lindgren, James. "Fall From Grace: *Arming America* and the Bellesiles Scandal (Part 1)." History News Network, August 27, 2002. http://hnn.us/articles/930.html, Excerpted from *Yale Law Journal* 111(June 2002):2195–2249.

Lindgren, James and Justin L. Heather. "Counting Guns in Early America." *William and Mary Law Review* 43(April, 2002):1777–1842.

Lott, John. *More Guns, Less Crime: Understanding Crime and Gun Control Laws*. Chicago: University Of Chicago Press, 1998.

Main, Gloria. "Many Things Forgotten: The Use of Probate Records in *Arming America*." *William and Mary Quarterly* 59:1(January 2002):212–216.

Merced, Michael de la. "Bellesiles Resigns as Fraud Investigation Ends: External Panel Asserts Guilt in July; Main Report Released Today." *Emory Wheel*, October 25, 2002, 1.

Morgan, Edmund S. "In Love with Guns." *New York Review of Books*, October 19, 2000, 30.

Rakove, Jack N. "Words, Deeds, and Guns: *Arming America* and the Second Amendment." *William and Mary Quarterly* 59(2002):205–210.

Robin, Ron T. *Scandals and Scoundrels: Seven Cases That Shook the Academy*. Berkeley: University of California Press, 2004.

Roth, Randolph. "Guns, Gun Culture, and Homicide: The Relationship between Firearms, the Uses of Firearms, and Interpersonal Violence." *William and Mary Quarterly* 59(2002):223–240.

Schrecker, Ellen. [Review, Wiener, *Historians in Trouble*] in *Academe* (American Association of University Professors) May, 2005. http://www.aaup.org/publications/Academe/2005/05so/05sobr.htm.

"Summary of the Emory Report on Michael Bellesiles." History News Network. November 2002. http://hnn.us/articles/1069.html.

Waldrep, Christopher and Michael Bellesiles. *Documenting American Violence: A Sourcebook*. New York: Oxford University Press, 2006.

Wiener, Jon. "Fire at Will." *The Nation*, November 4, 2002. http://www.thenation.com/doc/20021104/wiener.

Wiener, Jon. *Historians in Trouble: Plagiarism, Fraud, and Politics in the Ivory Tower.* New York: The New Press, 2004.

Wills, Garry. "Spiking the Gun Myth" *New York Times*, September 10, 2000, Book Review, 1.

Chapter 4

Gut-Based Discourse in the Age of the Internet

HAVING AUTHORED BOOKS with titles like *Fantasies of the Master Race* and *A Little Matter of Genocide*, Ward Churchill has been no stranger to controversy. However, until one winter weekend early in 2005, he had not made the short list of the *Wall Street Journal*, the O'Reilly Factor, and other ministers of truth in George W. Bush's world. What happened thereafter tells us much about the limits of permissible debate in the United States post 9-11, in our land of the free, where governors, legislators, and other political revelers in cheap rhetorical thrills seem ready to dump the Constitution's First Amendment in the toilet on a sound bite's notice.

Two eminently quotable words—"little Eichmanns"—scorched repeatedly on a right-wing grill, more than three years old and quoted out of context, earned Churchill, who heretofore had been known principally as a Native American scholar and activist, the hounding of his life by ideology-driven opponents. The University of Colorado, his employer, excused his remarks, however reprehensible, as protected speech. In the meantime, however, a number of other questions arose about Churchill's way of doing scholarly business, which culminated, almost a year and a half later, in an official report recommending that he be fired from his tenured post for academic misconduct, the first professor at his university to be disciplined in such a manner.

LIMITS OF PERMISSIBLE DEBATE

The Internet has changed the ways in which we handle information. In the old days, first drafts languished in our desks gathering dust, or were circulated among a few colleagues for review. These days they may be hung out on the Internet for everyone to see (including people we would rather not meet under other circumstances). There our drafts may lay like seeds in desert sand until, years later, long after our own thoughts have moved on, they may be drenched in unwelcomed attention. At that time, attention can be instant, incendiary, and overwhelming, as *everyone* goes for the gut.

Thus Ward Churchill, who took pride in the provocative nature of his discourse, found himself with more attention than he, or perhaps anyone, could handle. By calling the martyred victims of the World Trade Center attacks "little Eichmanns" in an Internet essay penned the day the Twin Towers fell, he offended a powerful new icon of U.S. civil religion. Three-plus years later, Churchill found himself pilloried like a witch in old-days Salem for violating the bounds of what linguist Noam Chomsky regards as the limits of permissible debate.

Those two words reaped for Churchill a whirlwind of recriminatory hatred that surged across the country within days, sped by the Internet and right-wing radio and television talk shows, quickly illustrating just how taut public opinion remained nearly four years after the World Trade Center attacks. Churchill's choice of words was incendiary and obscured his main point—that U.S. policies have provoked opposition (popularly characterized these days as "blowback"). This is not an argument novel to Churchill. It has been made in several books and other forums, and has informed legitimate opposition to policies of the George W. Bush administration in Iraq.

Churchill concluded later:

> The bottom line of my argument is that the best and perhaps only way to prevent 9-11-style attacks on the U.S. is for American citizens to compel their government to comply with the rule of law. The lesson of Nuremberg is that this is not only our right, but our obligation. To the extent we shirk this responsibility, we, like the "Good Germans" of the 1930s and 1940s, are complicit in its actions and have no legitimate basis for complaint when we suffer the consequences. This, of course, includes me, personally, as well as my family, no less than anyone else. (Churchill, Press Release, 2005)

Churchill's political analysis—that U.S. arrogance and power fosters terrorism—is hardly his alone. Consider the work of William Blum, an historian whose writing was praised by Osama bin Laden during an audio presentation released in January 2006. After bin Laden's blurb, his book *Rogue State: A Guide to the World's Only Superpower*, surged from 205,763 to 19 on Amazon.com's book-sales rankings within 48 hours. No "Little Eichmanns" for Blum, who told interviewers that he detested the 9-11 attacks even as he understood them as a retaliation against U.S. foreign policy. Blum joked that bin Laden's endorsement was "almost as good as being an Oprah [Winfrey] book" ("Historian Welcomes," 2006, 13-A).

A week after the furor blew open, Churchill said February 8, 2005 that he mourned for everyone killed on September 11, 2001, and conceded that he could have explained himself better. "I wouldn't retract it. I would explain it better," he told the Associated Press (Elliott, March 25, 2005). "If someone were to ask me,

'Do you feel sorrow for the victims of 9-11,' of course I do," he said. "Let's begin with the children. Yes, they were innocent. And I mourn them. But they were not more innocent than those half-million Iraqi children" (Elliott, March 25, 2005).

Poor judgment, yes. Inappropriate language, yes. Talking before he thought it out, certainly. Colorado's governor Bill Owens (among other political luminaries) indicated that while a bum on the street has a right to say just about anything he wishes, the same rights do not pertain to someone paid partially by the State of Colorado. That's where the ideological rubber meets the First Amendment road, and where the case gets interesting for any of us who draw a paycheck funded, ever so partially, by a government. Operated properly, the First Amendment to the U.S. Constitution gives all of us the right to make fools of ourselves—and not, as one Denver talk-show host thought (out loud, gutter-level, over the air), to be executed for treason. The attack on Churchill is an attack on anyone who "dares to question the myth of American imperial innocence" (Rothschild, 2005).

So exactly what is the far-left limit of freedom of speech in the United States, post 9-11? By any stretch of the legal imagination, the fiery destruction of tall buildings full of people by use of commercial aircraft full of innocent passengers is not an expression of symbolic political or religious speech. What, however, of describing (or even supporting) another's rationale for such things? Such expression may be repugnant to the vast majority of U.S. citizens, but is it protected under the First Amendment?

That was the initial question in this explosive debate. After mulling it for several months, the university that employed Churchill decided he had a constitutional right to his opinion. What remained were questions about Churchill's Native ancestry, which had played a role in his hiring. The university found that self-definition was appropriate here (as for all other affirmative action hires). Finally, Churchill's tenure rested on a number of debates regarding copyright law, asserted plagiarism, and interpretation of historical evidence. Churchill, formerly a journalist with a speedy pen and a talent for attention-grabbing phrases, had written more than 20 books and dozens of articles, mostly in the hotly contestable field of Native American Studies, which were scrutinized intensely by a troupe of critics. His printed record provided fertile ground for his many critics' intense search for scholarly malpractice. They were soon raked for errors in a manner suffered by few other scholars.

A CONTROVERSIAL LIFE

Ward Churchill, named after his grandfather, was born to Jack LeRoy Churchill and Maralyn Lucretia Allen in Urbana, Ill., during 1947. His father and mother divorced before his second birthday. Churchill's high-school classmates recalled him as "a friendly teen who liked to debate politics" (Curtin et al., 2005, A-1). He graduated from Elmwood Community High School in 1965, and was drafted a year later to serve a tour of duty in Vietnam as the war escalated.

Churchill has variously described his service in Vietnam as editor of an Army newspaper (on an employment application at CU in 1980), and as a member of an elite reconnaissance patrol (Curtin, et al., 2005, A-1). Churchill said he walked point during combat in Vietnam during a trial for disrupting Columbus Day parade activities in Denver, when he was arrested by Denver police, as he described the parade as a "celebration of genocide," which had caused millions of Indians' deaths with the advent of European colonization (Johnson and York, 2005). Denver has experienced the largest protests of Columbus Day in the world. In 2004, about 240 protesters, including Churchill, were arrested for blocking the parade's progress. Morris, Churchill, and six other leaders of the protest were later acquitted of failure to obey a police order to disperse in Denver County Court.

Service in Vietnam formed Churchill's politics hard left. After discharge, he burned a U.S. flag on the steps of the Peoria County Courthouse. He attended meetings of Students for a Democratic Society and became friends with Mark Clark, a Black Panther leader, who was killed in a shootout with police in Peoria. Churchill also became friends with Russell Means about the time of the 1973 siege at Wounded Knee, and wrote some speeches for him.

Churchill, who is 6-foot-5, smokes two to four packs of Pall Malls a day (Brennan, March 28, 2005, 23-A). Churchill's first teaching job was as an art instructor at Black Hills State College, Spearfish, S.D., in 1975 and 1976. Churchill, who was 58 in 2006, became a lecturer at the University of Colorado in 1978 and was granted tenure in Communications during 1991. After that, he transferred to Ethnic Studies.

A TEST FOR FREE SPEECH AT HAMILTON COLLEGE

Churchill's "Little Eichmanns" statement first reached the attentive ears of various right-wing media gatekeepers in January, 2005, after he was invited to Hamilton College, with a student body of about 1,750, which is housed in century-and-a-half old stone buildings near Utica, N.Y. Churchill had been invited as part of a panel discussion on the limits of free speech titled "Limits of Dissent." Very quickly, the real world intruded with an academic debate over how far an individual could take free speech.

Ian Mandel, a 21-year-old junior at Hamilton College majoring in government, editor-in-chief of the *Spectator*, the student newspaper, wrote a front-page piece January 21 headlined "Controversial Speaker to Visit Hill." Mandel had received his story idea in an e-mail from Hamilton professor Theodore Eismeier during the previous December. "I thought it would be an issue; I didn't realize how big it would be," he said later. Mandel grew up 18 miles from New York City in suburban Nyack, N.Y. When the Trade Center was attacked, he smelled the burning buildings from his parents' home.

On January 26, Mandel's *Spectator* story was picked up by the *Post-Standard*, in nearby Syracuse. A link to the article quickly was posted on Little Green Footballs, a widely read conservative blog, at 9:40 a.m. Eastern time the same day. Eleven minutes later, a reader posted a comment saying that Churchill deserved to be shot in the face. Just before 10 a.m., a different reader provided Churchill's e-mail address. Before 11 a.m., another reader announced she had just called the Colorado governor and had written letters to the *Denver Post* and the *Rocky Mountain News*. The same person followed up a few minutes later with contact information for the newspapers so that others also could write letters calling for Churchill to be fired (Smallwood, February 18, 2005, 10).

Within a few hours, 500 comments about Churchill's "Little Eichmanns" comment had been posted on Little Green Footballs. According to an account in the *New York Times*, "Readers linked to old news releases regarding squabbles between Churchill and the American Indian Movement. They linked to Hamilton news releases about alumni who were killed in the attacks. Someone requested the name of a September 11 widow from Colorado who might have political clout" (Smallwood, February 18, 2005, 10).

Within a few days, an editorial salvo in the *Wall Street Journal* lambasted Churchill, calling him "a cheerleader for the 9/11 attacks" ("There They Go," 2005, W-11). "His screeds usually attract little notice outside obscure Marxist Web sites and the like," the *Journal* opined ("There They Go," 2005, W-11). The editorial (in the Weekend Journal section, not the main editorial page) then suggested that alumni of Hamilton College refuse to contribute to the college's capital campaign until Churchill was "disinvited." Within hours after the *Journal* editorial hit the street, Hamilton College's switchboard and e-mail system were jammed with thousands of comments—mainly protests, although a small minority defended Churchill's freedom of speech.

Three days later, on February 1, Bill O'Reilly opened fire on Churchill and Hamilton College on his national television talk show and in his syndicated newspaper column, saying: "There's simply no way to justify allowing a man who hails terrorist killers to lecture on campus, and this free speech stuff is a canard. Hamilton wouldn't invite the Klan or a serial killer to lecture" ("Talking Points," 2005). O'Reilly also interviewed Churchill briefly, via video. Churchill said, in part:

> [George W.] Bush, at least in symbolic terms, is the world's leading terrorist. He absolutely thumbs his nose at the rule of law. He's the head of a rogue state by definition, and it's a rogue state that dispenses carnage on people presumed to be inferior in some set of terms, whether they be racial or national or religious or otherwise, on the one hand, and of no particular utility to the empire, on the other. . . . Try to have a little empathy and respect for other people and that will carry a long way, just in and of itself, towards alleviating the dynamic that produces 9/11, and, if things continue, undoubtedly and inevitably, we'll produce another one." ("Talking Points," 2005)

O'Reilly retorted:

> The problem with this guy is that he sees the U.S.A. as a country that persecutes people, a bad country. You just heard him say it. . . . He wants us to empathize with

Al Qaeda. Yet he has little empathy for his fellow countrymen who died on 9/11. He sees the U.S.A. as a racist country run by human rights violators. So, of course, any attack on America is justified in his mind. Churchill's view is beyond extreme. . . . Churchill's entitled to his opinion, and we are entitled to shun him. ("Talking Points," 2005)

For more than a month, from January 31, 2005 to mid-March, O'Reilly pounded Churchill night after night. Typically, on March 2, he said: "Churchill's viewpoint is just hateful. He believes the U.S.A. is an evil country and terrorists are justified in attacking civilians. Again, in my view, Churchill's simply a traitor, a disgrace to the University of Colorado, a man to be scorned" (O'Reilly, March 7, 2005).

Joan Hinde Stewart, Hamilton College's president, within three days, found herself in the midst of 6,000 angry e-mails, including those from alumni who said they would follow the *Wall Street Journal*'s advice to tear up their checks for the college's capital campaign. Some prospective students withdrew applications or refused to enroll. Some of the e-mails had been spurred by the *Wall Street Journal* editorial, but many more arrived after O'Reilly scorched Churchill repeatedly. The uproar at Hamilton College eventually did no long-range damage to its endowment, however. In late July, the college reported that its capital campaign (the one the *Wall Street Journal* had urged alumni to boycott) had raised a record $5.44 million ("Hamilton College Raises," 2005, B-3).

The tsunami of right-wing outrage stoked by incensed bloggers, the *Wall Street Journal*'s editorial writers, O'Reilly, and others also swamped Nancy Rabinowitz, the Hamilton professor who had invited Churchill to speak to the campus. On February 11, Rabinowitz resigned as director of the Kirkland Project for the Study of Gender, Society, and Culture "under duress," two weeks after the controversy erupted. She remained at Hamilton, teaching comparative literature.

Churchill's speech at Hamilton, scheduled for the evening of February 3, was canceled for security reasons, Hamilton officials said. Churchill had planned to speak that evening in a flak jacket, flanked by two bodyguards. Churchill said he and his wife, Professor Natsu Saito, had received more than 100 death threats (Healy, et al., 2002, C-17). In a telephone interview with the *New York Times*, Churchill called the threats against Hamilton College "American terrorism." He urged those making the threats to "take a look in the mirror" (Healy et al., 2002, C-17).

"His remarks about the victims of 9/11 are repellent, but our reaction to 'repellent' is how we test the right to free speech," Stewart said shortly before addressing the events with the Hamilton faculty, who gave her a standing ovation. "We did our best to protect the principles and the values that we believe in—the right to speak, to study, to teach freely—but the point came that I simply felt that this threat was too large for us to handle," said Stewart, who was told by campus security that even additional police officers could not ensure safety. Stewart said she alone received 6,000 messages, describing them as "ranging from angry to profane, obscene, violent," and asserted that Hamilton's actions had been mischaracterized by many of the writers, as well as by O'Reilly (Healy et al., 2005, C-17).

A PROXY FOR THE PROFESSORATE

Once the controversy over Churchill's remarks exploded, right-wing wags lost no time generalizing from him to all professors: "The reluctance of the University of Colorado to fire professor Ward Churchill is showing the public that colleges and universities are nests of subsidized radicals," trumpeted Phyllis Schlafly on the Copley News Service. "Churchill is no anomaly; like-minded professors hold forth on campuses all over the country" (Schlafly, 2005). She continued:

> Churchill's Ethnic Studies, Women's Studies, Gay and Lesbian Studies, and African-American Studies are not merely studies or departments; they are university-financed "movements" of the left. . . . Professorial bias against conservatives in general and President George W. Bush in particular is exceeded only by the bias against traditional morality. We are indebted to columnist John Leo for revealing the shockers at Wesleyan University: the naked dorm, the transgender dorm, the queer prom, the pornography-for-credit course, the obscene sidewalk chalking, the campus club named crudely for a woman's private part, and more. . . ." (Schlafly, 2005)

Within a week of O'Reilly's initial broadcast, self-righteous shock-jocks on right-wing radio talk shows in Bush country were trussing Churchill up like a pig on a spit, singing the praises of faggot-fires scorching the unholy. Dismissed in the scramble to condemn Churchill, the statements of Voltaire, among them: "I may disagree with what you say, but I will defend to the death your right to say it," said Barry Pritzker, an administrator at New York's Skidmore College. "The sad and horrible truth is that people like Jefferson, Sam Adams, Madison and half of the other 'Founding Fathers' would probably be vacationing at Guantanamo Bay if they were alive today" (Pritzker, 2005).

On February 2, the Colorado legislature laid aside its usual business and passed a resolution denouncing Churchill's remarks. The next day, the same state's Senate passed a similar resolution. Churchill said that his truck had been painted with swastikas as it sat in his driveway the previous evening. Colorado's governor, Bill Owens, a Republican, called on Churchill to resign, several times. Failing that, the governor called upon the university to terminate Churchill's tenure and fire him. Said Governor Owens: "No one wants to infringe on Mr. Churchill's right to express himself. But we are not compelled to accept his pro-terrorist views at state taxpayer subsidy nor under the banner of the University of Colorado. Ward Churchill besmirches the University and the excellent teaching, writing and research of its faculty" (Owens, 2005). Churchill gave up his chairmanship of the ethnic studies department the same week, and a spokeswoman said that the university's governing body, the nine-member Board of Regents, would meet Thursday to discuss his future (Healy et al., 2005, C-17).

Owens's and O'Reilly's assumption that Churchill is a state employee was something of a stretch. While O'Reilly railed that "the guy is being paid nearly $100,000 of taxpayer money . . ." (O'Reilly, February 11, 2005), as of 2005, the University of Colorado was receiving only 8 percent of its funds from state taxes.

Roughly 15 percent of Churchill's salary was being paid out of state taxes. The rest was being paid by tuition—three-quarters of that by students from out of the state (Spencer, 2005, B-1).

Thursday, February 3, CU-Boulder Interim Chancellor Phil DiStefano (with Arts and Sciences Dean Todd Gleeson and Law School Dean David Getches) initiated a 30-day review of Churchill's speeches and writings to determine whether he had overstepped the boundaries of academic conduct, and whether his conduct might be grounds for dismissal. This review of Churchill's "writings, speeches, tape recordings and other works," must find evidence of outright academic dishonesty, said R. L. Widmann, a professor of English and the chairwoman of the Academic Affairs Committee of the Boulder Faculty Assembly (Johnson and York, 2005). Once the review was completed, the administration had three possible courses of action: do nothing, declare intent to dismiss Churchill for cause, or forward the matter, which had come to include allegations of plagiarism and falsification, to a faculty research-misconduct committee.

HOW MUCH "INDIAN" IS HE?

The controversy over Churchill quickly spread from his right to engage in unpopular political commentary to other matters, including the nature of his ethnic identity. Questions about Churchill's ethnicity had dogged him for many years. During May 1994, he was granted an "associate membership," or honorary status, with the Keetoowah Cherokee. He would have had to show proof of one-quarter blood quantum to be granted full membership; he said that he has 3/16. In July that year, the Keetoowah Cherokee stopped issuing associate member-ships (Rave, 2005). Late in May, a revised statement from the United Keetoowah Band of Cherokee Indians asserted, according to a report in the *Rocky Mountain News* (Brennan, May 21, 2005), that it had found no legal records to indicate that Churchill is a federally recognized American Indian. The statement also clarified the group's reasoning behind its award to Churchill of an associate membership by the Tahlequah, Oklahoma-based tribe in 1994.

> He was not eligible for tribal membership due to the fact that he does not possess a 'Certificate of Degree of Indian Blood' (CDIB)—which is under the jurisdic-tion of the U.S. Department of Interior/Bureau of Indian Affairs. . . . However, Mr. Churchill may possess eligibility status for Cherokee Nation of Oklahoma, since he claims [at least] 1/16 Cherokee [blood quantum]. Because Mr. Churchill had genea-logical information regarding his alleged ancestry, and his willingness to assist the UKB in promoting the tribe and its causes, he was awarded an 'Associate Member-ship' as an honor. (Brennan, May 21, 2005)

Official certification of native status has long been a debatable credential. Many Native people resent having to prove their ethnicity (like a dog's breed, some complain) at the behest of a government agency created under U.S. law.

Some assert that the whole idea of classifying people by degree of blood is an Anglo-American notion born in the nineteenth century of a desire to divide people racially. Others have blood in Native groups that no longer have organized governments or government recognition. Because of all these factors, the entire debate over Churchill's degree of certified Native blood had an artificial air. Churchill lashed out against people who questioned his identity as "card-carrying Indians" and "blood police." For purposes of employment at the University of Colorado, so it turned out, ethnicity was self-identified, as it is for the U.S. Census.

Russell Means, a founder of the American Indian Movement, who is a friend of Churchill, said "We are the only ethnic group that has to prove our blood like the dogs and horses. Ward is my brother. Ward has followed the ways of indigenous peoples world-wide" (Flynn, 2005, 4-A). Churchill said his mother and grandmother told him he was part Indian, and he thought of himself that way while growing up in Illinois. "I'm not identifying as an Indian because of something out of cowboy and Indian movies," he said. "That's my family's understanding of itself" (Elliott, March 18, 2005).

Indian Country Today came down hard on Churchill for what its editors characterized as identity fraud: "the issue of Churchill's . . . [manufactured] identity [as] an American Indian and . . . a spokesman for Native peoples [which] gives the appearance of impropriety and perhaps even professional deception. . . . The professor is not in fact what he professes to be . . ." (Editors' Report, 2005). The newspaper then called upon Churchill to prove his Native ancestry. Any such argument can be blurred by lack of definition. In some cases, people with miniscule amounts of "quantum" (say, 1/32) have assumed legal Indian identities and acquired government-approved credentials.

Suzan Shown Harjo, a Cheyenne and Hodulgee Muscogee (Creek) who is president of the Morning Star Institute in Washington, D.C. and a columnist for *Indian Country Today*, wrote that "People began to check out Churchill's claims." Harjo, who called Churchill "horribly divisive, and . . . a thug" (Flynn, 2005, 4-A), continued: "Cherokee journalist David Cornsilk verified that Churchill and his ancestors were not on the Cherokee Nation rolls. Creek-Cherokee historian Robert W. Trepp did not find them on the Muscogee [Creek] Nation rolls. Then, according to Harjo, "He went tribe-shopping. He added [the] Metis, then [the] Keetoowah, variously claiming to be an associate member, an enrolled member or 1/16 or 3/16 Cherokee" (Harjo, 2005).

AN AVALANCHE OF HATE MAIL

While Harjo was trussing up Churchill on allegations of ethnic fakery, an avalanche of hate mail was racially raking for being *too* Indian. The University of Colorado Ethnic Studies Department, the chancellor's office, and Churchill himself received about 1,000 e-mails and dozens of phone calls *each day* at the height of the controversy during February 2005, many of which were explicitly racist.

These e-mails laid bare centuries-old racial hatreds. While Churchill was reviled for lacking government-issued proof of his Native American identity in some quarters, many authors of these e-mails denigrated him as a filthy, worthless Redskin. What follows is a tiny fraction of the messages received. Some of them were incoherent with hatred from a mixture of patriotism and racism that reminded some observers of the days after the Sand Creek Massacre, in 1864, when body parts of dead Indians were exhibited in Denver for an admission fee.

It's too bad that he is one Indian that got away. . . . Tell um Chief Ward Wigwam: Look like pale face who want um to be um red face is um disgraced. . . . My ancestors killed a lot of Indians and I'm proud of it . . . picket Univ. Of Colorado Prof. Ward Churchill at the fag-infested Kirkland Project of Hamilton College. . . . God Hates Fags! & Fag-Enablers! [and] Hamilton College, the sodomite whorehouse. . . . Why don't you take a silly-*ss Muslim name like Mohammed Mohammed Mohammed and wear a diaper on your head. . . . I'll keep this brief, one—too bad you weren't in the cockpit of one of those jets [at the WTC]. And two, with a comment like that, I'm glad the Indians were wiped out. . . . Your people are a lazy bunch of scum! . . . We The People have given Freedom to . . . Europe and Japan, and we are . . . trying to bring freedom to the Middle East. I will force you to become a piece of trash in the dust bin of history with the rest of your "ancestors." . . . Hey Chief—the "7th Cavalry" is coming after your worthless *ss. . . . YOU'RE A SICK MF AND HOPE YOU FRIGIN GET ANAL CANCER FROM YOUR HOMO STUDENTS. . . . I wouldn't expect a f*cking squaw pussy like you to understand. . . . F*ck you, go to hell. . . . GO PREACH YOUR BULLSH*T IN SAUDI ARABIA OR WHERE ELSE THERE ARE "SAND N*GGERS" BECAUSE YOU WILL BE PUT TO DEATH . . . AND MANY PEOPLE WOULD BE HAPPY. . . . Given my way, you'd be throw[n] into a dark cell for ten years, then [we'd] execute you after that, you homo. . . . You may be interested in knowing that my god son has killed over 30 ragheads, destroyed 15 tanks and 10 Toyota pickup trucks from his F-18. . . . Muslims and Arabs. Where is A. Hitler now that we need him? Even gas wouldn't handle this many vermin.

CHURCHILL SPEAKS IN HAWAII

The controversy evoked support as well as hatred for Churchill. He was invited to speak at the University of Hawaii (UH) at Manoa February 22, 2005 on "Speaking Truth to Power: Academic Freedom in the Age of Terror," by a broad group of UH and community organizations. Speaking to an auditorium that was filled to capacity with a mostly supportive crowd of more than 400 people (plus another 300 standing outside, listening on a video hookup), Churchill emphasized that he had not advocated an attack on the World Trade Center. Rather, he said, he insisted an attack was inevitable, given U.S. international policies and actions. "One does not advocate the volcano," he said. "It requires no advocacy from mere mortals. One points to the volcano and attempts to make sense of it" (Lee, 2005). Churchill spoke of U.S. atrocities in Japan, the Philippines, and in the United States against Hawaiians and American Indians.

A newspaper report said, "The crowd loved it when Mr. Churchill railed against 'the urinal sort of journalism.' They loved when he joked about Bill O'Reilly or Paula Zahn [of Cable News Network]. They laughed when he mocked Thomas Brown, a Lamar University professor who has charged that Mr. Churchill's research is fraudulent. Churchill dismissed the claim with one sentence: 'He found a footnote he disagrees with'" (Smallwood, March 4, 2005, 48).

A DEFENSE OF CHURCHILL'S FREEDOM FROM DAVID DUKE

Two evenings after Churchill was warmly received at the UH, Bill O'Reilly again made him an evening feature on national television. O'Reilly interviewed former Ku Klux Klan leader David Duke, who surprised O'Reilly by supporting Churchill's freedom of speech:

> DUKE: Well, you know, it's true. I was in the KKK about 30 years ago. I've also since that time been elected to the House of Representatives. I've been an elected Republican official in Louisiana, and that's not really what I'm about today.
>
> I'm about the preservation, obviously, of my people, I think our heritage is being really ethnically cleansed in the United States, Canada and Europe. The European-Americans are losing our way of life.
>
> Now, as far as Ward Churchill's concerned, I don't really know much about him, and the only way that we can know about an individual or his viewpoints is to allow those viewpoints to be heard.
>
> I do know that he's very anti-European-American. But I think that all viewpoints have a right to be heard in this country. I do believe in freedom of speech.
>
> I don't agree with what Ward Churchill said, not in one iota. I think it's terrible, the things—some of the things he said. But when you're in academia and when you have an opportunity to express yourself, I think people have a right to make statements. (O'Reilly, February 24, 2005)

A DEBATE IN WISCONSIN

Churchill's next guest-speaking engagement was scheduled for March 1 at the University of Wisconsin at Whitewater, about 50 miles southwest of Milwaukee. Several hundred alumni and others protested a decision allowing Churchill to speak there. Academic officials at the university stood by the decision despite the pressure, which included 700 to 800 e-mails addressing the Churchill controversy, with roughly 75 percent calling on the school to cancel his appearance (Held, 2005, 3).

The Wisconsin Assembly on February 22 passed a resolution condemning "anti-American hate speech" by a vote of 67 to 31, following the University of Wisconsin (UW) Whitewater's refusal to cancel the speech. The assembly's wording was similar to semantics used by Bill O'Reilly on his national talk show, where he kept up a steady drumbeat of anti-Churchill rhetoric. One Wisconsin newspaper commented:

> State Rep. Steve Nass, R-Palmyra, got his Assembly resolution passed last week rec-
> ommending that the UW-Whitewater cancel a scheduled address by controversial
> University of Colorado Professor Ward Churchill. In so doing, he proved that, while
> the State Capitol does not sit upon much of a rise, there are many fools on the hill.
> The Assembly vote on the resolution to condemn Churchill was 67 to 31. Thus, it
> can be said that two-thirds of the members of the lower house of the Legislature have
> confirmed that they do not understand, value or agree with the most basic of principles
> of free speech, free expression and democratic discourse. . . . Yes, the Colorado pro-
> fessor, who has been invited to speak on issues of concern to American Indians, is a
> radical. And, yes, he has said and written things that offend many Wisconsinites. But
> if there is a point to the First Amendment, then it is to protect speech that is radical
> and offensive. ("Fools," 2005, 6-A)

An account in the Madison *Wisconsin State Journal* called Churchill's anticipated appearance "the biggest media event in U.W.-Whitewater history" (Rivedal,
February 24, 2005, A-1). A week before the speech, the university issued 112
sets of press credentials (Rivedal, February 24, 2005, A-1). All 440 free tickets
for the speech were taken the same day they were offered (Rivedal, March 2,
2005, A-1).

At Whitewater, the crowd filed through metal detectors at UW-Whitewater's
Hamilton Center before entering a hall that had been swept by police K-9 units.
Churchill supporters gathered outside the campus' main gate, holding signs reading
"First Amendment Fan" and "Free Speech." Republicans down the sidewalk coun-
tered with signs that read "Wanted, Osama bin Laden, Dead Not Alive" (Associ-
ated Press, March 2, 2005). About 200 protesters gathered on Whitewater's Main
Street and later outside the lecture hall. About half opposed Churchill's appearance,
while those in the other half were interested in protecting his freedom of speech.

Characterized in a news report as "an imposing figure with a deep, booming
voice and black shoulder-length hair tinged with silver," Churchill called the
United States a fascist state that has built an empire on defiance of the rule of
international law. "I think we arrived at that a long time ago," Churchill said in a
fiery talk to a full house audience at the UW-Whitewater. "All the key ingredients
have existed for some time" (Brennan, March 2, 2005, 4-A). Churchill received
his longest, warmest applause when he described media mistakes and misinter-
pretations. "It's on you," Churchill thundered at the many media reporters in the
audience, bringing many in the crowd of nearly 500 to their feet (Rivedal, March
2, 2005, A-1).

Churchill had been invited to speak six months previously, before the "Little
Eichmanns" controversy erupted, as part of the university's third annual Native Pride
Week. Churchill touched only briefly on his original topic, "Racism Against the
American Indian," as he talked about the extermination of indigenous Americans
(Derby, 2005, 3-A). The Wounded Knee massacre of 1890 was just a "punctuation

mark," said Churchill, during an "uninterrupted stream of massacres—wholesale and retail." America's history has been a "continuous, felonious slaughtering of the brown-skinned other" and it has been a part of U.S. enterprise militarily and financially even before the United States existed, Churchill continued (Derby, 2005, 3-A). On the subject of racism, Churchill lashed out at opponents who sought to discredit him by challenging his ethnicity. "This crew can think of nothing worse to call me than a white man," said Churchill, "And they're all white men. Figure that one out." "My elders determine who I am. White journalists don't" (Brennan, March 2, 2005, 4-A).

After the speech, the audience gave Churchill a standing ovation. "I've got 24 books in print, 70 book chapters, about 100 journal articles, introductions, prefaces. . . . Of that, we are focused now on one less-than-20-page essay and within that essay, one phrase," he emphasized (Derby, 2005, 3-A).

THE BATTLE CONTINUES IN COLORADO

On February 28, roughly 200 University of Colorado faculty purchased a $4,000 full-page advertisement in the Boulder *Daily Camera* to maintain that the university should follow its own rules and defend the academic freedom of its faculty, including Churchill. Four days later, two Denver talk-show hosts, Dan Caplis and Craig Silverman, bought another full-page ad making their case that Churchill should be fired. Caplis and Silverman argued that Churchill had violated a loyalty oath to the U.S. and Colorado constitutions that is required of all CU professors:

> Churchill stands credibly accused of ethnic fraud, grade retribution, falsification of the nature of his military service, academic fraud, plagiarism, selling other artists' creations as his own and falsely accusing *Denver Post* columnist Diane Carman of inventing incendiary quotations. All this provides ample justification for termination pursuant to accusations of incompetence and lack of integrity. But it is Churchill's instructions on violence that demand immediate suspension followed by termination. Due process must be provided, but unless this accused can somehow suppress his own statements, he should ultimately lose his job. (Caplis and Silverman, 2005, 13-C)

On March 7, three days after she had warned Colorado University's faculty that a "new McCathyism" was stalking the country (Johnson, 2005), Elizabeth Hoffman announced that she would resign as CU president by June 30. Hoffman told Kirk Johnson of the *New York Times* that the Churchill case was not the main reason for her resignation, but that it had become a distraction that was hindering her ability to address a budget crisis at the university, instigated by erosion of state support (Johnson, 2005). "It was becoming increasingly difficult to be strong on the issues that were important in the long run because it kept coming back to questions about me," Hoffman said, "so I decided I had to take my future, my job, off the table." (Johnson, 2005).

The same day that Hoffman resigned, Bill O'Reilly was back on the air crowing about it:

> O'REILLY: . . . Hoffman blamed the Ward Churchill disaster on me and others in the media who she says are pushing a new McCarthyism. . . . That, of course, is ridiculous. . . . Hoffman is totally intimidated by Churchill. She should have called him into the office and told him to button it, that his offensive rantings . . . were making C.U. look bad. The sad truth is that the University of Colorado has been severely damaged on Hoffman's watch. She was smart to resign, showed a lot of class, much more than Ward Churchill would ever show. He'll take the entire University of Colorado down with him. . . . He's a traitor. He's calling for a violent overthrow of the country. He's a traitor. (O'Reilly, March 7, 2005)

On March 7, O'Reilly once again made Churchill his top story of the evening in an on-going political soap opera that provoked Churchill to joke that O'Reilly should change his talk show's name to "The Ward Churchill Factor." By the end of April 2005, O'Reilly had mentioned Churchill's name (and often much more than that) on 31 segments in three months (Labash, 2005).

Some of the right-wing press took a cut of the parody. The right-wing *Weekly Standard* characterized Churchill as "a nostalgia ride at the Aging Radicals Theme Park. . . . As on most days, he is denim'ed and boot'ed, his hair featuring two gray racing stripes down either side that tuck behind his prodigious ears, pushing them out as if he were trying to receive The O'Churchill Factor on twin satellite dishes. He has the lived-in and leathered quality of Nick Nolte in a post DUI-mugshot, and the Sunday-Morning-Coming-Down, outlaw Zen of a Kris Kristofferson" (Labash, 2005).

In mid-March 2005, Associated Press reporter Dan Elliott described Churchill at home in Boulder:

> Stacks of papers sit on a sun-drenched table in the home of University of Colorado professor Ward Churchill, some full of praise and others full of dark threats and unprintable insults. In one message, liberal scholar Noam Chomsky calls Churchill's achievements of inestimable value, while an e-mail in another pile warns: "If you ever come to Florida, I will personally bash your [expletive] brains in." (Elliott, March 18, 2005)
>
> Churchill . . . said he won't back down as the school investigates him to see if he can be fired. But he wearily acknowledged the uproar now dominates his life and makes it difficult to focus on his job as a tenured professor of ethnic studies. "I'm struggling desperately to be able to deliver to my students what they signed up for," Churchill said, slumped in a chair and chain-smoking Pall Malls. "All of my time is devoted to responding to gratuitous (expletive). Every day there's a new idiocy." (Elliott, March 18, 2005)

AN EXERCISE IN FREE SPEECH

On March 25, the same day that the Colorado regents ordered a review of the university's tenure system, the panel appointed to review Churchill's conduct found that his comments *vis a vis* the Trade Center attacks were an exercise of free speech not warranting revocation of his tenure. However, the same panel said that other allegations involving misrepresentation of his ethnic identity, misinterpretation of evidence, and plagiarism should be examined. Allegations that Churchill had violated copyright by free handing a piece of Thomas Mails's artwork did not figure in this report; perhaps because no one brought them to the committee, or perhaps because the incidence occurred before Churchill was employed at the University of Colorado.

As the University of Colorado investigated his record, Churchill's book *On the Justice of Roosting Chickens*, from Oakland-based anarchist publisher AK Press [developed from the original "Little Eichmanns" essay on the Internet (Churchill, "Some People Push Back, 2001)], briefly cracked Amazon.com's top 100 best-seller list. At about the same time, Churchill was invited to speak at the tenth Annual San Francisco Bay Area Anarchist Book Fair on March 26 in Golden Gate State Park, hosted in part by his Oakland publisher.

From San Francisco, *Rocky Mountain News* reporter Charlie Brennan described Churchill's keynote address at the book fair:

> The preacher found his choir. . . . Ward Churchill spent the weekend in the bosom of a community where his defiant, iconoclastic political message is mother's milk. The highlight of his tour was the 10th annual San Francisco Bay Area Anarchist Book Fair on Saturday at Golden Gate Park. You could have found it just by following the spiked Mohawks, the prodigious full-body tattoos and the hundreds of acolytes attired in every shade of black. . . . "This is great. I've never been to one of these before," said Churchill, who never took off his can't-see-through-'em wraparound shades during a 45-minute keynote address Saturday afternoon. . . . The fair's exhibits offered more than just books. There was clothing, including baby jumpers bearing the words "Future Queer" and T-shirts featuring a familiar fast-food franchise logo and the words "Murder King." There were even games to play, including "Pin the Molotov Cocktail on the Cop Car." (Brennan, March 28, 2005, 4-A)

At the book fair, the right-wing *Weekly Standard*'s Matt Labash characterized Churchill as "collecting five grand a throw to feed discontent to roomfuls of emaciated anarchists, when what they most need is a hot shower and a cheeseburger" (Labash, 2005).

> Churchill takes the dais, uncoiling his long frame like a python warming itself in the sun, and lets his pearl-buttoned denim shirt drop to the floor, giving it an angry kick. He's wearing a stained T-shirt. In an over-pronounced Indian cadence (what Indian activist and longtime Churchill nemesis Suzan Harjo calls his "Tonto talk"), he brings greetings from the elders of the Keetoowah band of Cherokee, and uncorks his customary tribute to Leonard Peltier. . . . (Labash, 2005)

From the same stage, Churchill needled Brennan, who had been assigned the Ward Churchill beat at the *Rocky Mountain News*:

> Brennan is in the audience, and the room turns to see him scribbling away furiously without looking up. "Yeah, Hi Charlie!" bellows Churchill. "Having a nice day now?

My turn. I got the high ground. . . . Are you still beating your wife, Charlie? Answer me yes or no, please. And remember, I got nine people who hate your guts and are going to comment on whatever it is you have to say." After demanding to see proof that Brennan is white (he'd probably never felt whiter), Churchill pushes the assault: "And you purport to be a man, . . . yet only one of your parents was, and you know it! . . . I'm practicing the journalist trade. . . . I expect a job at the *Rocky Mountain News* when I get back. (Labash, 2005)

PIT BULLS WITH LOCKJAW

By the end of March, the tidal wave of national media coverage had begun to ebb, although the *Rocky Mountain News* and Bill O'Reilly still couldn't seem to get enough of Churchill. One observer in Denver jested that the *Rocky Mountain News* "has printed enough words attacking longtime AIM provocateur Ward Churchill to fill a Harry Potter book" ("AIM Fire," 2005, n.p.). Regarding the media focus on his personal life, Churchill at one point growled: "I don't care. Show me some possible relevance to it. . . . I'm not running for f---ing office. I don't have to vet my life back to potty training stage" (Labash, 2005).

Churchill sometimes became emotional. Evoking concerns for his aging mother and stepfather as his life came under intense scrutiny. "I chose this life; they didn't," he said, noting that the names of his relatives had been published in newspapers. He called the uproar against him "nakedly hostile, racially hostile," "Maybe Hitler chose the wrong group of people to place in the ovens," read one of the e-mails he received. "Maybe he should have chosen the American Indians, starting with your great-great-grandparents," read another (Herdy, March 31, 2005, A-1).

Like a pit bull with an enduring case of lockjaw, Bill O'Reilly continued to hound Churchill on his Fox Network talk show. Should he live to be a hundred years of age, however, Churchill may never receive the treatment that O'Reilly meted out to Jane Fonda April 5, 2005. Never mind that Fonda's visit to Hanoi during the Vietnam war that provoked O'Reilly's tirade was almost four decades old. Never mind the fact that Vietnam now makes more Nikes than any other country, or that Americans today are being invited to recline in five-star Hanoi hotels. Never mind the fact that Fonda has since confessed that her advocacy of North Vietnam during the war was a monumental error of judgment. The "news" on the O'Reilly Factor April 5, 2005 was: "How should we feel about Jane Fonda? Some people think she makes Ward Churchill look like Patrick Henry" (O'Reilly, April 5, 2005).

During May 2005, Churchill won a student poll as University of Colorado students' favorite professor. The university's alumni association, which had sponsored the contest, withheld the award, finding itself in a public-relations lose-lose situation, due to Churchill's tendency to "antagonize and create enemies," according to the head of the association. "There are many things we say and do based on free speech," Kent Zimmerman, president of the alumni association, said. "But how we say them can make people more accepting of the message" (Herdy, May 27, 2005, B-1).

Churchill wasn't winning any popularity contests with members of a fundamentalist Christian group who marched on his office July 19, asserting that he is possessed by demons. "That's the power of Christ, to set the captive free from the lies and from those demons that are inhabiting Ward," declared Rev. Flip Benham, of Concord, N.C., to more than 100 members of Operation Save America who gathered outside CU's Ketchum Building, which houses Churchill's basement office (Morson, July 20, 2005, 6-A).

FORMAL INQUIRY INITIATED

On September 9, the University of Colorado decided to initiate a formal inquiry into charges of research misconduct against Churchill, including allegations that he had published work mischaracterizing blood-quantum requirements in the Indian Arts and Crafts Act of 1990 and the General Allotment Act of 1887; that he had repeatedly advanced a theory charging the U.S. Army with an act of genocide against the Mandans in 1837 by intentionally spreading smallpox; that he plagiarized the work of professor Fay Cohen of Dalhousie University in Nova Scotia, Canada, and that he had plagiarized a defunct Canadian environmental group's pamphlet on a shelved water-diversion project.

In his defense, Churchill said the allegations were trivial: "Out of dozens of accusations . . . ranging from treason to advocacy of violence to personal threats to misrepresenting his identity to plagiarism, all that remain are a handful of questions regarding historical interpretation and the conventions of citation or attribution," said Natsu Saito, CU associate professor of Ethnic Studies and Ward Churchill's wife (Saito, September 10, 2005). Churchill argued:

> On the whole, I submit that no scholar with a comparably extensive publication record would have fared better. Certainly, my accusers would not. The real question, then, is not the integrity of my scholarship. Rather, it is whether the University of Colorado is going to subject the writings of all its faculty to a degree of scrutiny similar in "rigor" to that visited upon mine. . . . (Churchill, May 16, 2006)

During February 2006, the committee asked for more time, until May 9. In an interim report to CU's Standing Committee on Research Misconduct, Marianne Wesson, CU professor of law and chairwoman of the five-person investigative committee, said that the group has met several times and interviewed many expert witnesses.

May 1, 2006, two weeks before the investigative report was made public, Saito resigned her position at CU. She charged that the university had become indifferent to ethnic studies and students of color in general, in "an environment hostile to people of color. The university has no commitment (other than a facade of 'diversity') to recruiting or retaining faculty and students of color," she said (Saito, 2006). "This may sound like boilerplate criticism," she said, but "It's a very different story when one spends hours, week after week, with students in tears, trying to help them muster the internal strength needed simply to face another day in an unrelentingly hostile environment" (Saito, 2006).

THE "CHURCHILL COMMITTEE" ISSUES ITS REPORT

The investigative committee's 125-page report, which was released to the public May 9, was a curious document. It began by questioning the context within which the committee was convened, as well as its scope and purpose, raising some of the same objections that Churchill himself had broached. Nevertheless, the committee found Churchill culpable on six of seven instances of plagiarism, falsification, and violation of academic research norms lodged before it, and called for suspension or termination of his employment.

The report answered Churchill's assertion that he had been over-scrutinized with a parable, suggesting that if a police officer stops a motorist because he objects to the content of a bumper sticker while he is violating the speed limit, the motorist is still guilty of speeding—for instance, the charges against Churchill raised in addition to his "little Eichmanns" statement were still valid, even as the committee went to great lengths to describe the statement itself as constitutionally protected free speech, in support of its devotion to "robust and free debate" (Wesson, 2006, 3). Most speeding tickets, however, are not adjudicated through a public shaming ritual in front of millions of people with the governor of one's home state calling for termination of the speeder's professional career.

The report's first section (pp. 3–12) wrung its hands over contextual matters that undoubtedly will figure in any future post-termination lawsuit by Churchill. The charges, for example, were several years old by the time the committee was convened; in at least one case, before the furor over the "Little Eichmanns" comment, the university already had declined to investigate the allegation. The committee observed that the charges against Churchill involved a very small fraction of his published work, which includes a dozen solely authored books and at least 100 other book chapters, essays, and reviews. The committee mulled whether Churchill's transgressions are a result of "occasional careless error . . . or form a pattern" (Wesson, 2006, 9). The report also acknowledged that Churchill "is one of the most widely read and influential writers in this country who deal with American Indian issues" (Wesson, 2006, 6).

The report then focused on specifics, often with exhaustive, legalistic intensity. Did Churchill mis-state some of the terms of the General Allotment Act (1887), notably a half-blood quantum, comprising what he took to be a "eugenics code," as alleged by Prof. John P. LaVelle of the University of New Mexico Law School? Yes, said the committee. The law contains no such specific requirement (it never defines "Indian"). The report found that Churchill repeated this statement at least 11 times. However (and here we get into nuanced territory generally ignored by media reports), the report acknowledged that "thirty years after the enactment of the General Allotment Act of 1887 . . . the Act was implemented with criteria like, but not identical to those Professor Churchill describes" (Wesson, 2006, 19).

The factual terrain here is immensely complex. Churchill seemed to have simplified and misrepresented a more complex history ("gross historical inaccuracies" is the report's phrase, on page 22) in an attempt to establish that the Allotment Act was eugenic in nature. The report also says that LaVelle distorts Churchill's allegations, and that Churchill was not engaged in a "general hoax," as LaVelle asserted (pp. 22–23). "Sloppiness," yes, but not "research misconduct" (p. 23). The committee found problems with Churchill's work on the subject of which LaVelle seemed unaware, however. In support of his case on this issue, for example, Churchill referenced book chapters under other peoples' names that he had written himself (Wesson, 2006, 24). Other references do not support his assertions (p. 25). By pages 26–27, adding all this up, the committee said that Churchill "has engaged in research misconduct . . . which . . . was deliberate" (Wesson, 2006, 26–27).

Professor LaVelle also alleged that Churchill misrepresented the Indian Arts and Crafts Act of 1990, claiming that anyone "not federally recognized as being Native American," defined as one-quarter blood quantum, may not offer for sale goods represented as Indian-produced under penalty of up to $5 million (Wesson, 2006, 28). The law contains no blood-level limit, but does require recognition of an artist by a federally recognized Native tribe or nation. While Churchill later described the act without mention of a blood-quantum requirement, he did so without explicitly retracting the original assertion (Wesson, 2006, 31), meanwhile again citing his own words in ghostwritten form (among other sources) in support. The committee concluded that Churchill again was guilty of "serious research misconduct . . . part of a general pattern of such misconduct in support of his political views" (Wesson, 2006, 31). Churchill also was criticized for refusing to engage LaVelle in a debate on the issue.

"Allegation C," in the committee's lexicon, took up allegations by Churchill that the smallpox virus was intentionally used as a vehicle of genocide, beginning with early settlement in New England, most notably by John Smith, of Jamestown, Virginia, during a visit to the Wampanoags in 1614. Smallpox is incredibly virulent. It spreads through the air, and killed many Native Americans from fishing boats offshore, often years before immigrants made landfall. By the time immigrants made contact, smallpox often already had done its work. It hardly needed human help. The committee found that while there is evidence of disease (*which* disease is not known) among New England Indians at the time, no direct evidence associates Smith with its introduction. Smith is on record as having favored using Indians as cheap labor; while he was brutal in his treatment of them, outright extermination did not seem to interest him, according to the committee's work. The report called Churchill's assertions about Smith and smallpox "falsification." "He fabricated his account, because no evidence—not even circumstantial evidence—supports it" (Wesson, 2006, 38).

"Allegation D" also examined allegations by Churchill that smallpox was deliberately spread, this time by the U.S. Army, among the Mandans at and near

Fort Clark, in present-day North Dakota, during 1837, initiating a regional epidemic that continued until 1840. The Mandan suffered a smallpox epidemic at the time; their population, 1,600 to 2,000 in June 1837, was reduced to 138 by October of the same year (Wesson, 2006, 44). During 1837 and 1838, the method of transmission may have been infected blankets from a military infirmary in St. Louis. Churchill's account was challenged by Prof. Thomas Brown of Lamar University. Brown asserted that Churchill's work cited work by Prof. Russell Thornton of UCLA, but Thornton concluded the opposite, that the story of intentional smallpox transmission "had no historical basis" (Wesson, 2006, 39). Thornton himself stated that Churchill misrepresented his work.

The fact that smallpox was conveyed up the Missouri on the St. Peter's, a supply ship, during 1837 has been well established. One man was reported to have been ill as early as April 29, when the ship docked in St. Joseph, Missouri. Several other passengers on the ship were ill by the time the ship reached Council Bluffs, Iowa, during early May. By that time, their illness had been positively identified as smallpox. (The report itself is not without errors. On page 43, the report states that the Missouri River from St. Joseph, Missouri to Council Bluffs is 600 miles. It's roughly a quarter of that.)

The ship arrived at Fort Clark during the third week of June, after which smallpox was transmitted to the Mandans. Published sources provide no evidence that the Army intentionally spread smallpox among Plains Native peoples during 1837, the committee found, after a painstaking examination of the evidence. What *did* provoke the massive smallpox epidemic was capitalist avarice: Bernard Pratte, Jr., the captain of the St. Peter's, and his partner in the shipping company Pratte, Chouteau & Co., should have turned around as soon as they realized that smallpox was on board, between St. Joseph and Council Bluffs. The captain should have returned to St. Louis, put the entire crew into quarantine, and burned all of the merchandise that was distributed to the Mandans, at considerable financial loss. Interviewed for an article in the *Missouri Republican* during 1879, 42 years later, at the age of approximately 75, Pratte was quoted as saying that "He supposed he was in some measure the innocent cause of this calamity" (Wesson, 2006, 52).

The committee found some vague assertions that the Army had spread smallpox in Native American oral histories, but then faulted Churchill for bringing these accounts into his argument during the investigation, only *after* he had allegedly fabricated a greater degree of detail and attributed it to written sources that did not support what he was writing. To the committee, this constituted disrespect of oral tradition. "Churchill," the report said, "has created myth under the banner of academic scholarship . . . [involving] falsification, fabrication, and serious deviation from accepted practices in reporting results from his research" (Wesson, 2006, 81, 82).

Regarding the smallpox epidemic, Churchill later told Amy Goodman on Democracy Now, on National Public Radio:

> With regard to the so-called Ft. Clark incident, the smallpox epidemic of 1837, I presented them with information that what I said had been said in print by prior authors.

They're right, they're wrong. But I could not have invented what was already in print. They disregarded that altogether. . . . They interviewed several people from a tradition of the peoples most directly affected by the 1837 smallpox epidemic, discovered to their dismay that the history of those peoples confirms essentially what I said. (Goodman, 2006)

The remaining three allegations before the committee dealt with assertions of plagiarism. The first, "Allegation E," involved a pamphlet by a Canadian environmental activist group, Damn the Dams Campaign, published during 1972, titled "The Water Plot." The publication alleged that Canadian officials were planning to divert fresh water and hydroelectricity to the United States from a project in Canada's far north that did not take place. The report called Churchill "a fluent and gifted prose stylist (Wesson, 2006, 83), as it expressed astonishment that he did not summarize the pamphlet and credit the source. Churchill asserted that the use of exact wording was authorized, but written permission was not obtained, and the authorizing person could not be traced years after the fact. The committee found, therefore, that plagiarism had occurred (Wesson, 2006, 87). The author of "Dam the Dams," John Hummel, was quoted in the Denver media as largely supporting what Churchill had done with his pamphlet, wishing he had done more. "Sounds like he 'confirmed permission'from where I'm sitting," Churchill said in an email (Churchill, December 20, 2006).

The second allegation of plagiarism involved a chapter, "Self-Determination and Subordination: The Past, Present, and Future of American Indian Governance," in *The State of Native America: Genocide, Colonization, and Resistance*, edited by M. Annette Jaimes (Boston: South End Press, 1992, pp. 87–121). This allegation was initially presented by Professor LaVelle. This was the one allegation of the seven that the committee did not affirm. It found that common wording was not long enough to constitute plagiarism. In addition, the chapter was actually ghost-written by Churchill himself, one of several noted in referencing problems under other allegations. Churchill himself told the committee that he wrote five chapters in the Jaimes book under other names.

Jaimes was Churchill's wife at the time; they divorced in 1995. In 2005, she was teaching at San Francisco State University. According to a report in the *Rocky Mountain News*, Jaimes called Churchill a "liar" and said he is trying to dodge a plagiarism charge by jeopardizing her career. "He's despicable," she said (Morson, June 7, 2005, 16-A).

While this instance was not held to be plagiarism, Churchill was criticized for research misconduct because he wrote scholarly non-fiction under the names of other people. Churchill argued that history provides precedent for such practice; while the committee found his argument "witty and provocative," its members were not persuaded (Wesson, 2006, 90).

The third and final charge of plagiarism involved work on fishing rights by Fay G. Cohen of Dalhousie University published during 1991 in *Critical Issues in Native North America*, an anthology edited by Churchill (Copenhagen: International Work

Group on Indigenous Affairs, pp. 154–175). Parts of the chapter were repeated, under Churchill's name, in *The State of Native America*, a year later. The University Secretary and Legal Counsel at Dalhousie described the use of this material as a case of plagiarism in 1997, and the Colorado committee agreed.

Churchill did not dispute what the committee called "robust similarities in language" when he was interviewed by the committee (Wesson, 2006, 91). Cohen's essay was referenced a few times in the 1992 chapter, but large passages of exact or similar text were not attributed. Churchill asserted that the chapter was placed under his name in error, and that he did not write it (Wesson, 2006, 92). The committee did not find this assertion convincing, in part because he was listed as author of the chapter on his internal annual report at the University of Colorado for 1991 (Wesson, 2006, 92). Churchill then denied having prepared the report, claiming that Jaimes (who declined an interview with the committee) or an un-named student assistant made an error. The report pointed out that Churchill signed the report, and thus became legally responsible for its contents. His excuse thus, in the report's words, "strains credulity" (Wesson, 2006, 92). The committee supported as credible statements by Cohen that she withdrew her essay from *The State of Native America* after editing disputes with Churchill, only to find that her name was removed but her words were used in "somewhat altered" form (Wesson, 2006, 93).

In addition to specific violations of research "norms," the report criticized Churchill for lacking a sense of scholarly nuance, of where scholarly advocacy ("profession") ends and unsubstantiated polemic begins. It acknowledged, however, that Churchill is one of many "scholar activists," some of whom (Howard Zinn and Noam Chomsky were mentioned as examples) are very well known and in no apparent danger of losing their livelihoods.

Based on its findings, four of five committee members (names were not provided) recommended that the university suspend Churchill without pay. Two suggested two years and two others recommended five years. The fifth committee member said the university should fire him. Two of the committee members who recommended suspension for five years agreed that Churchill's misconduct was severe enough that CU also could legally terminate his tenure and employment. Two said that dismissal was not warranted, "because they believe that his dismissal would have an adverse effect on the ability of other scholars to conduct their research with due freedom" (Wesson, 2006, 102).

SELF-ASSIGNED SEATS

Reaction to the report was so predictable that I could have been watching members of a class taking self-assigned seats; everyone was absorbed in his or her familiar role, riding well-worn tires on a familiar road. One, of course, was Churchill himself, who had lost none of his own talent for acerbic sound-bite reaction.

The day the report was made public, Churchill called it a "travesty," and a "pretext to punish me for engaging constitutionally-protected speech and, more generally, to discredit the sorts of alternative historical perspective I represent" (Churchill, May 16, 2006). "The upshot is that the committee's report is often self-contradictory. It frequently misrepresents or conflicts with the evidence presented. In many respects, it is patently false. . . . The entire procedure appears to be little more than a carefully-orchestrated effort to cast an aura of legitimacy over an entirely illegitimate set of predetermined outcomes. It follows that I reject and will vigorously contest each and every finding of misconduct," Churchill continued (Churchill, May 16, 2006). Churchill also said that the C.U. report did not include any of the evidence files he had submitted. "So there's no way for anybody to compare their findings with the information they had in hand" (Churchill, December 20, 2006).

The day the report became public, I checked pirateballerina.com, the most acerbic of many anti-Churchill Web sites, and was reminded that Jim Paine, its sponsor, is a master of the out-of-context quote, playing to his own audience in the Sound-bite Nation, letting three- and four-word bits of Churchill's first gut-level reaction resonate with his audience:

> 9News (Denver) has an exclusive interview with Churchill . . . in which Churchill broadcasts his responses to the investigative committee's report direct from Bizarro World. Our favorite quote happens to be his very first statement: "There is not a shred of evidence—and I'm not talking about convincing evidence, I'm talking about *any* evidence—to support the allegation of plagiarism." Toward the end of the interview, Churchill calls the members of the investigating committee "a bunch of devout non-Indians" and "a bunch of white academics."

Governor Bill Owens and a number of other politicians once again dusted off their vote-aggrandizing calls for the regents to fire Churchill, this time reinforced with references to the committee's recommendations.

David Lane, Churchill's attorney, took his own seat, threatening once again that he would sue the university for infringing his client's First Amendment rights—as if the courts in the racist empire that Churchill describes were going to snap to attention on his command. Vincent Carroll, editorial-page editor at *The Rocky Mountain News*, was in his usual and accustomed chair two days after the report came out, titling his "On Point" column "Ward's World: Fade Out," crowing that the academic wimps up in Boulder never would have gotten as far as they did without prodding from "the media," by which he meant his newspaper. "The larger point missed by the committee as it held its nose in proximity to the grubby press is that reporters, particularly at this newspaper, had already examined most of the issues in the C.U. report and had reached essentially identical, if not so detailed, conclusions. If it hadn't been for the news media blazing the investigative trail, Churchill's future at C.U. as its resident fraud would remain secure to this day" (Carroll, 2006, 44-A).

CHURCHILL'S DETAILED DEFENSE

Following his sound-bite reaction the day the report was released, Churchill issued a detailed rebuttal a few days later. While the investigatory committee's report stressed a focus on specific instances of research misconduct and maintained that Churchill's free-speech rights had been protected, his response said this was a smokescreen. He called the report "the latest step in CU's ongoing attempt to fire me for political speech and, more fundamentally, for scholarship which challenges the orthodox 'cannon' of historical truth" (Churchill, May 16, 2006, 1). Churchill maintained that the committee had abandoned "all semblance" of due process and equal protection under the law—phrases that could appear again in a lawsuit after the university terminates Churchill's employment based on the report's findings. Churchill's response also maintained that the committee "betrayed the most basic principles of academic freedom." He said that the committee, "unable to condemn my substantive conclusions . . . engaged in a detailed *post hoc* critique of my citations," to determine the "historical truth" about disputed matters.

Churchill asserted that the committee, acting as prosecutor and judge, had done "exactly what it accuses me of doing: it tailored its report to fit its conclusions" (Churchill, May 16, 2006). Churchill's books contain roughly 12,000 references by his count, and thus he argues that not even "any even marginally prolific scholar's publications could withstand the type of scrutiny to which mine has been subjected" (Churchill, May 20, 2006, 5–6).

The work under examination was "years, sometimes decades, old," Churchill argued (Churchill, May 20, 2006, 2). The university's public disclosure of the report violated confidentiality rules as well, he asserted. Churchill contended that the committee "included no one with expertise in my field," which he defined as "American Indian Studies—a subset of Ethnic Studies." His definition excluded legal experts; Robert N. Clinton, one of the committee's members, served as a justice on several reservation courts, coauthored a casebook on American Indian law and federal courts, *The Handbook of Federal Indian Law, Colonial and American Indian Treaties* (a collection on CD-ROM), and more than 25 law-journal articles on federal Indian law, American constitutional law and history, and federal courts.

Churchill said that the committee should have merely reported its findings, and avoided recommending sanctions. He also asserted that the committee exceeded its mandate by attempting to determine " 'truth' of disputed historical matters" (Churchill, May 20, 2006, 3). The report thus devotes 44 pages of historical fact-finding and analysis to two paragraphs that Churchill produced about the alleged transmission of smallpox by the Army at Fort Clark. In so doing, responded Churchill, "the committee retroactively imposed standards in ways that have never been applied to other scholars at C.U." (Churchill, May 20, 2006, 4). In many cases, Churchill said the committee took his lack of exact information and sources to be evidence of falsification when he admitted in the material under investigation that evidence was circumstantial. Churchill also took considerable umbrage at the committee's finding that he had disrespected Indian oral traditions while writing about the 1837 smallpox epidemic.

Churchill further asserted that "Damn the Dams" was happy to have had its material published, and credit for coauthorship was provided, only to be removed later by the publisher. Churchill later credited the group in footnotes. "For this I am charged with plagiarism," Churchill retorted (Churchill, May 20, 2006, 5). Regarding Fay Cohen's plagiarism allegations, Churchill said that he merely copy-edited the book, that Cohen never complained to the publisher, her university solicited the complaint, and that neither she nor Dalhousie University provided the committee any evidence that he had plagiarized her work. "On the record," wrote Churchill, "My denial that I did so stands uncontested" (Churchill, May 20, 2006, 5).

THE STANDING COMMITTEE ON RESEARCH MISCONDUCT CALLS FOR TERMINATION

On June 13, casting secret ballots, University of Colorado's Standing Committee on Research Misconduct accepted the special committee's report. Six of nine members who cast ballots (two were ex-officio, without voting authority) said he should be fired, saying he "has committed serious, repeated and deliberate research misconduct," including plagiarism and fabrication of material (Burnett, 2006).

The panel excoriated Churchill for "a pattern of intentional errors" in his work. "The [committee] acknowledges that any scholar can make an occasional mistake, particularly when producing the volume of writing that Professor Churchill claims. . . . We are forced to conclude, as did the Investigative Committee, that this is not a case of 'ordinary error,' but a pattern of repeated, intentional misrepresentation," the committee's report said. The report said that

> The SCRM strongly disagrees with critics of the Investigative Committee report who have suggested that Professor Churchill's violations were isolated, mundane, or trivial. To the contrary, we conclude that the violations are extreme examples of research misconduct, particularly in this area of study. Providing misleading or incorrect citations, bending accounts to fit one's desired interpretation, or simply making up information all strike at the foundation of scholarly historical work. (Rosse et al., 2006, 10)

"The pattern and the nature of the violations suggest that Professor Churchill's behavior was motivated not simply by a lack of awareness of academic standards, but in willful disregard of those standards," the report said, continuing:

> As one example, it is apparent that he is familiar with standards for citing references, and by his own statements (as noted by the Investigative Committee) about the importance of doing so—yet he repeatedly violated those standards. In the case of putting others' names on publications he wrote (and then citing these publications as support for statements he made in subsequent publications), we find incredible his claim that this is standard and accepted practice. His conduct and claims indicate deliberate misconduct, which we believe merits serious sanction. (Rosse et al., 2006, 11–12)

"We are drawn to the irresistible conclusion that Professor Churchill is unable, or at least unwilling, to acknowledge legitimate critique," the report concluded. "If he is unwilling to acknowledge critiques, we are pessimistic that he is likely to change his behavior" (Burnett, 2006).

The committee also recommended three changes of university policies: more thorough peer review of faculty members' research, and consistent application of policies for hiring and promotions, following allegations that Churchill was granted promotion and tenure without the usual seven-year review. The third recommendation asked the provost and chancellor to help restore the reputations of faculty members hurt by the investigation, particularly those in the ethnic studies department (Burnett, 2006).

The committee's 20-page report and recommendations were forwarded to Provost Susan Avery and Arts and Sciences Dean Todd Gleeson, who then send it to Interim Chancellor Phil DiStefano (who made the final decision, subject to approval by the Board of Regents). After DiStefano recommended on July 26 that Churchill be fired, he was entitled to one more review: an appeal to the university's Committee on Privilege and Tenure. During that appeal, Churchill was relieved of teaching assignments. DiStephano emphasized that his decision had nothing to do with Churchill's comments about the World Trade Center attacks, but was based entirely on the decisions of university committees that he had been guilty of plagiarism, misrepresentation of facts, and fabrication of scholarly work.

David Lane, Churchill's attorney, retorted that the committees' findings were a pretext for firing on freedom-of-speech grounds, and that a lawsuit on those grounds was being prepared. "It's window dressing," Lane said. "They want to make it look legitimate so then they can fire him and say, 'Look, it had nothing to do with free speech'" (Johnson, June 27, 2006).

An Emergency Summit of Scholars and Activists Defending Critical Thinking and Indigenous Studies met September 29 and 30 in Lawrence, Kansas. After a number of presentations, several dozen people, some of them nationally known, endorsed a resolution calling upon the Privilege and Tenure Committee to "stand up" and uphold Churchill's appeal of dismissal at C.U. The resolution said that the university was reinforcing "mainstream" truths' concerning the 1837 smallpox epidemic and other matters while accusing Churchill of 'disrespecting American Indian oral traditions,' and punishing his 'bad attitude' illustrated by his refusal to "recant his understandings of historical truth," thereby "chill[ing] the expression of counter-hegemonic truths to re-impose a 'consensus' history dictated by the perspective of the colonizers, and to fuel racist attacks on students and scholars of color" (Ward Churchill Update, November 6, 2006). The statement called upon the university to recognize that its report was flawed, rescind it, and restore Churchill to his post with an explicit recognition of "perspectives which challenge orthodoxy in pursuit of truth" (Ward Churchill Update, November 6, 2006). Signers included Russell Means, Noam Chomsky, Winona LaDuke, and Richard Falk.

"DEAD MAN WALKING"

The evening that Churchill's firing was recommended by DiStefano, Bill O'Reilly enthused on his national talk show: "Late this afternoon, Ward Churchill was deemed a dead man walking. . . ." (O'Reilly, June 26, 2006). Thus, by the time University of Colorado had exorcised Ward Churchill, his career as all-purpose political hate-object reached its apex in the world of gutter-level rhetoric, from the well-known world of right-wing pundits to the lesser-known precincts of the American Indian Movement's faction-ridden remains.

Representative of the latter, David Seals, Wyandot (Huron) and Welsh, an accomplished author of fiction (*Pow-Wow Highway* and *Sweet Medicine* are among his works) penned a vitriolic essay (Seals, 2006, 182–198) that may, someday, come up for examination by a committee of scholars as exacting as those who examined Churchill. Without evident proof, Seals's essay called Churchill a "poseur" (p. 184), an agent provocateur on the Federal Bureau of Investigation's payroll (p. 188), a purveyor of "over-footnoted anal academic speciousness" (p. 190), a *wink-tay* ("homosexual" in an unspecified Native language) (p. 192), and a "suck-up" to the Nicaraguan "contras" during the 1980s (p. 198)—all in the space of 17 printed pages. A court brief, this was not. As a novelist, Seals can be mesmerizing, but his aversion to the rituals of academic anality raise acute doubts over where his perception of reality ends and imagination begins—a common problem in the world of gut-level commentators, many of whom are much less skilled at their art than Seals. Thus did Churchill, once a proud, self-professed artist of gut-level rhetoric, become its victim.

REFERENCES

"AIM Fire: The American Indian Movement Targets *The Rocky*." *Denver Westword*, December 15, 2005, n.p. (in LEXIS).

Associated Press, Wisconsin State and Regional Feed, March 2, 2005 (in LEXIS).

Brennan, Charlie. "Churchill Says U.S. a Fascist State; Hundreds Turn Out to Hear Professor Speak in Wisconsin." *Rocky Mountain News*, March 2, 2005, 4-A.

Brennan, Charlie. "Churchill Finds Fans at Calif. Fest; C.U. Professor Gives Keynote address at Anarchist Book fair." *Rocky Mountain News*, March 28, 2005, 4-A.

Brennan, Charlie. "Tribe Clarifies Stance on Prof.; Milder Statement Explains Churchill's 'Associate' Label." *Rocky Mountain News*, May 21, 2005, 16-A.

Burnett, Sara. "C.U. Panel: Fire Prof; Churchill Should be Cut Loose, Say Six of Nine Who Cast Secret Ballots." *Rocky Mountain News*, June 14, 2006. http://www.rockymountainnews.com/drmn/education/article/0,1299,DRMN_957_4773332,00.html.

Caplis, Dan and Craig Silverman. "Churchill's Active Advocacy of Violence Demands his Firing." *Rocky Mountain News*, March 5, 2005, 13-C.

Carroll, Vincent. "On Point: Ward's World: Fade-out." *Rocky Mountain News*, May 18, 2006, 44-A.

Churchill, Ward. "Some People Push Back: On the Justice of Roosting Chickens." 2001. http://www.kersplebedeb.com/mystuff/s11/churchill.html, N.d. (accessed February 3, 2005).

Churchill, Ward. "Press Release." January 31, 2005, via e-mail forward.

Churchill, Ward. "Statement of Ward Churchill." May 16, 2006. Supplied by the author via e-mail.

Churchill, Ward. Personal Communication. December 20, 2006.

Curtin, Dave, Howard Pankratz, and Arthur Kane. "Questions Stoke Ward Churchill's Fire-brand Past." *Denver Post*, February 13, 2005, A-1.

Derby, Samara Kalk. "Churchill Defends 9/11-Nazi Link; Indian Issues Get Little Attention in U.W. Speech." *Capital Times* (Madison, Wisconsin), March 2, 2005, 3-A.

Editors' Report. "The Churchill Episode: Two Unfortunate Currents." *Indian Country Today*, February 10, 2005. http://www.indiancountry.com/content.cfm?id=1096410338.

Elliott, Dan. "AP Interview: Professor Says He Won't Back Down from Sept. 11 Comments, but Is Weary of Fight." Associated Press, March 18, 2005 (in LEXIS).

Elliott, Dan. "Indian or Not? Churchill Committee Faces Daunting Task." Associated Press, March 25, 2005 (in LEXIS).

Flynn, Kevin, David Montero, and Charlie Brennan. "Heritage, Writings Split Indian Activists." *Rocky Mountain News*, February 12, 2005, 4-A.

"Fools on the Hill." *Capital Times* (Madison, Wisconsin), February 28, 2005, 6-A.

Goodman, Amy. "Ward Churchill Defends His Academic Record and Vows to Fight to Keep His Job at University of Colorado." Democracy Now. National Public Radio. September 27, 2006. http://www.democracynow.org/article.pl?sid=06/09/27/146255.

"Hamilton College Raises $5.44M Despite Uproar." Albany *Times-Union*, July 28, 2005, B-3.

Harjo, Suzan Shown. "Why Native Identity Matters: A Cautionary Tale." *Indian Country Today*, February 10, 2005. http://www.indiancountry.com/content.cfm?id=1096410335.

Healy, Patrick D., Kirk Johnson, and Michelle York. "College Cancels Speech by Professor Who Disparaged 9/11 Attack Victims." *New York Times*, February 2, 2002, C-17.

Held, Tom. "Churchill Speech Protested." Milwaukee *Journal Sentinel*, February 12, 2005, 3.

Herdy, Amy. "CU [Colorado University] Prof Plans Tough Defense; Moves to Oust Him 'Vicious'; Ward Churchill Says Race and Politics are Motivating a Review of His Academic Credentials." *Denver Post*, March 31, 2005, A-1.

Herdy, Amy. "CU [Colorado University] Students' Vote Favors Churchill, but Award Withheld." *Denver Post*, May 27, 2005, B-1.

"Historian Welcomes Plug from Bin Laden." *Washington Post* in *Omaha World-Herald*, January 22, 2006, 13-A.

Johnson, Kirk. "University President Resigns at Colorado Amid Turmoil." *New York Times*, March 8, 2005. http://www.nytimes.com/2005/03/08/national/08colorado.html.

Johnson, Kirk. "University of Colorado Chancellor Advises Firing Author of Sept. 11 Essay." *New York Times*, June 27, 2006. http://www.nytimes.com/2006/06/27/education/27churchill.html.

Johnson, Kirk and Michelle York. "Incendiary in Academia May Now Find Himself Burned." *New York Times*, February 11, 2005. http://www.nytimes.com/2005/02/11/national/11professor.html.

Labash, Matt. "The Ward Churchill Notoriety Tour: The Worst Professor in America Meets His Adoring Public." *The Weekly Standard*, April 25, 2005, n.p. (in LEXIS).

Lee, Jeannette J. "Churchill Defends his Views in Hawaii; Hundreds Hear CU Prof's Speech; 20 Students Protest." Associated Press, February 23, 2005 (in LEXIS).

Morson, Berny. "1993 Essay Also Raises Questions; Churchill Says Pieces Credited to Others Are Actually His Work." *Rocky Mountain News*, June 7, 2005, 16-A.

Morson, Berny. "Christian Group Targets Churchill; Demons Destroying Prof., Minister Tells Abortion Protesters." *Rocky Mountain News*, July 20, 2005, 6-A.

O'Reilly, Bill. "Networks Ignore Churchill Story." The O'Reilly Factor. Fox News Network. Transcript, February 11, 2005 (in LEXIS).

O'Reilly, Bill. "The O'Reilly Factor: Interview with White Nationalist David Duke." February 24, 2005 (in LEXIS).

O'Reilly, Bill. "The O'Reilly Factor." Transcript, Fox Broadcasting, March 7, 2005 (in LEXIS).

O'Reilly, Bill. "The O'Reilly Factor: Is Jane Fonda a Traitor?" Fox News Network, April 5, 2005 (in LEXIS).

O'Reilly, Bill. "The O'Reilly Factor." Transcript, Fox News Network, June 26, 2006 (in LEXIS).

Owens, Bill. [Letter to the editor regarding Ward Churchill]. *Denver Post*, February 1, 2005. http://www.denverpost.com/Stories/0,1413,36%257E53%257E2686241,00.html#.

Pritzker, Barry. Personal communication (e-mail), February 1, 2005.

Rave, Jodi. "Reporter's Notebook: Controversial C.U. Professor Stretches Truth." Billings *Gazette*, February 6, 2005. http://www.billingsgazette.com/index.php?display=rednews/2005/02/06/build/nation/67-reporters-notebook.inc.

Rivedal, Karen. "In the Eye of the Storm: UW [University of Wisconsin] Whitewater Prepares for Speech by Controversial Colorado Professor." *Wisconsin State Journal* (Madison), February 24, 2005, A-1.

Rivedal, Karen. "Churchill says Media Misrepresented Him; He Says All Americans are Culpable for Abuses Overseas." *Wisconsin State Journal* (Madison, Wisconsin), March 2, 2005, A-1.

Rosse, Joseph, chair; Sanjai Bhagat, Mark Bradburn, Harold Bruff, Judith Glyde, Steven Guberman, Bella Mody, Linda Morris, Uriel Nauenberg, Ron Pak, and Cortlandt Pierpont. "Report and Recommendations of the Standing Committee on Research Misconduct Concerning Allegations of Research Misconduct by Professor Ward Churchill." June 13, 2006. http://denver.rockymountainnews.com/pdf/churchillfinalreport.pdf.

Rothschild, Matthew. Personal communication, February 14, 2005.

Saito, Natsu Taylor. "Update on University of Colorado's Investigation of Ward Churchill." September 10, 2005. (From author via e-mail.)

Saito, Natsu Taylor. "Resignation." May 1, 2006. From author via e-mail May 16, 2006.

Schlafly, Phyllis. "The Outrages Taxpayers and Parents Pay For." Copley News Service, Washington Wire, March 22, 2005 (in LEXIS).

Seals, David. "Nicaragua: What's Ward Churchill Got Against You?" in Marijo Moore, ed. *Eating Fire, Tasting Blood: Breaking the Great Silence of the American Indian Holocaust.* New York: Thunder's Mouth Press, 2006, 182–198.

Smallwood, Scott. "Inside a Free-Speech Firestorm." *The Chronicle of Higher Education*, February 18, 2005, 10.

Smallwood, Scott. "Aloha, Ward Churchill." *The Chronicle of Higher Education*, March 4, 2005, 48.

Spencer, Jim. "Whom Does Churchill Work For?" *Denver Post*, February 11, 2005, B-1.

"Talking Points Memo"; Top Story: Interview with Hamilton College Students Jonathan Rick, Matthew Coppo. The O'Reilly Factor [Transcript] Fox News Network, February 1, 2005 (in LEXIS).

"There They Go Again." Review and Outlook. *Wall Street Journal*, January 28, 2005, W-11.

Ward Churchill Update, November 6, 2006, from Natsu Saito via e-mail.

Wesson, Marianne, chair. *Report of the Investigative Committee of the Standing Committee on Research Misconduct at the University of Colorado at Boulder Concerning Allegations of Research Misconduct against Professor Ward Churchill*. May 9, 2006. www.colorado.edu/news/reports/churchill/churchillreport051606.html.

Chapter 5

Student and Faculty Rights (and Lefts)

Is AMERICAN ACADEMIA really in the thrall of a great left-wing conspiracy? Looking in from the outside, a notable number of non-leftists seem to think so. They have built a fortress of numbers to "prove" the point. We now have our own squad of very loud, single-minded thought police—Bill O'Reilly, David Horowitz, Ann Coulter, to name three—who have built careers on the purported pinheaded zaniness of the American academy. All of them need their looney leftists, as part of the formula "where attacking is the brand . . . your worst enemy is your best friend. . . ." (Lemann, 2006, 36). What, for example, would all of them do for work without their zoo of left-leaning, *New York Times*–reading, Marxist-coddling, peace-at-any-price academic airheads? Where would Ann Coulter be without her repetitive shelf of books attacking "Godless liberals?" Without them, the poor gal might starve to death, or find herself picking fruit and shining shoes for a living. I can imagine David Horowitz waking one day in an alternative universe without a single leftist professor to pillory. Would he celebrate the arrival of a perfect world—or panic?

All stereotypes grow from a nub of reality taken to extremes, of course. The academy is doubtless a more liberal place than the average boardroom of a Fortune 500 company, police station, or major-party national political convention. In a survey of 1,643 full-time faculty at 183 four-year schools in the United States, 72 percent identified themselves as liberals, and 15 percent as conservatives. About half identified themselves as Democrats, compared to 11 percent Republicans. The study, by political-science professors Robert Lichter of George Mason University, Neil Nevitte of the University of Toronto, and Stanley Rothman of Smith College, which was funded by the right-wing Randolph Foundation, had some right-wing pundits calling for affirmative action for their ideological mates on university campuses. Right-wing columnist Cal Thomas called American universities "re-education camps," where scholars with conservative views are routinely left without jobs by their left-of-center peers (Thomas, 2005, 7-B). I have seen no call for similar studies of corporation boards, the military, small-business owners, or talk-show hosts, where the right wing predominates.

Two other studies discuss the political leanings of professors at the University of California at Berkeley, and Stanford. One dealt with voter registration, concluding that in 2003 Democrats outnumbered Republicans 10-to-1 at Berkeley and almost 8-to-1 at Stanford (Schuman, 2005, E-1). The second study indicated that in social sciences and the humanities, Democrats outnumbered Republicans 7-to-1 at both institutions. The response rate for this study was only 31 percent, however, undercutting its credibility.

In November 2001, a report was released by the American Council of Trustees and Alumni, founded by Lynne Cheney, wife of Vice President Dick Cheney. The report, titled "Defending Civilization" as posted on the Internet, listed 117 statements by professors who were identified as "weak links" in the war on terrorism. The statements included such generic gems as "intolerance breeds hate" and "There needs to be an understanding of why this kind of suicidal violence could be undertaken against our country" (Maharidge, 2004, 76).

Until widespread disillusionment set in *vis a vis* the Iraq War, the hard right also had its shock troops in the student body—a vocal number of college students who proclaimed their unwillingness to endure what they regarded as a rain of liberal hell and brimstone on campus—a professoriate deemed so uniformly left wing that right-wingers' freedom to practice their own inclinations was said to have been compromised, sometimes on pain of their academic survival. Of late, however, I have noticed an abundance of long hair on men and left-leaning, anti-war political buttons on student backpacks that takes me back to the 1960s.

The right-wing faction is hardly dead, however. To some of these students I have jested that I'd gladly surrender half of academia to the Republican Party in exchange for half of the Standard and Poor's 500 chief executive officers. If they are feeling generous, the right wing may want to toss in half the U.S. Supreme Court. Do I have a deal? The campaign to make academia over in search of "balance" is being pursued at a time when most of our government and economic structure already has a definite rightward tilt. If we need affirmative action for ideological running buddies of Dick Cheney in English departments at major universities, how about quotas for professing Marxists and Green Party endowed chairs in global-warming studies at ExxonMobil?

As a professor, I tell students that they have a right to their opinions, and so do I. My job in the classroom is not to tell them *what* to think, but *how* to think. In a society in which some right-wingers spit the word "liberal" out like a slur, even Democrats have to earn a living doing something.

"HERO HANK" IN HIS DEN

As an undergraduate student about 1970, I recall the ideological shoe frequently having been fit to the other foot—students to the left, faculty to the right. Back then, leftist students sometimes loudly complained that their professors were hewing too far rightward. On February 11, 1970, for example (one incident I witnessed personally as a sophomore), five members of the Seattle Liberation Front invaded Professor Henry Buechel's 9:30 a.m. basic economics class of about 350 students at the University of Washington, interrupting his lecture in an attempt to "bring the [Vietnam] war home."

The abrasive but fatherly 62-year-old Buechel, white-haired, short, and stocky, wearing a Marine-style haircut, nursing diabetes, asked the students whether they thought he should continue his lecture. By a margin of roughly 90 to 10 percent, they indicated by a show of hands that they'd rather listen to Buecheel's economics over SLF current affairs.

Buechel then turned to the SLF members, and told them, as a senior professor to a group of rude students, to sit down and shut up, or leave. When they refused, Buechel advanced on the invading students, like a 150-pound lion in his den, and they left the room. The next day, Buechel's story was spread across the top of the *Seattle Times'* front page. A campus stringer for United Press International made a phone call and spread the story across the country.

During the days that followed, Buechel became something of a national hero. During the ensuing weeks, he received about 1,000 mostly supportive letters and telegrams. When it was over, however, he said he "wished it had never happened. Our lives—my wife's and mine—have been terribly disrupted" (Johansen, 1970, n.p.). He was standing on principle, however. "Not even the university president will take my classroom away from me," Buechel said afterward. "They would have to kick me out." If the class had not supported him that day, Buechel said later, "I would have walked out of that class. I would have never returned. . . . I would have gone into early retirement. That's a goddamned fact" (Johansen, 1970, n.p.).

At a time when opinion was split over the war in Vietnam, Buechel found himself celebrated and reviled coast to coast. One letter of support came from Hubert H. Humphery, a political science professor at the University of Minnesota following his loss in a close presidential election to Richard M. Nixon in 1968. Nixon also wrote: "The patience of the people is wearing thin with arrogant hooligans who intimidate and harass and bully speakers who they disagree with" (Johansen, 1970, n.p.). Buechel himself had advocated socialism during the 1930s; after starting his teaching career at the University of Washington after World War II, he became a liberal Democrat on domestic issues. On the Vietnam War, however, he was a hawk. His pugnacious conversations were laced with mild obscenities and occasional table pounding. He talked with his hands as well as his lips.

I wrote a detailed story on Buechel for the *University of Washington Daily*, after which he thanked me for dealing with him "competently and fairly," despite my obvious opposition to the war (Buechel, 1970) in that, my year of maximum exposure to the draft lottery. He sent a $5 check to the newspaper staff (which was densely populated with leftist student radicals at the time) and advised us to have a beer on him. Shortly thereafter, before we cashed the check, Professor Buechel died.

RIGHT-WINGERS NEED NOT APPLY?

Right-wing activists seeking leftist excess at universities rarely have to expend much shoe leather. In one "infamous case" during 2002, according one account, "a University of California-Berkeley course on 'The Politics and Poetics of Palestinian Resistance' warned, 'Conservative thinkers are encouraged to seek other sections.' The graduate student instructor was forced to remove the notice after a national outcry" (Goldberg, 2003).

On the other hand, Jonathan Cole, a former Columbia University administrator, complained that "a rising tide of anti-intellectualism and intolerance of university research and teaching that offends ideologues . . . is putting academic freedom—one of the core values of the university—under more sustained and subtle attack than at any time since the dark days of McCarthyism" (Schuman, 2005, E-1).

Some students who believe that they have been marginalized in class, even graded down, for refusing to embrace a professor's political views, don't agree. Consider:

> Marissa Freimanis, a junior at California State Long Beach, said that she lost her perfect grade-point average when her less-than-leftist political convictions infuriated an English professor, who flunked her paper on Michael Moore's *Fahrenheit 9/11* because she "missed the point of the film."

> Three incoming freshmen at the University of North Carolina sued over a reading assignment they said offended their Christian beliefs. They lost their legal case, but the university removed the word "required" from the reading.

> Gerald Wilson, a history professor at Duke University, apologized for his answer to a student's question in class, "Do you have any prejudices?" to which he had joked: "Republicans."

> University of Oregon senior Anthony Warren said, "Professors nowadays are too liberal and cross the line from teaching to political preaching in the classroom." He was one of about 50 students responding to an informal questionnaire e-mailed to students at the University of Oregon, Stanford University, Washington State University, Willamette University, Northwest Christian College, Humboldt State, and the University of Minnesota (Schuman, 2005, E-1).

Jennie Mae Brown, an Air Force veteran, was attending a Pennsylvania Republican Party picnic when she told her state representative, Gibson C. Armstrong, that a physics professor at the York campus of Pennsylvania State University routinely used class time to criticize President George W. Bush and the Iraq war. Brown complained that such comments were not appropriate (Janofsky, 2005).

Brown's complaint evolved into an official legislative inquiry into political bias among professors in Pennsylvania's state universities—with hardly an exception, the purported left-of-center biases of professors foisted on right-of-center students. A committee of the Pennsylvania legislature convened hearings during November 2005, in Pittsburgh, and January 9, 2006 in Philadelphia to debate whether the political bias should be banned at 18 schools in the state that receive state tax funds. The committee issued a final report and recommendations for legislative remedy late in 2006.

The Pennsylvania inquiry is one of several pursued by David Horowitz, whose Center for the Study of Popular Culture has been lobbying more than a dozen state legislatures to pass an "Academic Bill of Rights" that he says would encourage free debate and protect students against discrimination for expressing their political beliefs (Janofsky, 2005).

Russell Jacoby, a history professor at the University of California, Los Angeles, criticized Horowitz to his face during a debate in the summer of 2004, saying that his "student bill of rights" calls for committees or prosecutors to monitor the lectures and assignments of teachers. "This is a sure-fire way to kill free inquiry and whatever abuses come with it" (Janofsky, 2005).

Horowitz's efforts usually produced more debate than action. Colorado and Ohio agreed to suspend legislative efforts to impose an academic bill of rights in favor of pledges by their state schools to uphold standards already in place. Georgia passed a resolution discouraging "political or ideological indoctrination" by teachers, encouraging them to create "an environment conducive to the civil exchange of ideas." Similar bills had failed in three other states, and other measures were pending in 11 others by 2006. In Congress, the U.S. House and Senate committees passed general resolutions during 2005 encouraging American colleges to promote "a free and open exchange of ideas" in their classrooms and to treat students "equally and fairly" (Janofsky, 2005). The measures were debated in both bodies during 2006.

According to an account by Michael Janofsky in the *New York Times*, Nathaniel Nelson, a former student at the University of Rhode Island and a self-described conservative, said that a philosophy teacher there referred often to his own homosexuality and made clear his dislike for President George W. Bush. A graduate student at the University of Connecticut told Janofsky that this teacher frequently called on him to defend his conservative values. "On the first day of class, he said, 'If you don't like me, get out of my class,'" Nelson said. "But it was the only time that fall the course was being offered, and I wanted to take it" (Janofsky, 2005).

Many universities' faculty handbooks address classroom ideological bias. The Oregon University system, for example, specifies that professors "are entitled to freedom in the classroom in discussing subjects. . . ." It continues: "in the exercise of this freedom of expression, faculty should manifest appropriate restraint, should show respect for the opinions of others" (Schuman, 2005, E-1). A University of Oregon student who believes that a professor has violated these guidelines may address the faculty member on an individual basis ("informally") or file a grievance. The process is confidential, and may include sanctions as severe as termination.

In 1940, the American Association of University Professors issued a "Statement of Principles," that cautioned them "not to introduce into their teaching controversial matter which has no relation to their subject" and to "remember that the public may judge their profession and their institution by their utterances" (Schuman, 2005, E-1).

UP AGAINST THE WALL: "LEFTIST TOTALITARIANISM"

Proposals for student "bills of rights" often cite high-minded objectives, urging "diversity" in lectures and course readings, and awards of tenure to faculty with a "plurality" of methodologies and perspectives. Some of these bills require grading students at public universities on merit, not political or religious beliefs; hiring and promoting professors based on expertise, not ideology; and establishing reading lists with dissenting viewpoints (Schuman, 2005, E-1). Who would be against such things? This is, with very few exceptions, how academic life operates today.

Scratch the surface of such proposals, however, and what often emerges is a complaint process designed to staunch unpopular points of view, especially those well to the left of center. Many of the "bills of rights" would introduce various forms of legislative oversight into the daily operations of university-level teaching and learning. Routine oversight for thousands of classes would be impossible, however. The trigger usually would be a complaint by students who assert that their own points of view (usually right of center) have been criticized, de-emphasized, or satirized.

Under pressure from some voters, state legislators in Arizona proposed a bill allowing college students who believed that a college reading, writing, or thinking assignment was "personally offensive," to create another assignment, more in tune with their beliefs or practices in sex, morality, or religion. Ron Roat, a columnist at the Evansville (Indiana) *Courier-Press*, remarked:

> In other words, if a student finds "personally offensive" an assignment to read *The Grapes of Wrath* because it contains sex, violence, and disparaging remarks about capitalism, then he can read something friendlier, such as *The Bible*. It contains only sex, violence, genocide, and war. Or, perhaps, he could write the epistemology of a peanut-butter sandwich. That should offend no one. (Roat, 2006)

The Arizona proposal never emerged committee.

Republicans on the Florida House of Representatives Choice and Innovation Committee voted along party lines March 22, 2005 to pass a bill that aimed to stamp out "leftist totalitarianism" by "dictator professors" in the classrooms of Florida's universities. The so-called Academic Freedom Bill of Rights, sponsored by Rep. Dennis Baxley, Republican of Ocala, passed 8-to-2 despite strenuous objections from the only two Democrats on the committee (Vanlandingham, 2005). Promoting the bill, Baxley said a university education should be more than "one biased view by the professor, who as a dictator controls the classroom," as part of "a misuse of their platform to indoctrinate the next generation with their own views" (Vanlandingham, 2005). The Florida bill was written to create a statewide standard prohibiting punishment of students for professing beliefs with which their professors disagree. Under the proposed law, professors also would be advised to teach alternative "serious academic theories" that may disagree with their personal views (Vanlandingham, 2005).

According to a legislative staff analysis of the bill, as a law, it would give students who think their beliefs are not being respected legal standing to sue professors and universities. A student who believes that a professor is singling him or her out for "public ridicule"—for instance, when professors use the Socratic method to compel student response in class—they also would be given the right to sue. "Some professors say, 'Evolution is a fact. I don't want to hear about intelligent design . . . and if you don't like it, there's the door,'" Baxley said, citing one example when he thought a student should sue (Vaughan and Vanlandingham, 2005). Rep. Dan Gelber, D-Miami Beach, warned of lawsuits from students enrolled in Holocaust history courses who believe the Jewish Holocaust never happened.

Similar suits could be filed by students who don't believe astronauts landed on the moon, who believe teaching birth control is a sin, or by medical students who refuse to perform blood transfusions and believe prayer is the only way to heal the body, Gelber added. "This is a horrible step," he said. "Universities will have to hire lawyers so our curricula can be decided by judges in courtrooms. Professors might have to pay court costs—even if they win—from their own pockets. This is not an innocent piece of legislation" (Vanlandingham, 2005).

During the committee hearing, Baxley cast opposition to his bill as the work of "leftists" struggling against "mainstream society." "The critics ridicule me for daring to stand up for students and faculty," he said, adding that he was being called a McCarthyist. Baxley later said he had a list of students who were discriminated against by professors, but refused to reveal names because he believed they would be persecuted (Vanlandingham, 2005). Baxley compared the state's universities to children, saying the legislature should not give them money without providing "guidance" for their behavior.

By late 2005, legislators in 20 states had introduced measures incorporating language from the Students for Academic Freedom's "Bill of Rights." Students for Academic Freedom, founded by David Horowitz of the Study for Popular Culture in Los Angeles, by that time had chapters of varying sizes on more than 100 U.S. college and university campuses. "Instead of racial minorities, women and gays," wrote Sharon Schuman in the Portland *Oregonian*, "the legislative measures promoted by Horowitz are aimed at protecting a new campus minority—conservatives" (Shuman, 2005, E-1). Horowitz has made the exposure of radical leftists on campus his life's work. He seems to have forgotten that few activities are as comforting (or as unproductive) as listening to opinions with which one already agrees.

HOROWITZ'S HORRID HUNDRED AND ONE

Horowitz himself is not a scholar; he produces no original work of his own. Instead, he feeds off right-wing resentment of others, always leftists, in an entirely predictable and repetitive way. Like Rush Limbaugh, Coulter, O'Reilly, and others, without liberals and leftist radicals to slime, Horowitz would be nobody. He never tires of bragging about the born-again nature of his anti-leftist zeal. He was, after all, not a garden-variety radical as a young man. He was a radical household word as editor of *Ramparts*, something of a far-leftist "bible" during the 1960s.

Thus, enter Horowitz's Horrid Hundred and One, describing America's "most dangerous" professors. Four hundred fifty pages of the same old stuff. Are we scared yet? Reflecting the predictable nature of his work, Horowitz starts his screed with a punching-bag exercise aimed at—who else?—Ward Churchill. The first sentence of Horowitz's introduction characterizes Churchill as "a figure of national revulsion" (p. vii) who is no "marginal crank" (p. vii), but an unusually vocal representative of "abhorrent views" (p. xx) expressed by thousands of professors. Horowitz's Horrible Hundred are "but the tip of the academic iceberg" (p. xxv). He could easily have profiled thousands of similar creatures (p. xxv), the wretched spawn of anti-Vietnam war activists, he writes, who stayed in school to become PhDs, then "tenured radicals" (a phrase Horowitz loves so much that he repeats it many times), spreading out from dens in Black and women's studies (Peace studies, too—250 programs! p. xxv) to colonize traditional fields such as English, history, and law (p. xi).

Of 617,000 college and university teachers in the United States (p. xlv), Horowitz very loosely estimates that about 25,000 to 30,000 are noxiously leftist—about 5 percent. Not one of his "dangerous" crew is a right-winger. Horowitz describes his efforts on behalf of "intellectual diversity" as "nonpartisan," although *all* of his complaints are directed against liberals and other left-wingers. They are advocates of Marxist-feminism, radical economics, peace studies, African-American studies and—most notably in these Muslim-militant-ridden days—Middle Eastern or Islamic studies (his list is heavy on the officer roster of the Middle Eastern Studies Association).

Some of Horowitz's names are familiar (Victor Navasky, Noam Chomsky, Angela Davis, bell hooks, et al.) but many are not well known at all. Having a member of the Communist Party two generations back (e.g. a red-diaper baby twice removed) is enough to ramp up one's profile in Horowitz's book. Bear in mind the ideological company in which Horowitz runs. He and his compatriots believe that Joseph McCarthy was soft on communism, that he "underestimated the extent of Soviet infiltration in the American government." And that "virtually all individuals called before congressional committees [on Un-American activities] were involved in a conspiratorial network controlled by the Kremlin" (Horowitz, 2006, 294).

According to Horowitz, deep-leftist professors are enforcing a reign of "intimidation" against the "silent majority" of academics, manipulating their fear of being labeled "racist, sexist, or reactionary" (p. xxvii). Many university administrators and the American Association of University Professors (a labor union) assert that Horowitz is overstating the magnitude of the supposed bias. By seeking legislative intervention, they say, it is Horowitz who is forcing political ideology into classes. "Mechanisms exist to address these glitches and to fix them," said Joan Wallach Scott, a professor at the Institute for Advanced Study in Princeton, N.J., and former chairwoman of the Professors Association Committee on Academic Freedom, in testimony at the Pennsylvania legislature's first hearing. "There is no need for interference from outside legislative or judicial agencies" (Janofsky, 2005).

Horowitz's standards for inclusion on his list seemed so loose that I cooked up an ersatz press release asking why I hadn't been included, then posted it on the Internet:

> A University of Nebraska professor has complained that David Horowitz left him off his list of the nation's 101 most dangerous professors. "It's probably sloppy research on his part," asserted Bruce E. Johansen, professor of communication and Native American Studies at the University of Nebraska at Omaha. "Just last fall," said Johansen, "I was accused of being a 'stooge' and a 'cheerleader' for Ward Churchill," Johansen said. "That, alone, should have been enough to make his list. The *Rocky Mountain News* called Ward Churchill Bruce Johansen's brain—and Horowitz missed it. Senator McCarthy's got to be turning over in his grave."
>
> Johansen said he would really like to sell some books, and that publicity from Horowitz might help. "It's frustrating to have run under his radar for so long. My *bona fides* are in order. I'm sure that, as an author, he can empathize."
>
> "Look, David," Johansen emphasized. "I have been dutifully filling my students' minds up with global warming. I write about atrocities perpetuated on American Indians for the last 500 years. I ride a bicycle to work. What does it take?" Johansen said that he even improves the attendance of students who idolize George W. Bush by telling them he'll turn other students into Bush-bashing zombies if the Bush supporters skip classes.
>
> "C'mon, Dave, get it while it's hot," Johansen bragged. "I write for Z Magazine. That makes me a running dog of Noam Chomsky. I'm a steady at *The Progressive*, too. I read the *New York Times* every day, and I believe in evolution. When I go to church, I do it as a Unitarian. I'm sure that after you've done a little research, you'll come to know me as just the kind of leftist pond scum that has made you famous. Am I good to go in the second edition? Come on, Horowitz, slime me. Please." (Johansen, 2006)

THE "ROYAL RUMBLE"

Horowitz may have ignored me, but he had no such problems with Churchill. He even engaged him April 6, 2006, in a "Royal Rumble" at George Washington University in Washington, D.C. The idea for the debate was Churchill's, but it was hosted by Horowitz's supporters. It was sponsored by Horowitz's Center for the Study of Popular Culture and Young America's Foundation. The subject was whether politics can or should be removed from teaching.

Rob Capriccioso, writing for *Inside Higher Education,* called the two-hour debate "relatively substance-free," and quoted Jamie Horwitz, a spokesman for the American Federation of Teachers: "I think they both would have gotten a failing grade in a high school debate class" (Capriccioso, 2006).

The name of the debate ("Academia's Royal Rumble") may have brought to mind the World Wrestling Federation, but the *Rocky Mountain News* stressed the civility and verbal gymnastics of the two: "If people expected to see a bloody clash between a fire-breathing leftist and a ranting right-winger,that was some other monster movie. Instead, two equally controversial men . . . put on a genial display of good manners and polysyllabic brilliance . . ." (Sprengelmeyer, 2006, 4-A).

"Like so many heavyweight bouts, this one didn't live up to the hype," wrote Scott Smallwood in the *Chronicle of Higher Education.* "It was, instead, a tame and civil discourse, interrupted only briefly by booing and catcalls" Smallwood summed up the subject matter and the participants' positions in 30 seconds worth of words: "The two debaters had starkly different takes on the central topic: "Can Politics Be Taken Out of the Classroom and Should It Be? Mr. Horowitz said bluntly: "Yes, it should, and of course it can." Mr. Churchill was equally curt: 'They cannot'" (Smallwood, 2006). The rest was, shall we say, duck soup.

Much of Horowitz's speech seemed so well rehearsed as to be practically an exercise in intellectual sleepwalking. As usual, Horowitz lambasted the liberal elite that he believes has hijacked academia, denouncing women's-studies programs as platforms for "radical feminists," and "social justice" teachings as socialist indoctrination. "Whole fields have developed," Horowitz argued. "They are ideological fields. They are not academic fields." Churchill replied that teaching critical thinking requires professors to inject opinions. "There is no consensus. There is no homogeneity. There is no truth, and that is what the issue here is. . . . The purpose of a professor is to profess—not simply to impart information" (Sprengelmeyer, 2006, 4-A).

FREEDOM THE *LIBERTAS* WAY

The Young Americas Foundation and its magazine, *Libertas,* regularly coaches conservative college students on "Embracing the Ronald Reagan Model of Activism" Coyle, 2006B, 6). "Learning how to respond appropriately to a biased, leftist professor is a rite-of-passage for every conservative activist," advises the magazine's Patrick X. Coyle, who holds the title "director of campus programs." Coyle coaches students in provoking debates with liberal professors and left-leaning students in class, including exposing such professors to local right-wing talk-show hosts, especially if a case can be made that they use subjective grading policies to enforce ideological conformity. The YAF has published a book, *Conservative Guide to Campus Activism,* which promises "Secrets of Surviving and Prevailing on Your Left-wing Campus." It advises: "Successfully defending conservatism in class can be one of the most rewarding experiences of your college career" (Coyle, 2006B, 6).

Libertas lists college courses that its editors suspect advance leftist points of view. Anything describing Marxism, racism, homosexuality, environmentalism, or women's rights in historical context will do. Thus, the winter, 2006 issue contained capsule descriptions of Harvard's "Marxist Concepts of Racism," Princeton's "Cultural Production of Early Modern Women," and Duke's "History of Socialism and Communism" (7–8). Amherst College's "Taking Marxism Seriously" gets star billing, as does "Gay and Lesbian Studies 201," and "Feminist Theory," as well as "Environment and Equity in North American History" (Koebensky and Custer, 7–9).

The magazine lionizes students who campaign against leftist influences on campuses, such as Trey Winslett, who was offended when he was instructed, as an incoming freshman at the University of North Carolina (Chapel Hill), to read Barbara Ehrenreich's book *Nickel and Dimed*, "that encourages socialist policies[,] including a living wage and other outmoded economic concepts" (Coyle, 2006A, 23).

"BOUNTIES" ON LEFTIST PROFESSORS AT UCLA

By 2006, a right-wing alumni group at the University of California Los Angeles was offering as much as $100 per class to students who provided video tapes and notes about professors they regarded as excessively leftist. On its Internet site www.uclaprofs.com/profs/profsindex.html, the Bruin Alumni Association said that its members were most concerned about professors who use lecture time to advocate political positions contrary to those of President George W. Bush, the U.S. military, and multinational corporations, among others ("'Radical' UCLA," 2006). The site included a list of what the group believes to be the university's 30 most radical professors. Positions taken in support of the president, the military, and corporations did not qualify as biased. An examination of the Web site revealed none.

A professor can attain a ranking on the Bruin Alumni Association list for many offenses other than bad-mouthing George W. Bush. Supporting Native American gambling is good enough, as is signing the wrong petition. The site keeps score of which petitions have been signed by whom. Having dyed one's hair red rates a rant, as does too-frequent declamation on the works of Malcolm X. Beverly Hills is a keen address, as long as one isn't a Marxist, in which case it's a violation of self-professed class consciousness. As with Horowitz, red-diaper pedigree counts; if you have a father who was hounded by Senator Joseph McCarthy, welcome to the "The Dirty Thirty: Ranking the Worst of the Worst."

Jewish professors who oppose Zionism seem to be a perennial favorite of the rankers who hand out "Power Fists" to alleged radicals—especially, as in the case of Sondra Hale, if the site's authors also can accuse a professor of being a women's studies advocate (e.g., "hardcore feminist"), which they seem to read automatically as "lesbian." The list seems to feast on accusatory generalities. Even being "too thoughtful," theoretical and "shy" (oh, my!) earned Power Fists for Russell Jacoby, although a low one, at No. 28. The authors of the Dirty Thirty pointed out that, in their opinion, "Jacoby has all the ideological ammo he'll need to indoctrinate his students. Now, the only question is whether he'll *use* it" ("The Dirty Thirty," 2006). Thus, even *failure* to make hay of one's ideological credentials in the classroom can earn a spot among the Dirty Thirty.

"Any sober, concerned citizen would look at this and see right through it as a reactionary form of McCarthyism," said education professor Peter McLaren, whom the Web listed No. 1 on its "Dirty Thirty" ("'Radical' UCLA," 2006). Following some professors' allegations that it was engaged in a witch-hunt, the group's president and founder, Andrew Jones, a 2003 UCLA graduate and former chairman of the student Bruin Republicans, said: "We're just trying to get people back on a professional level of things. Having been a student myself up until 2003, and then watching what other students like myself have gone through, I'm very concerned about the level of professional teaching at UCLA" ("'Radical' UCLA," 2006).

The association's decision to name targets and pay students for information led to the resignation of at least one of its 20-plus advisory board members. Stephan Thernstrom, a former UCLA professor (later at Harvard) who was a member of the alumni group's advisory board resigned after he learned of the "Dirty Thirty" campaign. "That just seems to me way too intrusive," he said. "It seems to me a kind of vigilantism that I very much object to" ("'Radical' UCLA," 2006).

CORPORATIONS' RIGHT TO RECRUIT

If students and professors of both the left and the right should enjoy free access to ideas on campuses, what about corporations and government agencies desiring to recruit employees—notably the military during an increasingly unpopular war? The military wants access to law schools on the same basis as other potential employers seeking to recruit students, while some of the schools insist that only those employers that pledge not to discriminate (most notably against gays) may recruit.

According to an account by Linda Greenhouse in the *New York Times*:

> For more than ten years, the two sides have circled one another as Congress pulled the noose ever tighter in the form of a threatened withholding of federal money from noncompliant universities. A showdown in the Supreme Court appeared inevitable, and on [December 6, 2005] it finally took place. The justices appeared strongly inclined to uphold a federal law known as the Solomon Amendment, which withholds federal grants from universities that do not open their doors to military recruiters 'in a manner at least equal in quality and scope' to the access offered civilian recruiters. John G. Roberts Jr. put it succinctly: "It says that if you want our money, you have to let our recruiters on campus." (Greenhouse, 2005)

The U.S. Supreme Court in *Rumsfeld v. Forum for Academic and Institutional Rights*, No. 04-1152, thus parsed the issue as a free speech and association matter under the First Amendment to the Constitution, very differently from the intellectual framework used by a federal appeals court in Philadelphia, which had ruled during 2004 on a lawsuit brought by about three-dozen law schools. The appeals court had rejected enforcement of the "Solomon Amendment" on grounds that it forced the schools to "propagate, accommodate and subsidize the military's expressive message" of disapproving homosexuality despite the law schools' commitment to equal rights for their gay students (Greenhouse, 2005).

The American Association of Law Schools—which includes 166 of the 188 accredited law schools—since 1991, has required its members to insist that prospective employers adhere to nondiscrimination policies that include sexual orientation. As law schools began refusing access to military recruiters, Congress responded with a series of amendments to military spending bills that allowed access for military recruiting. "While the measures were addressed to universities, and not specifically to law schools," wrote Greenhouse, "it was the law schools that were the source of resistance" (Greenhouse, 2005).

Speaking before the Supreme Court, the law school coalition's attorney, E. Joshua Rosenkranz, supported the appeals court's ruling that the Solomon Amendment amounted to "compelled speech" in that it forced the law schools to convey the military's message. Chief Justice Roberts disagreed fundamentally. "I'm sorry, but on 'compelled speech,' nobody thinks that this law school is speaking through those employers who come onto its campus for recruitment," the chief justice said. "Nobody thinks the law school believes everything that the employers are doing or saying" (Greenhouse, 2005).

U.S. Solicitor General Paul D. Clement told the court that, in his legal analysis, the Solomon Amendment permitted law schools to oppose the military's policy. Asked by Justice Ruth Bader Ginsburg what a law school "could do concretely while the recruiter is in the room," Clement replied that as long as the school granted equal access, "They could put signs on the bulletin board next to the door. They could engage in speech. They could help organize student protests" (Greenhouse, 2005).

Opposing the Solomon Amendment, the universities found themselves on shaky legal ground, indicated by skeptical questioning they faced from several of the justices during oral arguments. The justices indicated that universities "should allow equal, unfettered access to their students by any employer whose policy with regard to sexual orientation is legal, so long as that policy is disclosed. The issue is not what the universities think about "don't ask, don't tell"—they have made that clear—but how their students view it" (Schuck, 2005).

Peter Schuck, writing on the op-ed page of the *New York Times*, agreed with Chief Justice Roberts:

A university's moral and pedagogical duty to its students is to cultivate their capacity for independent thinking, explain its own view (if it has one) and then get out of the way. The students' duty is to listen carefully—and then make their own decisions. (Schuck, 2005)

URBAN ANTHROPOLOGY AND TENURE POLITICS AT YALE

David Graeber, who speaks Malagasy, French, and Spanish, earned his PhD at the University of Chicago in 1996. He was teaching anthropology at Yale University when he "came out" as an anarchist, shortly before his crucial hurdle to tenure, and suddenly found himself unemployable, despite a worldwide reputation and a long publication record. No one *really* knows why—the faculty who made the decision was under no obligation to justify the decision.

David Graeber, 45 years of age in 2006, son of a seamstress and a print plate stripper, still lives in the same New York City co-op ("Socialist housing," he calls it) where he grew up.

Graeber conducted his doctoral research in Madagascar, in a rural community that was divided between descendants of an andriana ("noble") clan and descendants of their former slaves. His dissertation was titled *The Disastrous Ordeal of 1987: Memory and Violence in Rural Madagascar*. Soon thereafter, Graeber became fascinated by the contemporary global resurgence of anarchism (or, as worded on his *curriculum vitae*, "The Ethnography of Direct Action"). His fascination led to articles in *New Left Review*, various books, and other publications. His inquiry initially was funded by a Yale Junior Faculty Fellowship, Fall 2001-Spring 2002. Graeber also participated in major "actions" (e.g. protests) in Washington, D.C., Philadelphia, New York, Quebec City, Genoa, Italy and Ottawa, among others places.

Graeber's first three years at Yale went well, and he was given a second three-year contract. By then, he had become involved in direct political action. Graeber said that he found the large protests against globalization in Seattle and Washington, D.C. "transformative," as he found himself amidst 30,000 people with no leadership. "People coming to a consensus without anyone running the show. You wouldn't think it could happen, but it does. And it's compelling," Graeber said (Arenson, 2005, B-1).

Graeber joined groups such as the Direct Action Network, and his political activity became more visible. He was an organizer and spokesman for the protest against the World Economic Forum in New York in 2001, as well as one of several hundred people arrested during a protest against the International Monetary Fund in Washington, D.C. during 2002. When word of his activism got around at Yale, Graeber found that some colleagues would not talk to him. Three years later, he was given two years instead of a standard four-year contract and told to contribute more and be more careful about things like arriving at classes on time. "I was told I was unreliable," he said (Arenson, 2005, B-1).

Graeber said that after this critical review, he directed a colloquium series, took part in more meetings, and was more careful about promptness in class. His political disagreements with some senior colleagues continued, however, including one defense of a student who had been active in the graduate student unionization movement. Yale then declined to extend an offer of tenure to Graeber, effectively terminating his career there.

After Yale's refusal to rehire him, more than 4,500 people signed petitions in Graeber's support. Maurice Bloch, a noted anthropologist at the London School of Economics, who said that Graeber is "the best anthropological theorist of his generation," called on Yale to rescind the dismissal (Arenson, 2005, B-1).

Graeber said:

> One thing that was repeatedly stressed to me when I was preparing my material for review is that no one is really taking issue with my scholarship. In fact, it was occasionally hinted to me that if anything I publish *too much*, have received *too much* international recognition, and had *too many* enthusiastic letters of support from students. All that might have actually weighed against me. Again, I have no way of knowing if that's really true, because everything is a secret. (Frank, 2005)

"I'm both more productive intellectually than they are and I'm having more fun. It must drive them crazy," he said. "I'm publishing like crazy. I'm all over the place. I try hard not to rub it in" (Apuzzo, 2005).

> I'd be willing to say this much. What happened to me was extremely irregular—almost unheard of, really. It happened despite the fact that I'm one of [the] best published scholars and most popular teachers in the department. Does it have anything to do with the fact that I'm also one of the only declared anarchist scholars in the academy? I'll leave it to your readers to make up their own minds. (Frank, 2005)

Graeber said that not all of Yale's senior anthropology faculty froze him out.

> There are some amazing, wonderful scholars amongst the senior faculty. We're really just talking about three, maybe four, who are atrocious bullies. I have five colleagues who were just awesome, and who fought as hard as they could to defend me. It's just that the bullies never give up—they're willing to throw all their time and energy into these battles, since after all, most have long since given up on any meaningful intellectual life—and of course since everything's secret, there's no accountability. (Frank, 2005)

Graeber appealed the decision, and Yale offered him a paid sabbatical which ended June 1, 2007 if he would drop the challenge. He accepted.

In an e-mail, Graeber reflected on the contradictions of academia:

> I'm . . . hoping I will get a permanent job someday. Academia is so odd. Formally I'm getting every honor conceivable: endless keynotes . . . my *Fragments* book is coming out in nine languages. . . . An invitation to the London School of Economics, to give its annual Malinowski lecture [an offer reserved for the world's most promising young anthropologists]. On one level, I'm a star. On another, I'm unemployable: I didn't even make it onto any short lists this year [2005]. I could easily get a job in Europe or even China I think, but the United States is a totally different story (and I've been so busy taking care of a very sick mother that moving overseas hasn't seemed a realistic option). (Graeber, 2006)

"One thing that I've learned in academia," said Graeber, is that "No one much cares what your politics are as long as you don't do anything about them" (Frank, 2005).

CAN A HIGH SCHOOL GEOGRAPHY CLASS BE *TOO* RELEVANT?

The right-wing radio host Sean Hannity regularly broadcasts complaints about professors he regards as biased, as he urges students to take recording devices to classes to gather evidence. While urging students to squeal on professors for expressing their opinions, Hannity freely admits that he campaigns for Republicans both on and off the job. Washington *Post* media critic Howard Kurtz reported that:

> Some liberals have been dismissing Fox News commentator Sean Hannity as a Republican flack following word that he is attending fundraisers for GOP Sen. Rick Santorum of Pennsylvania. "Sean Hannity, conservative, an on-air advocate for conservatives—it's a shock that I support a conservative and want him to get elected?" Hannity asks. "What's the big deal? Rick is a great conservative. I believe he's a great senator." But isn't there a difference between a commentator voicing support and actively working with a campaign? Hannity says he has helped raise money for other candidates and campaigned for President Bush in 2004. "I'm in the opinion business. I do none of this in secret," he says. (Kurtz, 2006)

While Hannity's own freedom of expression seems sacrosanct, he seems to believe that political opinion in the classroom—most notably, *liberal* opinion—should be forbidden. Thus, with Hannity's help, we can see into a future when teachers stare into a battery of MP3 recording devices, realizing that any 16-year-old with a grudge may soon plug his or her words into the Internet—as well as nationally broadcast television, if Hannity likes what he sees. George Orwell's telescreen will have arrived, hand-held and *en masse*, and Hannity and Bill O'Reilly, et al. will never run out of academic canon-fodder for their talk-shows. Indeed, they may drown in it.

An MP3 player was present in an Overland High School geography class in the Denver suburb of Aurora early in February 2006, when teacher Jay Bennish, age 28, very loosely compared President George W. Bush's rhetoric to the speeches of Adolf Hitler, provoking copious motor-mouthing on several national talk shows. Both Hannity and O'Reilly jumped on this one, along with Rush Limbaugh and NBC's *Today Show*. It took Bennish less than one class period to enrage the usual Rocky Mountain Front Range thought police (Vince Carroll, Caplis/Silverman, and others), providing a brief reprieve from their year-long feast on Ward Churchill. Without loose-lipped leftists, what would these folks do for work?

The most notorious lecture of Bennish's life was delivered February 1, a day after Bush's State of the Union address, as Sean Allen, a 16-year-old sophomore, used his MP3 player to record it. The student's father then complained to school officials, and sent the recording to KOA radio talk-show host Mike Rosen, who put it on the Internet and played parts of it on his radio program. The school district promptly suspended Bennish, concluding that, at a minimum, his comments may have breached a policy requiring teachers to be "as objective as possible and to present fairly the several sides of an issue" when tackling subjects with religious, political, economic, or social implications (Vaughan and Doligosa, 2006, A-4).

Bennish said that in Bush's State of the Union speech, the president was, in effect, "threatening the whole planet." "Sounds a lot like the things that Adolf Hitler used to say—we're the only ones who are right, everyone else is backwards," Bennish said. He told students he was "not saying that Bush and Hitler are exactly the same. "But," he said," there's some eerie similarities to the tones that they use" (Vaughan and Doligosa, 2006, A-4). And who has more weapons of mass destruction than any other nation, Bennish asked—the United States of America.

Right-wing sensibilities screamed. Bennish had called the United States "probably the single most violent nation on planet Earth" (Vaughan and Doligosa, 2006, A-4). He even said that the United States has more weapons of mass destruction than any other country on Earth. Without calling anyone a "little Eichmann," Bennish described the World Trade Center bombings in terms similar to Ward Churchill's "Roosting Chickens" critique:

> You need to understand something—that when al-Qaida attacked America on Sept. 11, in their view they're not attacking innocent people. The CIA had an office in the World Trade Center. The Pentagon is a military target. The White House was a military target. Congress is a military target. The World Trade Center is the economic center of our entire economy. The FBI, [which] tracks down terrorists and so on and so forth around the world, has offices in the World Trade Center. Some of the companies that work in the World Trade Center are these huge, multinational corporations that are directly involved in the military industrial complex, in supporting corrupt dictatorships in the Middle East. (Vaughan and Doligosa, 2006, A-4)

Bennish hired Ward Churchill's lawyer, David Lane, who announced that "I know about 10 federal judges who are more than willing to teach the Cherry Creek School District what the First Amendment is all about" (Vaughan and Doligosa, 2006, A-4).

Carroll, editorial-page editor of the *Rocky Mountain News*, who is never at a loss for invective *vis a vis* teachers who seem as opinionated on the left as he can be on the right, quickly slapped his ultimate insult on Bennish, calling him a "Ward Churchill wannabe" (Carroll, March 3, 2006, 38-A). Bennish's lecture also included some harsh words about capitalism, U.S. foreign policy, and the invasion of Iraq—quite a dose of relevance in an academic setting that sometimes puts students to sleep, judging by their knowledge of geography after the fact. Carroll couldn't get enough, as the news columns of "The Rocky" kept up a daily drumbeat. "The only question is how many more of his ilk are hectoring our kids," Carroll intoned (Carroll, March 9, 2006, 38-A). Keep those MP3 players running, kids. Fame awaits if you can bag a "liberal."

March 2, after Bennish was suspended, hundreds of students—estimates varied from 200 to 700—walking out of Overland High, crowding a nearby pedestrian bridge, chanting, "Freedom of speech, let him teach." "It's not fair," said Stacy Caruso, a 17-year-old junior. "He spoke his mind. We have Christian groups in school, and they're not censored" (Vaughan and Doligosa, 2006, A-4). Some wore duct tape over their mouths. A few others took the side of the student who recorded Bennish's talk, writing "Teach, don't preach" on their T-shirts. Five days later Bennish's father, who lives in Detroit, said that his family had been receiving numerous telephone calls—some of them death threats—since his son's comments became public. John Bennish of Beverly Hills, Mich., said at least 12 people have called his home and threatened his life and the lives of his family.

In the meantime, the younger Bennish (who also said that his life also had been threatened several times by over-enthusiastic self-described patriots), cut off his Rasta-style locks and flew to New York City to appear on NBC's Today show. He maintained that that the recorded section of his class was out of context because it didn't provide his other statements that day, that he tries to get students to think by making provocative statements and that he did nothing wrong. Bill O'Reilly invited Craig Silverman, the Denver talk-show host, to help him verbally dismember Bennish on his national talk show March 7, drumming the Hitler/Bush comparison just as he had Churchill's "Little Eichmanns" remark a year earlier. It fit the "Factor" formula finely—find a left-winger, add a buzz-phrase, then flail both mercilessly in front of a right-wing audience.

The entire affair blew over inside of two weeks, as the Cherry Creek School District cleared Bennish's return to the classroom as of March 13. "Jay Bennish has promise as a teacher," Superintendent Monte Moses said in a two-page state-ment, "but his practice and deportment need growth and refinement." *Rocky Mountain News* editorial-page director Carroll fumed over "The legal difficulties in getting rid of incompetent teachers these days," confusing (as he often does) competence and difference of opinion—one more example of the right wing's inability to extend rights of speech to those with whom its members disagree ("Unsatisfying End," 2006, 12-C).

Such a controversy would not have been complete without a cameo appear-ance by David Horowitz, who scored a rather late hit, on March 23 (10 days after Bennish resumed teaching) with a bulk e-mail to his supporters, soliciting contributions to buy advertising in Denver daily newspapers critical of Bennish. Horowitz said that Bennish should have been suspended without pay after the first incident. "A year's suspension would have been merciful," Horowitz said (Morson, 2006). As usual, Horowitz upheld his own right to opinion, while denying the same rights to others. In his e-mail, Horowitz wrote that he is trying to raise $28,000 in 72 hours to pay for the ads. The fund-raising campaign failed, but it was good for a new column-inches on the news pages. "As the Jay Bennish episode demonstrates, our children are abused daily by teachers who routinely and self-ishly ignore their primary job, that is, to educate young people so they can survive in the world," Horowitz wrote (Morson, 2006).

A COMPARISON UNFAIR TO HITLER?

About a year after the Bennish controversy in Colorado, an instructor at the University of Wisconsin–Madison came under attack for comparing President George W. Bush to Hitler in an essay that he required students to buy for his course. Kevin Barrett's essay, "Interpreting the Unspeakable: The Myth of 9/11," was contained in a $20 book of essays by several authors titled *9/11 and American Empire: Muslims, Jews, and Christians Speak Out.* Barrett, a part-time instructor, did not require the students to read his essay for the course, "Islam: Religion and Culture."

"Like Bush and the neocons, Hitler and the Nazis inaugurated their new era by destroying an architectural monument and blaming its destruction on their designated enemies," Barrett wrote in the essay (Antlfinger, 2006). Barrett, holder of a doctorate in African languages, literature, and folklore from the University of Wisconsin–Madison, has taken part in Scholars for 9/11 Truth, whose members assert that U.S. officials, not Al-Qaeda terrorists, instigated the September 11, 2001 attacks. Barrett compared the 9-11 attacks to the burning of the German Reichstag, in 1933, which helped the Nazis solidify power. "That's not comparing them as people, that's comparing the Reichstag fire to the demolition of the World Trade Center, and that's an accurate comparison that I would stand by," he said. He added: "Hitler had a good 20 to 30 I.Q. points on Bush, so comparing Bush to Hitler would in many ways be an insult to Hitler" (Antlfinger, 2006).

After Barrett was assigned the course, 61 Wisconsin state legislators denounced him. One county board cut its funding for the University of Wisconsin Extension by $8,247, equal to Barrett's pay for the class, a move that had no budgetary impact on the course or his paycheck (Antlfinger, 2006). Both candidates for governor of Wisconsin, incumbent Democrat Jim Doyle and Republican Mark Green, said before the November 2006 election that Barrett should be fired. Provost Patrick Farrell retained Barrett, however, following a review of his lesson plans and qualifications. He said Barrett could present his ideas during one week of the course as long as students were allowed to challenge them. Farrell said faculty might assign readings that may not be popular to everyone. "I think part of the role of any challenging course here is going to encourage students to think of things from a variety of perspectives," he said. Provost Farrell did, however, tell Barrett to quit seeking publicity for his point of view.

Barrett's views were featured on the O'Reilly Factor October 11 and 12, 2006. O'Reilly's rhetoric was as one would expect. Unlike the explosion that followed O'Reilly's drilling of Ward Churchill, these shows were followed by very little press coverage. Said O'Reilly:

> So your opinion is that Bush murdered everybody on 9/11 to seize control and make him the dictator of America, or whatever the crazy thing is. And my opinion is: You're nuts. . . . If I were Bush, I'd take a look at you . . . just like Sami al-Arian [See Chapter 6]. I'd put the FBI on you . . . nutty Barrett, and find out what the hell you guys are up to. . . . (O'Reilly, October 12, 2006)

SUBSIDIES FOR RELIGIOUS STUDIES

D. Michael Quinn, an outspoken dissident scholar of Mormon history, was expelled from the church in 1993 when some of his writings contradicted doctrine. He also resigned a professorship at Brigham Young University (BYU), the largest academic institution owned by the church, during 1998, where he had taught since 1976. Although he was denied access to documents and travel funds, BYU officials said that they did not force Quinn out. Nevertheless, his writings sparked controversy, especially when he asserted that Mormon elders had winked at polygamy after officially forbidding it.

Quinn, a seventh-generation Mormon on his mother's side, in 1996 declared his homosexuality in the face of Mormon doctrine that condemns it. Between 1994 and 1998, he also published four books on Mormon history with assistance from fellowships and research grants obtained from secular sources. During 2003, when Quinn was a visiting professor at Yale University, the Mormon Church threatened to withdraw funding from a conference on Mormonism that it was co-sponsoring with Yale if Quinn was allowed to speak. Yale defended Quinn's right to speak, but canceled his presentation of a scholarly paper and assigned Quinn to introduce a keynote speaker instead (Golden, 2006, A-8).

By 2004, with six books on his curriculum vitae, Quinn could not get an academic job in Mormon history anywhere, in large part because most professorships in the growing field, even at secular schools, were being endowed by the church and Mormon donors—a state of affairs that effectively blunted critical examination of its history or doctrines. "At this point, I am unemployable," said Quinn, 62 years of age in 2006 (Golden, 2006, A-1). He was living with his mother in Rancho Cucamonga, east of Los Angeles.

Even secular schools in Utah shied away from hiring Quinn. In 2004, he was ranked as the only finalist for a job at the University of Utah, but was not hired out of fear (widely rumored but officially unconfirmed) that the Mormon-dominated state legislature might cut the state school's budget. This wouldn't work as a legal reason to refuse someone employment at a public university. Robert Newman, dean of humanities at the university, told the *Wall Street Journal* that most of Quinn's books were not published by university presses (Golden, 2006, A-8). After the religious-studies department at Arizona State University recommended Quinn be hired for a one-year appointment in 2004–2005, the administration reversed the decision.

Public universities' acceptance of private donations to fund chairs in study of various religions began during the 1970s in Judaic studies, and spread within 30 years to many other faiths. In 1999, the Roman Catholic Aquinas Center endowed a chair in the study of that church at Emory University, for which the university hired Mark Jordan, who is homosexual, and who had written critically of the Church's attitude toward sodomy. When the Aquinas Center complained, the university shifted Jordan to a line that it did not fund, and gave up on plans for the chair. Harvard University in 2006 was arranging financing for a position in evangelical Christian studies funded by Alonzo L. McDonald, a practicing evangelical who stipulated that whoever holds the position should be "understanding and empathetic" toward traditions of his faith (Golden, 2006, A-8).

WHAT'S A PROFESSOR TO DO?

Given pressure to bend to various political, ideological, and religious winds, what is a professor to do, other than "profess?" The preferred dictionary definition of "to profess" is "To affirm openly, declare, or claim" (Morris, 1969, 1,044). Alfie Kohn wrote in the *Kappa Delta Pi Record* (Kappa Delta Pi is an international academic honor society for education):

> It's neither possible nor desirable for the field of education to be value-free, and it's never been more important to take a stand than in these dark days of test-driven instruction. . . . The assumption that it is possible, or even obligatory, to avoid taking a moral stand in one's work is partly due to the persistent and rather desperate attempt of many social scientists to align themselves with the natural sciences and snub the humanities, which are regarded as soft, subjective, and less substantive. This alliance manifests itself in different ways, ranging from the belief that everything can (and should) be reduced to numbers, to the current fashion for supporting certain pedagogical practices by certifying them as "brain-based." The attempt to bask in the reflected glory of the hard sciences helps to explain why many professors refuse to profess. After all, values are tantamount to biases, something to be excluded or denied. The scientist's job is simply to discover. (Kohn, 2003)

Can we, in this contentious time, still agree to disagree in the interest of a devotion to freedom and discovery, in the academy, and elsewhere?

REFERENCES

Antlfinger, Carrie. "UW [University of Wisconsin] Instructor Compares Bush to Hitler." Associated Press, October 11, 2006. (in LEXIS).

Apuzzo, Matt. "Professor Points to Politics as Yale Fails to Renew Contract." Associated Press, October 23, 2005. (in LEXIS).

Arenson, Karen W. "When Scholarship and Politics Collided at Yale." *New York Times*, December 28, 2005, B-1.

Buechel, Henry. Personal correspondence, March 11, 1970.

Capriccioso, Rob. "David Horowitz vs. Ward Churchill." *Inside Higher Education*, April 7, 2006. insidehighered.com/news/2006/04/07/debate.

Carroll, Vincent. "On Point: Teacher on the Fringe." *Rocky Mountain News*, March 3, 2006, 38-A.

Carroll, Vincent. "On Point: Molding the Future." *Rocky Mountain News*, March 9, 2006, 38-A.

Coyle, Patrick X. "Activist Challenges the 'Peoples Republic of Chapel Hill.'" *Libertas*, Winter, 2006, 23. (Coyle, 2006A).

Coyle, Patrick X. "The X-Files: Answers to Your Activism Questions." *Libertas*, Winter, 2006, 6. (Coyle, 2006B).

"The Dirty Thirty: Ranking the Worst of the Worst." Bruin Alumni Association. January 9–24, 2006. www.uclaprofs.com/profs/profsindex.html.

Frank, Joshua. "An Interview with David Graeber: Without Cause: Yale Fires An Acclaimed Anarchist Scholar." *Counterpunch*, May 13, 2005. counterpunch.org/frank05132005. html.

Goldberg, Michelle. "Osama University?" Salon.com, November 6, 2003. salon.com/news/feature/2003/11/06/middle_east/index_np.

Golden, Daniel. "In Religious Studies, Universities Bend to View of the Faithful; Scholar of Mormon History, Expelled from Church, Hits a Wall in Job Search." *Wall Street Journal*, April 6, 2006, A-1, A-8.

Graeber, David, personal communication, March 10, 2006.

Greenhouse, Linda. "Supreme Court Weighs Military's Access to Law Schools." *New York Times*, December 7, 2005. www.nytimes.com/2005/12/07/politics/07scotus.html.

Horowitz, David. *The Professors: The 101 Most Dangerous Academics in America.* Washington, D.C.: Regnery Publishing, 2006.

Janofsky, Michael. "Professors' Politics Draw Lawmakers Into the Fray." *New York Times*, December 25, 2005. www.nytimes.com/2005/12/25/national/25bias.html.

Johansen, Bruce. "A Rap Session with 'Hero Hank.'" *University of Washington Daily*, March 6, 1970, n.p.

Johansen, Bruce E. "Nebraska Professor Asserts That David Horowitz Missed Him on List of Dangerous Professors." Interactivist Information Exchange, September 30, 2006. info.interactivist.net/article.pl?sid=06/02/08/1417212.

Koebensky, Jessica and Roger Custer. "Comedy, Tragedy, and Today's College Classroom." *Libertas*, Winter, 2006, 7–9.

Kohn, Alfie. "Professors Who Profess: Making a Difference as Scholar-Activists." *Kappa Delta Pi Record*, Spring, 2003. www.findarticles.com/p/articles/mi_qa4009/is_200304/ai_n9210167.

Kurtz, Howard. "Steady as He Goes; In the Anchor Chair, Bob Schieffer Buoys CBS." Washington *Post*, March 6, 2006, C-1. www.washingtonpost.com/wp-dyn/content/article/2006/03/05/AR2006030501190_pf.html.

Lemann, Nicholas. "Fear Factor: Bill O'Reilly's Baroque Period." *The New Yorker*, March 27, 2006, 32–38.

Maharidge, Dale. *Homeland*. New York: Seven Stories Press, 2004.

Morris, William, ed. *The American Heritage Dictionary of the English Language.* Boston: Houghton-Mifflin, 1969.

Morson, Berny. "Bennish in New Spotlight; Calif. Activist Wants to Run Newspaper Ads Criticizing Teacher." *Rocky Mountain News*, March 22, 2006, 6-A.

O'Reilly, Bill. "The O'Reilly Factor." Fox News. Transcript. October 12, 2006. (in LEXIS).

"'Radical' U.C.L.A. Professors Targeted by Alumni Group" January 18, 2006. Associated Press. (in LEXIS).

Roat, Ron. "Dumbing Down 101." Evansville (Indiana) *Courier-Press*, May 12, 2006. www.courierpress.com/ecp/news_columnists/article/0,1626,ECP_747_4693818,00.html.

Schuck, Peter. "Fighting on the Wrong Front." *New York Times*, December 9, 2005. www.nytimes.com/2005/12/09/opinion/09schuck.html?pagewanted=print.

Schuman, Sharon. "Picked on by Their Profs." *The Sunday Oregonian* (Portland, Oregon), October 30, 2005, E-1.

Smallwood, Scott. "In a Clash of Academic-Freedom Titans, Civility Reigns." *Chronicle of Higher Education* 52:33(April 21, 2006): n.p. (in LEXIS).

Sprengelmeyer, M.E. "Churchill, Horowitz on Their Best Behavior; Liberal Professor, Conservative Author Keep Discourse Civil." *Rocky Mountain News*, April 7, 2006, 4-A.

Thomas, Cal. "Study's Results Hardly Shocking; College Faculties Lean Leftward." Omaha *World-Herald*, April 11, 2005, 7-B.

"Unsatisfying End to Bennish Affair; What Was the Punishment?" *Rocky Mountain News*, March 11, 2006, 12-C.

Vanlandingham, James. "Capitol Bill Aims to Control 'Leftist' Profs; The Law Could Let Students Sue for Untolerated Beliefs." University of Florida *Alligator*, March 23, 2005. www.alligator.org/pt2/050323freedom.php.

Vaughan, Kevin and Felix Doligosa Jr. "High School in Turmoil over Teacher's Remarks; Controversial Lecture Thrusts Overland into National Spotlight." *Rocky Mountain News*, March 3, 2006, 4-A.

Chapter 6

Terrorology 101

WITHOUT A DOUBT, the most difficult test of academic freedom—and freedom of inquiry generally—since the attacks of September 11, 2001—have involved people of Middle Eastern heritage (or who specialize in studying the region) who have expressed support for Palestinians and Islamic fundamentalists. Attempts have been made to regulate academic inquiry in Middle Eastern studies as the conflict has sharpened. Visas also have been denied to scholars from other countries, some of them prominent scientists, on groundless suspicion of terrorism. Some prosecutions under the "Patriot Act" have involved a fuzzy line between unpopular speech and advocacy of illegal action. The most unpopular type of advocacy—acting as "spiritual advisor" of young men play-acting jihad in the woods of Falls Church, Virginia, earned one scholar a sentence of life in prison without parole.

The federal government of the United States has never heretofore imposed regulation ("oversight") of an academic field for two major reasons: the First Amendment to the Constitution prohibits strictures on freedom of expression and (more practically) nearly all public higher education is maintained at the state level, but with some federal funding. After the attacks of September 11, 2001, however, the U.S. House of Representatives almost eagerly abandoned this tradition in an attempt to establish control of Middle Eastern Studies on the assumption that the field had become riddled with radical Islamic influence.

The traditional notion that ideas—even irritating information that challenges cherished assumptions—can be used to constructive ends (such as learning something about other cultures) seemed to have no place in this debate. Ideological conformity was the unabashed goal in this instance. The road of a scholar who championed Islamic interests in our Land of the Free became studded with ideological nails post 9-11.

The late Palestinian American scholar Edward Said, who died of leukemia in October 2003, wrote *Orientalism* (among many other books), in a groundbreaking effort to explore Western fantasies about the Middle East. *Orientalism* asserts that Westerners arc inherently unable to fairly judge, or even grasp, the Arab world. Instead of trying to understand this world, critics dismissed Said. In the toxic atmosphere post 9-11, even *quoting* Said with proper attribution could raise questions about one's patriotism.

Some of Said's statements provided fat targets for neoconservatives. For example, in 1999, he called for Bill Clinton, Madeleine Albright, and Wesley Clark to stand trial for war crimes, along with Slobodan Milosevic. He also dismissed the U.S. Constitution as a law written by and for wealthy, European-descended, slave-holding Anglophilic men. After Said died, Ze'ev Chafet even sneered in the *New York Daily News*: "As an Episcopalian, he's ineligible for the customary 72 virgins, but I wouldn't be surprised if he's honored with a couple of female doctoral graduates" (Fisk, 2003).

"Is 'Palestinian' now just a dirty word? Or is 'Arab' the dirty word?" asked Robert Fisk in the London *Independent* (Fisk, 2003). Where we once had witches, or bad Indians, or Communists, the hate-object Arab is now the generic barbarian at our gate.

CULTURE WARS IN MIDDLE EASTERN STUDIES

The terrorist attacks of September 11, 2001 enhanced long-running campus "culture wars" that pitted hard-line supporters of Israel, aided by neoconservatives in the Bush administration who now dominate the American right wing, against many academics who specialize in the Arab and Muslim world. Following the ascension of Arab as stereotypical bogeyman after the 9-11 attacks, Michelle Goldberg wrote in Salon.com that the U.S. right wing sensed an opportunity "to accuse Middle East academics not just of biased scholarship but of representing a kind of intellectual fifth column" (Goldberg, 2003).

Middle Eastern academics who expressed points of view similar to Edward Said's were denounced in testimony to the U.S. Congress by Dr. Stanley Kurtz, who asserted that the presence of "post-colonial theory" in academic circles has produced professors who refuse to support or instruct students interested in joining the State Department or American intelligence agencies. Congress then proposed to set up an "oversight board"—with appointed members from Homeland Security, the Department of Defense and the U.S. National Security Agency—that will link university department funding on Middle East studies to "students training for careers in national security, defense and intelligence agencies . . ." (Fisk, 2003).

Post 9-11, Palestinian American faculty members faced increasing discrimination. This held true not only in the United States, but also in Australia. There, a determined effort was mounted to prevent the Palestinian scholar Hanan Ashrawi from receiving the 2003 Sydney Peace Prize. Ironically, Ashrawi never favored suicide bombings in Israel. She spoke out emphatically against them, even as Sydney University withdrew the use of its Great Hall for presentation of the peace prize and the Lord Mayor of Sydney, Lucy Turnbull, dissociated the city, a sponsor of the prize, from the presentation.

What a difference a couple of decades can make in the world of convenient political alliances, especially regarding U.S. diplomacy in the Middle East. During the 1980s, the United States allied with the Afghani *mujahideen*, forerunners of the Taliban, when they were resisting a Soviet invasion. At one point, President Ronald Reagan compared Afghani "freedom fighters" to the Founding Fathers of the United States. Reagan's administration also approved the sale of chemical weapons to Saddam Hussein's Iraq, at the time an ally of the United States in a war with Iran, where hostages had been held at the U.S. Embassy a few years earlier. The United States also sold Iraq helicopters for "crop dusting," some of which were used to spray chemical weapons on recalcitrant Kurds, killing 3,000 to 5,000 people in Halabja during 1988. Fifteen years later, George W. Bush used nonexistent weapons of mass destruction as a pretext for invasion of Saddam's Iraq.

The same day that the United States invaded Iraq, TomPaine.com, an on-line public-interest journal, placed an advertisement in the *New York Times* with Osama bin Laden in the style of the "Uncle Sam" Army recruiting poster, saying: "I want YOU . . . to Invade Iraq," continuing: "Go ahead . . . Your bombings will send me a new generation of recruits and fuel their hatred and desire for revenge. So go ahead. Squander your wealth on war and occupation . . ." (Berman, 2006, 218).

A CONFLICT AT COLUMBIA

Witness the troubles of Prof. Joseph Massad, among other Arab-American professors who teach Middle Eastern Studies at Columbia University. Massad, an untenured junior faculty member in the department of Middle Eastern and Asian Languages and Cultures (MEALAC) became a major target for a campaign designed to intimidate academics critical of Israel and U.S. foreign policy in the Arab world. In a "special report" by the *New York Daily News* on November 21, 2004, Massad's entire department was accused of "promoting an I-hate-Israel agenda, embracing the ugliest of Arab propaganda, and teaching that Zionism is the root of all evil in the Mideast" (Feiden, 2004). Arguing that "Columbia has been infected with a contingent of faculty members whose hatred for Israel has eclipsed any academic mission that makes sense," a November 19, 2004 *New York Sun* editorial went so far as to demand that Columbia University investigate "the content of the scholars' research" ("Bollinger Whitewash," 2004). At least one Congressman, Rep. Anthony Weiner, called for Professor Massad to be fired.

The conflict at Columbia began to jell during 2001 and 2002, when several Jewish groups met to discuss what they believed to be a marked increase in anti-Israel activity there. The Israel on Campus Committee (ICC), a partnership of Hillel and the Charles and Lynn Schusterman Family Foundation (which gave the group

$1 million), formed after those meetings. Members of the group then resolved to "take back the campus," through lectures, political pressure, and Internet publicity (Doumani, 2006, 28–29).

Massad was attacked in a short film, *Columbia Unbecoming*, produced by The David Project, a Boston-based anti-Palestinian group formed in 2002. In the film, students affiliated with Lionpac, the University's pro-Israel student club, accused Massad of intimidating students who expressed views sympathetic to Israel. None of the students interviewed in the film had filed any kind of complaint against Massad or the MEALAC. Few had even taken a class with him. Students supportive of Professor Massad and appreciative of his classroom instruction were not interviewed by the filmmakers.

The half-hour film featured 14 students, of whom six presented first-hand complaints against professors Massad, as well as George Saliba and Hamid Dabashi. *Columbia Unbecoming* identified two interactions with students attributed to Massad. In one, Tomy Schoenfeld, a former member of the Israeli Defense Forces, asked Massad a question that he reportedly refused to answer until Schoenfeld told him "How many Palestinians [he had] killed" (Eisenberg, 2004, 300). In the second episode a student, Noah Liben, asked Massad whether he had understood a point he had made defending the treatment of Sephardic Jews by the Ashkenazi majority in Israel. According to Liben's account, Massad said he did not understand, and "smirked" (Eisenberg, 2004, 300). In the film, Massad was accused of describing Israel as "a racist state that does not legitimately represent Jews" (Eisenberg, 2004, 300).

Massad called the David Project and the film part of a "witch hunt that aims to stifle pluralism, academic freedom, and the freedom of expression on university campuses" (Eisenberg, 2004, 301). He also said that Schoenfeld was not a student of his, and that he had never met him. Massad also asserted that the makers of the film had distorted ("lied") about his purported assertion that Israel could be equated with Nazi Germany, calling such a characterization "abhorrent." "I never made such a reprehensible equation," he said (Eisenberg, 2004, 301).

Even in an unfriendly portrait, Massad seemed to be a rather benign aggressor. Columbia student Adam Sacarny wrote in the school's newspaper upon seeing the film: "Much like the electoral campaigns, it uses talking points in place of pesky verifiable facts," adding, "The film's case is so shoddy that I fail to see how any critical viewer could leave the theater convinced that [the department] has violated academic integrity standards" (Alam, 2005). Even the generally sympathetic Israeli daily *Haaretz* said that, "The movie fuses few solid examples of intimidation—only some of which involved professors and the students they were teaching—with generalized complaints of anti-Israel and anti-Semitic statements and behavior on campus" (Alam, 2005). Despite these students' claims of being "silenced," "intimidated," and "denied" (their own words), none said their grades were affected (Alam, 2005).

Some students complained that Massad's classes had been seeded with auditors whose sole purpose seemed to be disruption. The auditors, said one student, John Taplett, often attempted to dominate class discussion with personal statements "unrelated or extremely loosely related to the course material." "To my amazement," one student was quoted as saying, "[Massad] allowed each and every student in the class an opportunity to speak, regardless of their familiarity with the class subject matter and required course material" (Alam, 2005).

Hitesh Manglani, another student, said that Massad was openly critical of all religions, including Islam, so his criticism of Israel should not have been taken as anti-Semitic. Having criticized Israel, said Manglani, Massad also critically examined the actions of Yasser Arafat and the Palestine Liberation Organization. "In general," said Manglani, "He maintained a tone of critical scholarly inquiry." Benjamin Wheeler, who also is Jewish, said that he wrote a term paper criticizing Palestinian nationalism's support of violence, and "despite Massad's supposed bias, he gave me an 'A'" (Schwartz, 2004).

A letter from the New York Civil Liberties Union to Columbia University's president, Lee C. Bollinger, on the Massad case said "Students can expect to be treated with respect. They cannot expect that their professors will trim the cut of their convictions as not to offend the sensibilities of their students. The notion of a system of free expression embraces the commitment to speech that is wide-open, unfettered, and robust" (Eisenberg, 2004, 303). The screening of professors' ideas according to ideological disagreements could "Descend into an inquisition into the ideological or political views of the professors who have been accused," the letter said (Eisenberg, 2004, 305). Moreover, "trying to impose balance from outside the Department might well violate academic freedom principles of self-governance [and constitute an] assault on academic freedom" (Eisenberg, 2004, 306).

A faculty panel appointed by Bollinger later found no evidence of anti-Semitism or political bias in the university's Middle Eastern Studies Department in grading students' work. The panel did criticize a "climate of incivility" on both sides of the debate ("Academia Assailed," 2005, 1).

"A MILLION MORE MOGADISHUS"

Columbia faced another test of free speech on Middle Eastern issues at about the same time. Columbia University held a teach-in March 26, 2003, during which 30 professors spoke to about 3,000 students. One of the professors, Nicholas de Genova, an untenured instructor who taught Latino Studies, spoke for 15 minutes, advocating "fragging" of U.S. soldiers, and stated "I personally would like to see a million more Mogadishus," in Iraq, a reference to bloody carnage that killed 18 U.S. soldiers in Somalia during 1993. The event inspired the movie *Black Hawk Down*.

Very quickly, New York City talk radio came alive with demands that de Genova be fired, as 78 New York State legislators signed a letter condemning his statements. Gov. George Pataki questioned his fitness to be a professor. Columbia President Bollinger then received a letter signed by 104 mainly Republican members of Congress demanding that de Genova be fired. In contrast, when Ann Coulter, a well-known right-wing pundit, told George Gurley of *The New York Observer*

"My only regret with Timothy McVeigh [who was convicted of bombing the Oklahoma City Federal Building] is that he didn't go after the *New York Times* building," none of the aforementioned lawmakers batted an eyelash (Maharidge, 2004, 166). Apparently, advocating fragging of the *New York Times* qualifies as free speech.

The entire professional anti-leftist troupe—Rush Limbaugh, the bloggers at Free Republic, Accuracy in Academia, and many, many more—jumped to attention with fuel and faggots to fan the fire under de Genova: a phrase or two of their favorite anti-leftist knee-jerkery, and a flood of phone calls and e-mails inundated Columbia University's central switchboard, President Bollinger's office, and de Genova's department. As with Ward Churchill's "Little Eichmanns," a few inflammatory words ignited a firestorm.

The next day, Ron Howell, the same reporter from New York *Newsday* who had first published de Genova's incendiary quote, called Eric Foner, also a speaker at the rally, who characterized de Genova's "million Mogadishus" remark as "idiotic." Foner told the reporter, "I thought that was completely uncalled for. We do not desire the deaths of American soldiers" (Horowitz, 2003).

Columbia faculty members other than Foner who spoke at the teach-in expressed nearly unanimous opposition to the Iraq war, but some quickly distanced themselves from de Genova's incendiary sound-bite. According to an account in *Accuracy in Academia* by Sara Russo, Jean Cohen, a professor of political philosophy and one of the event's organizers, asserted that de Genova had not originally been invited to speak at the event, but stepped in at the last minute when one of the other participants was unable to attend. "He and the press have hijacked this teach-in, and I'm very, very angry about it," she told the *Columbia Daily Spectator*. "It was an utterly irresponsible thing to do. And it's not innocent . . . this was a planned undermining of this teach-in" (Russo, n.d.).

Following the remark, platoons of right-wing bloggers slammed de Genova hard, heavy, and often. He was called "garbage," "terror teacher," and worse. One blogger, who was hardly unrepresentative, said:

> Nicholas de Genova certainly has the First Amendment right (protected, incidentally, by the men and women whom he is hoping will be killed by his Iraqi friends) to say this, just as I have the First Amendment right to express my wish that de Genova had been in the World Trade Center on September 11, 2001—or, even better, on one of the airplanes that Al Qaeda crashed into the towers. I will leave it to Rudyard Kipling, however, whose eloquence far exceeds mine, to answer this two-legged piece of garbage. (Rudyard, 2003) [Kipling is older than this, of course, but the source is a web page p[osted in 2003.]

His reference was to Kipling's poem "Tommy," the story of a soldier who was refused service at a bar, in which the blogger had bold-faced the words:

> Yes, makin' mock o' uniforms that guard you while you sleep Is cheaper than them uniforms, an' they're starvation cheap; An' hustlin' drunken soldiers when they're

goin' large a bit Is five times better business than paradin' in full kit. Then it's Tommy this, an' Tommy that, an' 'Tommy, 'ow's yer soul?' (Rudyard, 2003)

Or, as supporters of the U.S. military in Iraq often phrased it in briefer but less elegant language: "Freedom ain't free."

David Horowitz landed on de Genova with all fours in *Front Page Magazine*, March 31, 2003. Horowitz recalled that de Genova's audience at the teach-in did not initially react to the Mogadishu remark; Horowitz speculated that they were too geographically challenged to understand the reference. They applauded loudly, however, when de Genova said, "If we really [believe] that this war is criminal . . . then we have to believe in the victory of the Iraqi people and the defeat of the U.S. war machine." In the late 1960s, Horowitz recalled, when he was editor of *Ramparts*, "the largest magazine of the New Left . . . I edited a book of anti-American essays with the . . . title, *Two, Three, Many Vietnams*," desiring a world of quagmires for U.S. troops (Horowitz, 2003).

When the Mogadishu remark was made, Horowitz wrote, "It was as if the devil had inadvertently exposed his horns, and someone needed to put a hat over them before others realized it. That someone was the demonstration organizer, Professor Eric Foner, the prestigious head of Columbia's history department. Actually, when Foner spoke, following de Genova, he failed to find the Mogadishu remark offensive. Instead, Foner dissociated himself from another de Genova comment to the effect that all Americans who described themselves as "patriotic," were actually "white supremacists" (Horowitz, 2003).

A feature on de Genova in the *Chronicle of Higher Education*, April 18, 2003, was headlined: "The Most Hated Professor in America." It began: "If you call Columbia University's main switchboard and ask for Nicholas De Genova, you will not be connected to his office. Instead, you will hear a recording of a statement by the university's president, Lee C. Bollinger, saying he is 'appalled' by his 'outrageous comments'" (Bartlett, 2003, A-56). Outraged he may have been, but Bollinger, a noted First Amendment scholar, also defended de Genova's First Amendment rights, even as some alumni promised to withhold donations until de Genova was ditched.

President Bollinger said that he usually refrains from commenting on faculty members' statements, but in this case he could not let de Genova's stand unchallenged. "Because of the University's tradition of academic freedom, I normally don't comment about statements made by faculty members. However, this one crosses the line and I really feel the need to say something," said Bollinger, "I am especially saddened for the families of those whose lives are at risk. . . . Assistant Professor Nicholas De Genova was speaking as an individual at a teach-in. He was exercising his right to free speech. His statement does not in any way represent the views of Columbia University" (Russo, n.d.).

De Genova's comment was not a flip provocation. He asserted in a letter to the *Spectator* that the scandal-happy media were responsible for blowing his remarks out of proportion by taking them out of context, by which his beliefs were "remarkably decontextualized [in an] inflammatory manner." De Genova said he was quoted as wishing for a million Mogadishus, with no indication whatsoever of the perspective that framed his remark. He wrote:

> My rejection of U.S. nationalism is an appeal to liberate our own political imaginations such that we might usher in a radically different world in which we will not remain the prisoners of U.S. global domination. "In my brief presentation, I outlined a long history of U.S. invasions, wars of conquest, military occupations, and colonization in order to establish that imperialism and white supremacy have been constitutive of U.S. nation-state formation and U.S. nationalism," de Genova wrote to the *Spectator*. (de Genova, March 27, 2003)

In that context, he stressed the necessity of repudiating all forms of U.S. patriotism. He also emphasized that the disproportionate majority of U.S. troops come from racially oppressed and working-class backgrounds, finding themselves in the military because they lack prospects for a decent life. "Nonetheless," he wrote, "I emphasized that U.S. troops are indeed confronted with a choice—to perpetrate this war against the Iraqi people or to refuse to fight and contribute toward the defeat of the U.S. war machine" (de Genova, March 27, 2003).

De Genova believes that Iraqi liberation can be attained only by Iraqis themselves, by resisting and defeating the U.S. invasion as well as overthrowing a regime whose brutality was long sustained by U.S. policy and aid. "Such an anti-colonial struggle for self-determination might involve a million Mogadishus now," he concluded, "but would ultimately have to become something more like another Vietnam . . . a stunning defeat for U.S. imperialism" (de Genova, March 27, 2003).

De Genova's explanation hardly quieted his critics, who were not in a mood for political context. A week after he made the remark, *Accuracy in Academia's* Sara Russo described "hundreds of patriotic students wearing yellow ribbons and waving American flags" rallying to support the troops in front of Columbia's Low Library. "While several of the rally's speakers criticized De Genova's remarks," Russo wrote, "the demonstration's main focus was on America's soldiers. The names of the soldiers who had been killed or declared missing or imprisoned in Iraq were read aloud while students listened in silence." Columbia College Republicans President Megan Romigh opened the event by leading the Pledge of Allegiance, noting in her address, "We are not here to debate the politics of this war, but rather to celebrate the efforts of our troops" (Russo, 2003).

De Genova tried to contextualize his remarks again in the *Chronicle of Higher Education.* "I was referring to what Mogadishu symbolizes politically," de Genova told interviewer Thomas Bartlett.

> The U.S. invasion of Somalia was humiliated in an excruciating way by the Somali people. And Mogadishu was the premier symbol of that. What I was really emphasizing in the larger context of my comments was the question of Vietnam and that historical lesson. . . . What I was intent to emphasize was that the importance of Vietnam is that it was a defeat for the U.S. war machine and a victory for the cause of human self-determination. (Bartlett, 2003, A-56)

In that context, Bartlett asked, "Just so we're clear: Do you welcome or wish for the deaths of American soldiers?" De Genova replied: "No, precisely not. That's one of the reasons I am against the war" (Bartlett, 2003, A-56). De Genova said he opposed the war because it was needlessly wasting soldiers' lives. De Genova did admit that had he known that a newspaper reporter was in the audience, "I certainly would have selected my words somewhat more carefully. But I would not have changed the message (Bartlett, 2003, A-56).

De Genova did receive some support. Historians Against the War, for example, started an electronic petition favoring his freedom of speech rights, which stated:

> We write out of concern for and in solidarity with Professor Nicholas De Genova, an assistant professor in anthropology and Latino Studies at Columbia University. In recent days, Professor De Genova has been attacked by the national media, physically threatened (including over 1,000 death threats), and institutionally reprimanded for remarks that he made at a Columbia University teach-in on March 26, 2003 which have been quoted, sensationally, with minimal account of the context in which they were made. We believe that this event raises urgent and compelling issues of free speech, the right of public dissent without fear of recrimination, and academic freedom. These issues, which are especially important in emotionally charged times of war, concern all of us, regardless of one's position on the war or on the content of Professor De Genova's comments. (Wilder, 2003)

More than two and a half years after de Genova made his incendiary comment, on December 21, 2005, Bill O'Reilly's "Factor" (whose audience of two million comprised the largest talk-show venue in the United States) compared him to that universal constant in O'Reilly's world of professorial perfidy, Ward Churchill, another professor with a sharp-left analysis and a talent for the headline-grabbing phrase (O'Reilly, 2005).

Joining O'Reilly on the show, Matthew Continetti, a reporter for the right-wing *Weekly Standard*, characterized American academia as a cesspool of radical leftist agitation *a la* Churchill and de Genova.

> Well, the funny thing about academic freedom in this body of tradition that's allowed professors to speak their mind[s] [is that] when you go on campuses, you find that there's a conformity of thought that's always to the left. The real free expression would be somebody who supported the war in Iraq, for example. But when Professor de Genova made those comments at the anti-war rally in 2003, he was speaking to an echo chamber. It was complete conformity. (O'Reilly, 2005)

By the time O'Reilly found him, de Genova was rather accustomed to his role as a right-wing punching bag. He also had become accustomed, at times, to lecturing flanked by security guards.

What amazed some observant academics was that de Genova could coin such a headline-grabbling phrase out of a general vocabulary so dense that even PhDs in his own field sometimes had trouble deciphering it. His professional biography on Columbia's Web site was instructive in this regard:

> The central concerns of my research and teaching include: labor and class formation, racialization, the production of urban space, nationalism, the politics of citizenship, and transnational social processes, especially migration. My ethnographic research explores the social productions of racialized and spatialized difference in the experiences of transnational Mexican migrant workers within the space of the U.S. nation-state. More specifically, I examine transnational urban conjunctural spaces that link the U.S. and Latin America as a standpoint of critique from which to interrogate U.S. nationalism, political economy, racialized citizenship, and immigration law. This work contributes to a reconceptualization of Latin American, Latino, and "American" (U.S.) Studies. Likewise, I am interested in the methodological problems of ethnographic research practice and the limits of anthropological disciplinary forms of knowledge and modes of representation. My current research concerns the politics of race and immigration in relation to the Homeland Security State and the so-called "War on Terrorism." (de Genova's web page, 2005)

The same site contained a sampling of de Genova's published work, excerpted here.

> 1998. "Race, Space, and the Reinvention of Latin America in Mexican Chicago," in Latin American Perspectives, Volume 25, Number 5.

> 2002. "Migrant 'Illegality' and Deportability in Everyday Life" in *Annual Review of Anthropology* #31.

> 2003. "Latino Rehearsals: Racialization and the Politics of Citizenship Between Mexicans and Puerto Ricans in Chicago" (coauthored with Ana Y. Ramos-Zayas) in *Journal of Latin American Anthropology*, Volume 8, Number 2.

> 2005. *Working the Boundaries: Race, Space, and "Illegality" in Mexican Chicago* (Durham, NC: Duke University Press).

> 2006. *Racial Transformations: Latinos and Asians Remaking the United States* (edited, with an Introduction, by Nicholas de Genova).

CONGRESS VOTES TO "OVERSEE" MIDDLE EASTERN STUDIES

Conflicts regarding U.S. policies in the Middle East quickly spread from Columbia to national venues. Following the events at Columbia, the neocons enlisted Congress in this crusade. On October 21, 2003, the U.S. House of Representatives passed HR 3077, the International Studies in Higher Education Act, which required university international studies departments to show more support for American foreign policy or risk their federal funding. The bill was referred to a committee in the Senate, where it died. Prof. Michael Bednar who teaches in the history department at the University of Texas/Austin said, "The possibility that someone in Homeland Security will instruct college professors . . . on the proper, patriotic, American-friendly' textbooks that may be used in class scares and outrages me" (Fisk, 2003).

The amount of federal funding at stake in this debate amounted to a few hundred thousand dollars annually at each university, not much in the world of large-university funding. The federal funding often is important to these centers' budgets, however. The important line of conflict here is ideological, rather than monetary. A number of Middle Eastern studies professors believe that such a committee could be controlled by the same neoconservatives who have promoted its creation.

Neoconservative critics have argued for years that tax money should not be spent on activities at universities whose faculty advocate Edward Said's (and others') left-wing ideas. Some of the neocons believe deeply that many Middle Eastern studies departments are dominated by "apologists" for the Arab world's rising tide of fundamentalist Islam, which they take to be terroristic on its face. At about the same time, Martin Kramer, editor of the right-wing *Middle East Quarterly*, published a book called *Ivory Towers on Sand: The Failure of Middle Eastern Studies in America*. He asserted that many academics in that field were preaching radical ideologies.

Also during 2003, Daniel Pipes, a colleague of Kramer's, initiated Campus Watch (www.campuswatch.org), a Web site that monitors Middle Eastern studies departments for signs of purported anti-Americanism as well as anti-Israeli bias on Middle Eastern issues. Once more on the model of Senator Joseph McCarthy, Pipes published files listing what he regarded as professors' lack of patriotic vigor. Pipes also asked students to squeal on their professors by reporting "inappropriate" remarks in or out of class. Pipes's "Campus Watch" has assailed Massad, as well as Columbia professors Rashid Khalidi and Hamid Dabashi. Khalidi held the Edward Said Chair of Arab studies at Columbia University.

Kramer, an American-born Israeli citizen with a PhD in Near Eastern Studies from Princeton, proposed legislation overseeing Middle Eastern Studies in *Ivory Towers on Sand*. He also had been director of the Moshe Dayan Center for Middle Eastern and African Studies at Tel Aviv University. Returning to the United States, he joined the same network of conservative think tanks that nurtured defense intellectuals like Richard Perle and Paul Wolfowitz. A journal he edited, *Middle East Quarterly*, is published by the Middle East Forum, whose director is Pipes. Kramer's book was published by the Washington Institute for Near East Policy, a staunchly pro-Israel think tank whose board of advisors includes Perle and former CIA Director James Woolsey. Wolfowitz resigned from the board when he joined the administration (Goldberg, 2003).

Passage of HR 3077 was initiated following hearings the previous summer at which some members of Congress listened to a testimony about the allegedly pernicious influence of Edward Said's philosophy in many Middle Eastern studies departments, which were often described as enclaves of debased anti-Americanism. Stanley Kurtz, a research fellow at the Hoover Institution, a right-wing think tank, testified, "Title VI-funded programs in Middle Eastern Studies (and other area studies) tend to purvey extreme and one-sided criticisms of American foreign policy" (Goldberg, 2003).

Had it been passed by the Senate and signed by President Bush (as of 2006, it had not reached that point), the International Studies in Higher Education Act would not have granted the federal government power to exclude any given point of view from Middle Eastern Studies departments, but it *would* have given the government a role in defining which views included in the academic mainstream. The bill provided for a seven-member board to provide Congress with recommendations regarding how the centers might better "reflect the national needs related to the homeland security," and make sure that programs "reflect diverse perspectives and represent the full range of views on world regions, foreign languages, and international affairs" (Goldberg, 2003). Two members of the board would be drawn from national-security agencies, while others would be appointed by Congress and the administration.

This proposed board was endowed with "extraordinary investigative authority, with no requirement that it report to the Secretary of Education. Despite a sentence added at the last minute prohibiting meddling with curriculum, this advisory board would set a precedent for federal intrusion into the conduct and content of higher education" (Doumani, 2007, 219–220). Khalidi believes that the threat HR 3077 posed to Middle Eastern studies in America was "deadly serious." The bill, he said, would have "impose[d] the teaching of one twisted version of Middle East reality, what I call 'terrorology,' impose[d] it at the taxpayers' expense as one central element in the way the subject is taught. Or, by subjecting self-respecting universities to conditions they will not under any circumstances accept, it would curtail the teaching of the Middle East" (Goldberg, 2003).

"An assumption implicit in the neo-con line," wrote Michelle Goldberg on Salon.com, "maintains that if most established experts believe American Middle East policy is bad, the flaw lies with the experts, not the policy" (Goldberg, 2003). "There's the threat that centers will be punished for not toeing the official line out of Washington, which is an unprecedented degree of federal intrusion into a university-based area studies program," said Zachary Lockman, a New York University history professor and director of the school's Hagop Kevorkian Center for Near Eastern Studies (Goldberg, 2003).

The bill also would have required Middle Eastern studies centers to allow government recruiters full access to students. In the past, some professors in the field have declined to cooperate with national security agencies, contending that students associated with these agencies could be targeted as U.S. agents while studying abroad.

The American Council on Education decided to support the bill after language was added to prohibit the board from reviewing specific course syllabi or otherwise interfering with curricula. However, several Middle Eastern studies professors expressed fears that a federal oversight committee might exceed any mandate to deal only with grant-making authority, and could be controlled by the same neoconservatives who advocated the idea to begin with. During 2003, for example,

David Wurmser, a key neoconservative scholar known for his close ties to the Israeli right, was appointed as a Middle East advisor to Dick Cheney's national security team headed by Lewis "Scooter" Libby, Cheney's chief of staff, who was forced to resign late in 2005 after he was indicted in the "outing" of CIA agent Valerie Plame (Goldberg, 2003).

Juan Cole, a professor of Middle Eastern History at the University of Michigan, worried that the International Studies Act could give the field's most adamant critics an institutional niche. "One of the subtexts is they don't like criticism of Ariel Sharon and want to shut it down," said Cole, who formerly directed the school's Center for Middle Eastern and North African Studies, which could have its funding threatened under the act (Goldberg, 2003).

The United States has 17 Middle Eastern studies centers, including Harvard, Columbia, New York University, and the University of Chicago, which receive grants for graduate-student fellowships as well as community outreach and education— activities like training high-school teachers about Middle Eastern issues and information for mass media. None of the money is used for professors' salaries (Goldberg, 2003).

Some neoconservatives object that many (too many, for their tastes) Middle Eastern studies scholars are non-white and non-Western. David Horowitz, the right-wing pundit who has spent much of his career on a single-minded crusade against what he regards as academia's leftist tilt, has asserted that while in 1979, 3 percent of Middle Eastern scholars were non-Western, by 2003 that proportion had grown to 50 percent. Horowitz attributes the change (as he does with most other trends in academia that do not please him) to leftist control of hiring. To restore what they regard as "balance" to Middle Eastern studies, right-wingers have proposed a sort of ideological affirmative action for like-minded scholars, a proposal that resonates with the creation of a federal oversight board in Middle Eastern Studies.

TOO WELL-KNOWN FOR YALE?

During the spring of 2006, Juan Cole found himself rejected for a post in Middle Eastern history at Yale University, provoking widespread criticism that Yale denied his application not because he was unqualified, but because he was *too* well known. Cole, a professor of history at the University of Michigan and president of the Middle East Studies Association, as well as a trenchant critic of U.S. and Israeli policies, has one of the largest audiences of Middle Eastern studies experts through his blog, "Informed Comment," on which he publishes numerous updates about events (Jaschik, 2006). Postings on the blog were cited by his critics who sought to block his appointment at Yale.

No one was commenting officially on the position in early June when a blog critical of Cole, Power Line, reported that a senior appointments committee at Yale had turned down his application. The item was reported as "today's good news," and reportedly confirmed by a professor with close knowledge of the search (Jaschik, 2006).

Zachary Lockman, a professor of Middle Eastern studies at New York University, called the campaign against Cole "an assault on academic freedom and the academic enterprise." Lockman, as president-elect of the Middle East Studies Association stressed that he was speaking for himself, not the group, and that he didn't have first-hand knowledge of the Yale search. Lockman said that Cole is "one of the preeminent historians of the modern Middle East and he's been attacked on political grounds—because he's critical of the Bush administration and Israel." Given Cole's reputation and the departmental backing for his appointment, Lockman said of the decision to reject Cole: "Universities seem to be willing to kowtow to pressure from outside interest groups" (Jaschik, 2006).

Cole's political statements have been criticized by some major right-wing media, including the *New York Sun, National Review*, and the *Wall Street Journal*. They say his positions display a willingness to blame the United States and Israel inappropriately. Critics also maintain that he is spending too much time on blogging and questioning his output of serious scholarship. Usually, critics ignore his lengthy vita of publications in prestigious scholarly journals. Campus Watch, a pro-Israel group, maintains a long list of articles about Cole, most of which it endorses for their criticism of him (Jaschik, 2006). Cole said that critics were "motivated by a desire to punish me for daring to stand up for Palestinian rights, criticize Israeli policy, criticize Bush administration policies and, in general being a liberal Democrat" (Jaschik, 2006).

"TERRORISM": IS IT SPEECH OR ACTION?

For anyone concerned with civil liberties in the United States, the biggest problem with the U.S. Patriot Act is its transformation of previously constitutionally protected advocacy into criminal activity linked to terrorist causes—most notably if one is a noncitizen (especially one of Middle Eastern descent) and an outspoken supporter of political causes that government prosecutors deem unworthy (e.g. terroristic).

Sami al-Arian, a former Florida professor and a Palestinian-born academic in the United States on a permanent resident visa lost his job following federal indictment during 2003 on terrorism charges. He was found not guilty in Tampa, Florida federal district court late in 2005, when a jury failed to convict on any of the 51 charges brought against him and three codefendants by federal prosecutors.

Al-Arian's support for militant Palestinian causes had placed him under intense federal-government surveillance since the early 1990s. By the mid-1990s, news coverage of his public statements rejecting Israeli occupation of the West Bank and Gaza Strip led some critics to label the University of South Florida "Jihad U." At the same time, al-Arian enjoyed enough support from Muslims in the area to make him a political figure deemed worthy of brief meetings with presidents Bill Clinton and George W. Bush. After the September 11, 2001 attacks, however, opposition to al-Arian's statements hardened and, with passage of the Patriot Act, became subject to investigation as criminal activity. Al-Arian appeared on Fox News Channel's "O'Reilly Factor," where he was confronted with statements he had made years earlier calling for "death to Israel" (Lichtblau, December 7, 2005).

After deliberating for 13 days, the jury found al-Arian not guilty on eight criminal counts alleging support of terrorism, perjury, and immigration violations, including a charge of conspiring to kill people overseas. It deadlocked on the remaining nine counts against al-Arian, and did not return any guilty verdicts against three other defendants. Linda Moreno, an attorney for al-Arian, said that interviews with several jurors indicated that, the jury as a whole was leaning strongly toward acquittal on the deadlocked counts (Lichtblau, December 8, 2005, 34).

David Cole, a law professor at Georgetown University who had represented al-Arian's brother-in-law in an earlier deportation case, said the government "stood down" and abandoned a retrial of al-Arian on the eight remaining charges. "It's consistent with a general pattern of overcharging in terrorism, and being unable to come up with the evidence to bear out their initial charges," Cole said. He noted that authorities first sought to imprison al-Arian for life (Hsu, 2006, A-3). Cole said, "If he decides he wants to stay in the country, it will be a contentious immigration case, because . . . [the government is] trying to deport a permanent resident who has not been convicted of any crime, based on his political affiliations alone, and that raises serious constitutional questions" (Lichtblau, December 8, 2005, 34).

Federal officials continued to shade the line between speech and action where alleged terrorism was involved. Thus, the verdict surprised them. "We remain focused on the important task at hand, which is to protect our country through our ongoing vigorous prosecution of terrorism cases," said Tasia Scolinos, a spokeswoman for the Justice Department. "While we respect the jury's verdict, we stand by the evidence we presented in court against Sami al-Arian and his co-defendants" (Lichtblau, December 7, 2005).

The verdicts were interpreted as a major defeat for government prosecutors, who could not convince the jury that the case involved action, rather than speech protected under the First Amendment. The five-month trial was a crucial test of the boundary between verbal support of Palestinian independence *vis a vis* illegal support for terrorists.

The charges described al-Arian as ringleader of a North American front for Palestinian terrorists. The prosecution case alleged that al-Arian had helped finance and direct terrorist attacks in Israel, the Gaza Strip, and the West Bank, using his faculty position teaching computer engineering as cover. The case enabled use of the U.S. Patriot Act to present years of wiretaps in a criminal context that previously would not have been admissible in court. Even so, as legal doctrine, the jury in this case flunked the Patriot Act. While al-Arian was well known as a fiery advocate of Palestinian causes and an acerbic critic of Israel, his behavior was nearly totally an exercise of free speech that pre-Patriot Act would have been protected under the late, great First Amendment.

According to media reports, the prosecution's wiretaps recorded conversations in which al-Arian "was heard raising money for Palestinian causes, hailing recently completed attacks against Israel with associates overseas, calling suicide bombers 'martyrs' and referring to Jews as 'monkeys and swine' who would be 'damned' by Allah" (Lichtblau, December 7, 2005). Many of the recorded conversations predated the 1995 designation by the United States of Palestinian Islamic Jihad as a terrorist group, which prohibited U.S. citizens from supporting it.

"This was a political prosecution from the start, and I think the jury realized that," said Linda Moreno, one of al-Arian's defense lawyers. "They looked over at Sami al-Arian; they saw a man who had taken unpopular positions on issues thousands of miles away, but they realized he wasn't a terrorist. The truth is a powerful thing" (Lichtblau, December 7, 2005). Cole said that the verdict amounted to a rejection of the government's "sweeping guilt by association theory" (Lichtblau, December 7, 2005).

The jury verdict was interpreted as a victory by al-Arian, his family, and the other three defendants, Sameeh T. Hammoudeh, Ghassan Ballut, and Hatim Fariz, many of whom wept in court as the verdicts were read. Muslims in the Tampa area planned a prayer service and celebration at the local mosque that al-Arian had helped to found (Lichtblau, December 7, 2005). Al-Arian "loves America, and he believes in the system, and thank God the system did not fail him," his wife, Nahla al-Arian, said outside the federal courthouse as throngs of family members, supporters and lawyers celebrated the results (Lichtblau, December 7, 2005).

Having investigated him for more than a decade (holding him in jail during the last three years), compiling more than 20,000 hours of taped conversations from wiretaps on al-Arian and people with whom he spoke and worked, having spent millions of tax dollars failing to make any of its charges stick, prosecutors then hounded al-Arian into a plea-bargained guilty plea on *one* charge. District court judge James S. Moody, Jr., then sentenced al-Arian to 19 more months in prison—*more* than the prosecution had requested—and allowed the government to deport him.

Judge Moody also accused al-Arian of acts for which he had not been found guilty by the jury. The judge continued to upbraid al-Arian, calling him a "master manipulator." During the judge's speech, al-Arian's wife left the courtroom in tears (Steinhauer, 2006). Describing horrific bombings in Israel, Judge Moody said, "Anyone with even the slightest bit of human compassion would be sickened. Not you. You saw it as an opportunity to solicit more money to carry out more bombings. . . . The only connection to widows and orphans is that you create them" (Steinhauer, 2006).

"I have been visiting with Sami al-Arian every week in the jail for the last 14 months," said the Rev. Warren Clark, pastor of the First United Church of Tampa. "I will tell you that the Sami al-Arian that I know is very different from the Sami al-Arian the judge described" (Steinhauer, 2006).

As a noncitizen on a permanent resident visa, al-Arian continued to be held in jail on an "immigration detainer," as federal officials debated where to deport him, possibly Egypt, where he has family. The immigration charges required a lower burden of proof than the terrorism indictment, in part because Congress during 2005 made association with a banned or terrorist group a deportable offense. Al-Arian's wife's brother, Mazen al-Najjar, had been deported from Florida in 2002 for associating with people believed by the government to be Palestinian militants.

U.S. Attorney General Alberto R. Gonzales hailed the effort to deport al-Arian. "We have a responsibility not to allow our nation to be a safe haven for those who provide assistance to the activity of terrorists," Gonzales said in a written statement. "Sami al-Arian has already spent significant time behind bars and will now lose the right to live in the country he calls home" (Hsu, 2006, A-3).

The Patriot Act was becoming an expensive consumer of federal legal time and talent that was failing, more often than not, to pass muster in the courts. Nationwide, in 30 attempts to convict defendants of conspiring to contribute money to a terrorist organization under the Patriot Act by 2005—one of the charges against al-Arian—28 were dismissed, according to the Terrorism Research Center at the University of Arkansas (Steinhauer, 2006). "This case almost reached the level of seditious conspiracy," Brent Smith, director of the center, said. "And historically, we have been very unsuccessful at trying those cases" (Steinhauer, 2006).

LIFE IN PRISON FOR JIHADI BRAGGADOCIO?

Mouthing off about killing Americans in the service of militant Islamism is obviously rather tactless in polite American company, but is it worth life in prison plus 70 years without parole? Ali al-Timimi, a biologist and Islamic scholar, during 2005 found out where a jury drew the line on free speech—even for a man, who, his defense maintained, never touched a weapon, much less carried out a *bona fide* terrorist act. According to the Justice Department, under cover of the U.S. Patriot Act, acting as a "spiritual advisor" to a group of would-be Virginia jihadis was terroristic enough. When play-acting jihad with a sharp tongue and real ammunition, the old adage that the First Amendment gives all of us the right to make fools of ourselves seems no longer to apply.

On April 26, 2005, al-Timimi was convicted in the U.S. District Court for the Eastern District of Virginia on charges of conspiracy, attempting to aid the Taliban, soliciting treason, soliciting others to wage war against the United States, and aiding and abetting the use of firearms and explosives. On July 13, 2005, he was sentenced to life in prison plus 70 years without parole. Al-Timimi's attorney, Jonathan Turley, early in 2006 appealed the case on grounds that the National Security Agency spied on al-Timimi without a warrant.

Born in Washington, D.C., al-Timimi's father, an attorney, worked at the Iraqi embassy. His mother was a scholar of psychology. At age 15, al-Timimi moved with his family to Saudi Arabia, and started a scholarly career studying Islam. By age 17, again in the United States, al-Timimi attended George Washington University. He also lectured often at the Center for Islamic Information and Education in Falls Church, Virginia, a southern suburb of Washington. He was a founding member of the center, which is also known as Dar al-Arqam ("Ali al-Tamimi," n.d.)

At a dinner meeting on September 16, 2001, five days after the World Trade Center attacks, al-Timimi lectured some men in a rag-tag group that called itself the Virginia Jihad Network regarding their "Muslim duty" to fight for Islam overseas and to defend the Taliban in Afghanistan against U.S. forces, according to testimony at his trial. In an Internet message posted during 2003, he described the destruction of the space shuttle Columbia as a "good omen" for Muslims in an apocalyptic conflict with the West.

For these and other statements, the Justice Department pursued al-Timimi as the "spiritual leader" of the Virginia jihadis as they practiced their martial skills in woods near Falls Church. Al-Timimi was prosecuted as a coconspirator with the group, nine of whose members were convicted of training with paint guns as well as various firearms, rocket-propelled grenades, and explosives. Most of this amounted to play-acting with live ammunition. Even so, no actual terrorist acts were consummated, although the jihadis certainly pounded their chests mightily in phone calls, social occasions, and e-mails.

In contrast to government portrayals of him as a terrorist, friends of al-Timimi characterized him as a scholarly, gentle soul (although one with strong political convictions), and a prolific reader with about 4,000 books in his personal library (Dwyer, 2005). He earned degrees from George Washington University and the University of Maryland, as well as (in 2004) a doctorate from George Mason University in computational biology, specializing in cancer and genes.

Members of the Washington, D.C. Muslim community who knew al-Timimi asserted that he was a victim of overzealous prosecution. "Ali never opened a weapon or fired a shot," said Shaker El Sayed, a member of the executive committee of the Dar Al Hijra mosque in Falls Church, "and he is going to get life imprisonment for talking. What kind of country are we turning the United States into today?" (Dwyer, 2005).

Sayed said that the jury must have been unable to distinguish between the lectures al-Timimi delivered and charges against him. "The government alleged Ali incited people to buy arms and take them overseas to fire against people, but they never presented anything at the trial to show any facts relevant to any evidence. They only relied on Ali's lectures" (Dwyer, 2005). Al-Timimi's political persuasions were hardly state secrets. Al-Timimi recorded more than 500 hours of lectures and seminars that he had presented at the Center for Islamic Information and Education, some of which were made available on the Internet.

Al-Timimi was characterized by Muslims and other supporters as a political prisoner, who had been made an example by a government intent upon silencing dissent, aided by anti-Muslim paranoia in U.S. society generally, and on the jury that convicted him in particular. "That which is exploited today to persecute a single member of a minority," al-Timimi admonished Judge Leonie Brinkema at his sentencing, "will most assuredly come back to haunt the majority tomorrow" (Smolla, 2005).

During the Virginia Jihadis' trial in 2004, some of them turned state's evidence and portrayed al-Timimi as a militant Muslim who taught his students that the September 11, 2001 attacks were justified. Fighting words, yes—but worthy of life in prison without parole? Mahdi Bray, executive director of the Muslim American Society Freedom Foundation, said that al-Timimi's conviction bodes ill for the First Amendment. "What he said was perhaps repugnant and inflammatory, but was it really his intent to have people go and take his words and translate that into going and killing other human beings, specifically Americans?" Bray asked. "If that was the case, then the jury evidently felt like he was shouting 'Fire!' in a crowded building." He said that the bar for what constitutes free speech has shifted since the September 11 attacks and that al-Timimi might have been a victim of that change (Dwyer, 2005).

Some legal scholars argued that society's right to protect itself outweighed al-Timimi's free-speech rights, and that he had crossed the line from speech to action. Rod Smolla, dean of the University of Richmond School of Law and a specialist in the First Amendment, said that al-Timimi's statements had crossed "A line . . . [that] has been drawn in the cornerstone decisions of modern First Amendment law—seeks to separate mere abstract expression from the concrete use of expression to effectuate evil." This broad distinction played out in several ways, Smolla asserted:

> One may not be punished for merely being a member of a group that allegedly adheres to a violent agenda—the Klan, the Communist Party, or the Virginia Jihad. But one may be punished for participating in group meetings to plot the execution of that agenda. One may not be punished for merely preaching and teaching the desirability of terror or treason, but one may be punished for training and instructing others in terrorist techniques. One may not be punished for rhetoric that is "threatening" in the vague sense of generating fear and loathing, but one may be punished for words that make a threat to do real harm. Aiding and abetting, an ancient concept in criminal law, may be accomplished by equipping someone with physical tools, like explosives or radios. It may also be accomplished by training someone with intellectual tools—providing information and instruction for the purpose of assisting someone to perpetrate a crime. (Smolla, 2005)

Thus, al-Timimi's rhetoric by itself may not have been a criminal offense, even in the context of national grief over the 9-11 attacks. According to Smolla's analysis, al-Timimi's own analysis of the situation—that America and Islam are at war—should have provided a clue that he was asking for legal trouble. Given the circumstances, according to Smolla, al-Timimi crossed the "speech-action" line by advocating armed resistance with "Islamic" men from the Washington, D.C., area who had repeatedly watched bloody jihad videos, owned assault rifles, participated in military training exercises, and took target practice at firing ranges, even if al-Timimi did not take an active role in the action himself, and even if it comprised play-acting with no specific targets at any specific time. To Smolla, al-Timimi's conduct was "at the cusp of incitement and aiding and abetting, blending elements of both" (Smolla, 2005).

Was the sentence of life in prison without parole appropriate for an offense that resulted in no actual physical injury? Smolla said that the judge had little discretion, given federal sentencing guidelines. He maintained that for al-Timimi's conviction to be valid "We must assume that he intended for his disciples to wreak death and destruction. None of his students appear to have succeeded, but others like them do. The severe punishments that the law metes out for such conduct seek to deter terrorism by punishing teachers like al-Timimi for steeling others to engage in it" (Smolla, 2005). There you have it—life in prison with no parole for intent to engage in terrorism backed up by some young men with guns play-acting in the woods. Smolla asserted that while the First Amendment's legal context did not change after 9-11, the context in which terrorism is defined and evaluated did change. That's what it takes to turn a relentlessly driven tongue aided by an overactive imagination into a conspiracy to wreak death and destruction.

In a more tolerant time, al-Timimi's rhetoric might have been fobbed off as a harmless exercise of imagination. In the aftermath of the 9-11 attacks, with airports under guard and even carry-on bottled water sometimes forbidden in carry-on luggage, the practicing definition of legally tolerable speech has, indeed, changed. Whether this change indicates a long-term preference for security over liberty is still at issue. In the meantime, watch your mouth (and your propensity for acting out your desires) in the "land of the free"—especially if you are a militant Muslim.

ISLAMIC FOOTBALL?

Muammar Ali led New Mexico State University's football team in rushing until October 9, 2005—the day he was kicked off the squad. That day, he "received a message on his phone answering machine at his home that his jersey was being pulled and that he was released," according to a letter to the university from his attorney, George Bach, of the American Civil Liberties Union of New Mexico (Rothschild, 2005). The letter, dated October 25, alleged that Head Coach Hal Mumme had engaged in religious discrimination.

"Coach Mumme questioned Mr. Ali repeatedly about Islam and specifically, its ties to Al-Qaeda," the letter stated. This made Ali uncomfortable. After New Mexico State's first game, "despite being the star tailback for several years, Mr. Ali was relegated to fifth string and not even permitted to travel with the team," the letter said. Two other Muslim players on the team also were released. Bach's letter added that the coach "regularly has players recite the Lord's Prayer after each practice and before each game" (Rothschild, 2005).

Ali's father, Mustafa Ali, said the trouble started at a practice during the previous summer when the coach told the players to pray, and "My son and two other players who were Muslim . . . were praying in a different manner, and the coach asked them, 'What are you doing?' They said, 'We're Muslims. This is how we pray'" (Rothschild, 2005). Mustafa Ali said that the coach later called his son to his office and "questioned him about Islam and Al-Qaeda" Ali told his father that the meeting "'was very weird. . . .'It disturbed him quite a bit. He didn't understand why it had anything to do with football."

After that meeting, the coach "never spoke to my son again," Mustafa Ali said (Rothschild, 2005). After that, Ali noticed that his role on the team declined—he wasn't called on to play as often or, if he played, he wasn't getting the ball. "In 2004, he was honorable mention All American in his sophomore year," Mustafa Ali said. "He was the fastest, strongest, quickest person on the team." When his son was cut, said Mustafa Ali, "He was upset; he was upset. The coach never gave a reason. None." (Rothschild, 2005).

HOLOCAUST DENIAL AND IRAN'S NUCLEAR AMBITIONS

On February 7, 2006, Bill O'Reilly, always on guard for political incorrectness among the professorate, told his audience that he had found a tenured professor who had embraced an Iranian president's denial of the Jewish Holocaust.

"Move over Ward Churchill," O'Reilly crowed. "Northwestern University Professor Arthur Butz might be as irresponsible as you are. Butz told the press in Iran . . . that its president is right, the Holocaust never happened. Six million Jews and millions of other Europeans were not slaughtered by the Nazis. Somewhere in hell, Hitler was smiling" (O'Reilly, February 7, 2006).

The script was familiar: a professor makes an incendiary statement as authorities at his university find themselves frozen in the headlights of tenure. "Northwestern President Henry Bienen calls Butz's comments a contemptible insult but the engineering teacher has tenure so the university can't fire him," O'Reilly told his audience of about two million (O'Reilly, February 7, 2007). Deborah Lipstadt, who teaches modern Jewish and Holocaust studies at Emory University, told O'Reilly that she had been following Butz since the late 1970s, as a racist anti-Semite who asserts that the Jews invented the Holocaust and then drumbeat the myth for sympathy and money.

As a professor of electrical engineering (tenured at Northwestern since 1974), Butz might be interested in the historical fact that the Nazis were working on an electrical shower floor at Auschwitz when the Allies rolled in near the end of World War II. While teaching in Poland, I came away from a visit to that camp in 2005 appreciating the historical value of the Japanese attack on Pearl Harbor. If the Japanese had not booted the United States into the war, the Nazis might have had time to install their electric showers.

O'Reilly couldn't help but compare Butz to Churchill, although Churchill never denied the Jewish Holocaust. Lipstadt asserted that Butz shouldn't be teaching, despite the fact that his subject matter—electrical engineering—has nothing to do with the Jewish Holocaust. She advised Butz's university to refrain from assigning Butz teaching, and assign him to sit in his office and write his "twaddle." "These aren't ideas," said Lipstadt. "These are lies" (O'Reilly, February 7, 2007). Butz promotes his views through his Northwestern-affiliated Web site, including a link to his 1976 book, *The Hoax of the 20th Century: The Case Against the Presumed Extermination of European Jewry* (Cohen, 2006).

Iran's semi-official Mehr News Agency and the English-language Tehran *Times* published Butz's comments, promoting him as an important scholar who supported Iranian president Ahmadinejad's view of history. While Butz denied the Holocaust, he did not address the Iranian president's opinion that Israel should be "wiped off the map."

Northwestern University president Henry Bienen said February 6, 2006 that Butz's comments were "a contemptible insult to all decent and feeling people" (Cohen, 2006). Bienen did his best not to blow a moon-is-made-of-green-cheese argument out of proportion. "While I hope everyone understands that Butz's opinions are his own and in no way represent the views of the university or me personally, his reprehensible opinions on this issue are an embarrassment to Northwestern," Bienen said in a statement that was e-mailed to Northwestern students, faculty, and staff (Cohen, 2006). Bienen said that Butz is entitled to express his personal views, and the university will not take action against him as long as he represents them as his own and does not discuss them in class. He also noted that the university has a professorship in Holocaust studies and offers several courses on it (Cohen, 2006).

Northwestern's chapter of Hillel, the Jewish student organization, purchased a full-page advertisement, published February 7 in the *Daily Northwestern* student newspaper. "We're frustrated because we feel forced to take action, but we don't want to dignify his lunacy with a response," the ad said. Hillel also called for a community meeting the same night to address the topic: "Why does the Holocaust matter? How do we ensure that 'never again' means never again?" (Cohen, 2006).

Butz told the Chicago *Tribune* that he e-mailed comments to the Mehr News Agency after he was approached by an Iranian journalist. Butz wrote that the Holocaust is a "deliberately contrived falsehood" and that its promulgation was motivated by the desire to create a Jewish state in the Middle East. About Ahmadinejad, he wrote: "I congratulate him on becoming the first head of state to speak out clearly on these issues and regret only that it was not a Western head of state" (Cohen, 2006).

FEAR, FASCISM, AND FREEDOM

Fear—most notably, after the September 11, 2001 attacks, of terrorism—is the primary incubator of a fascistic willingness to forsake freedom of expression in search of illusionary security.

Consider: On September 15, 2001, Dan Gutherie, a columnist at Oregon's Grant Pass *Daily Courier*, wrote of heroics by the firefighters at the Twin Towers. At the end of his column, however, Gutherie opined that President George W. Bush had fled the White House on Air Force One the day of the attacks, displaying cowardly behavior. "The kid has lived a pampered life of privilege. . . . His first time under real pressure, he bolted," Gutherie concluded (Maharidge, 2004, 75). For this opinion, Gutherie received hundreds of negative calls, letters, and e-mails. One man suggested he should be fed to crabs. Gutherie's job as a columnist was spiked and he was put to work on the copy desk for two weeks. At that point, publisher Dennis Mack, not one to paddle upstream in defense of the First Amendment, fired Gutherie. The newspaper apologized for the offending column on its front page.

In early October 2001, Dave "Davey D" Cook interviewed a California member of Congress, Barbara Lee, on his radio show "Street Knowledge" on San Francisco's KMEL-FM radio. Rep. Lee, the lone vote in the house against a grant of "unlimited military response power" to President Bush following the 9-11 attacks, said over the air, in part, "As we act, let us not become the evil we deplore" (Maharidge, 2004, 76). Days later Cook, in his eleventh year at the station, was fired, as general manager Joe Cunningham insisted he was let go for economic, not political, reasons.

CENSORSHIP BY VISA

Steady tightening of immigration policies under the George W. Bush administration has excluded from the United States many scientists, humanists, and artists. It has become virtually impossible to hold a major international conference, colloquium, or symposium in the United States. Such scholarly meetings are now increasingly being moved to Canada, the Caribbean, or Europe out of necessity.

It is equally difficult to invite notable scholars and artists of the world to take up academic posts in the United States, to the detriment of American students, and the general U.S. cultural milieu. Distinguished non-U.S. invitees have run the gauntlet of assistant U.S. consuls, only to emerge from their ordeals without visas, dismaying many U.S. cultural and educational institutions, which would so richly benefit from mutual collaboration with the great minds and talents of the planet. What would Thomas Jefferson, who started our system of state universities in Virginia, have thought of this?

On the supposition of fighting terrorism, the U.S. Patriot Act requires that universities in the United States monitor the activities of foreign students to determine whether they are sufficiently engaged in course studies, to dispel suspicion of terrorist activities. The federal government also has created a "nightmare of red tape" that has prevented many students from receiving (or renewing) visas, sending large numbers to study in other countries, leading to major enrollment declines at major research universities. "In an effort to exclude a dangerous few," Josesph S. Nye, Jr., wrote in the *New York Times*, "we are keeping out the helpful many" (Johnson, 2005, 478).

Shortly before the 2004 presidential election, Tariq Ramadan, a Muslim scholar, was denied a visa to give a keynote address to scholars at George Mason University's Arlington campus, who watched his speech on a DVD. Ramadan, who was to have been received as Henry R. Luce Professor of Religion, Conflict, and Peace-building at Notre Dame's Kroc Institute of Peace Studies, had visited the United States dozens of times before, and had never endorsed terrorism. "We very much want him here," said a Notre Dame spokesman (Johnson, 2005, 480).

Ramadan was granted the requisite visa to enter the United States by the State Department, seemingly a routine case. He then rented a house, shipped furniture and other possessions, and enrolled his children in schools. Unknown to Ramadan, however, his file had come to the attention of the Department of Homeland Security, whose minions subjected it to intense scrutiny, finding that, between 1998 and 2002, he had contributed roughly $770 to a French charity, which was suspected by the U.S. government of supporting the Palestinian liberation group, Hamas.

The charity had been placed on a State Department blacklist in 2003, *after* Ramadan's donations, but that seemed not to matter. His visa was revoked on allegation that Ramadan had violated the Patriot Act, which denies a visa to anyone who has given "material support" to a terrorist organization. Additionally, mission creep had the government denying visas, as well, to anyone it suspected of "irresponsible expression of opinion," a very broad definition indeed when interpreted by standards of the Homeland Security Department's gumshoes (Packer, 2006, 59).

In 2006, Ramadan's case was still in limbo, and the Luce chair was still unfilled, as Notre Dame, the American Civil Liberties Union, and several other groups sought to reverse his visa revocation. Commented George Packer in *The New Yorker*: "Barring Ramadan makes the country that claims to represent the side of freedom . . . appear defensive, timorous, and closed" (Packer, 2006, 60).

Ramadan said that while he had sometimes criticized specific U.S. policies, he was not anti-American. He had never espoused terrorism—on the contrary, he was one of 199 Muslim signatories to a petition rejecting terrorism, and had spoken out against the use of the Koran to justify murder. The contributions to Palestinian charity were made "to provide humanitarian aid to people who are desperately in need of it" (Rothschild, 2006, 17).

Many of the immigration restrictions bore the ham-handed trademark of a bungling bureaucracy. A British journalist, Elena Lappin was denied entry to the United States at Los Angeles International Airport, detained, handcuffed, body-searched, fingerprinted, photographed, and interrogated for four hours. Twenty-six hours after landing, she was sent back to England for no evident reason. The British novelist Ian McEwan, landing in Vancouver, British Columbia on his way to give a speech in Seattle, was detained for 36 hours. The British consulate, two members of Congress, an immigration lawyer, and the sponsors of his lecture intervened to get McEwan into the country, where he started his talk by thanking the Department of Homeland Security "for protecting the American public from British novelists" (Johnson, 2005, 481–482).

FENCING OUT FOREIGN STUDENTS

The number of foreign graduate students enrolled in U.S. universities rose in 2005, compared to 2004, but remained far lower than in 2002. According to the

Institute of International Education, 565,000 foreign students were enrolled during 2004 at U.S. colleges and universities. The largest number, 80,466, came from India, with China in second place at 62,523 (Shane, 2005).

"Foreign graduate students, particularly those who study science or engineering, are a boon to the American economy and education system. They are critical to the United States' technological leadership in the world economy," wrote Stuart Anderson, executive director of the National Foundation for American Policy, and executive associate commissioner for policy and planning at the Immigration and Naturalization Service from 2001 to 2003 (Anderson, 2005).

According to a study by Keith Maskus, an economist at the University of Colorado, for every 100 international students who receive science or engineering doctorates from U.S. universities, the country gains 62 future patent applications. International students have founded many of America's most innovative companies, including Sun Microsystems and Intel (Anderson, 2005). Without international students, certain science and engineering programs could not be offered at many American universities, Anderson contends, "because the foreign students populate classes and serve as teaching assistants. They also go on to supply faculty for those programs. About one-third of America's engineering professors are foreign-born" (Anderson, 2005).

While the United States has tightened immigration policies, screening out academic talent as well as potential terrorists, several other countries, among them Britain and Japan, and the rapidly expanding economies of China and India, have become increasingly competitive in the educational marketplace, and more than willing to offer places to students turned away at U.S. borders.

Anderson argues that the United States makes it exceedingly difficult for foreign-born science and engineering students who earn their doctorates in the United States to stay in the country, "where they might work in our private sector, conduct research in our labs or teach at our universities. It can take two years or more to gain permanent residency, and there are significant backlogs in applications for employment-based green cards" (Anderson, 2005). Anderson believes that Congress should eliminate the requirement that visa-seekers pursuing advanced degrees in the United States demonstrate that they will return to their home countries.

U.S. universities warned late in 2005 that rules proposed by the Defense Department and the Commerce Department could hurt research by limiting the ability of foreign-born students and technicians to work with sensitive technology in laboratories. One target of the proposed rules may be China. More than 60,000 Chinese citizens are studying in the United States as Chinese intelligence officials are strongly seeking U.S. technology for military use (Shane, 2005).

Universities submitted hundreds of comments criticizing the proposed rules, arguing that tighter restrictions on research by foreigners could hurt national security by hindering scientific progress. "The impact on research could be very serious," Barry Toiv, a spokesman for the Association of American Universities, said.

"The bottom line is that research that benefits both our economy and our national security just won't happen" (Shane, 2005). The Commerce Department, whose inspector general recommended tighter regulations during 2004, was expected to propose the new rules by the end of 2005. The Defense Department proposed new regulations in July and produced final rules during 2006.

The rules govern use of software, equipment, or technical data that has military applications and cannot be legally exported to certain countries without a license. A similar permit, called an export license, is required when the same sensitive technology is used by a foreign citizen in an American laboratory, on grounds that such people might return home and reproduce the technology (Shane, 2005). Many noncitizen researchers are exempted from the licensing requirement because their basic research is intended for publication that will be shared widely to advance science.

The Commerce Department's inspector general, Johnnie E. Frazier, has warned that present regulations do not adequately protect secrets from potential spies. The new rules would use the country of birth of a foreign laboratory worker, not current citizenship, to determine whether a license is required. The report said, for example, "that an Iranian-born Canadian citizen who held dual citizenship would be considered a Canadian under the current regulations and would therefore not be subject to the licensing requirement" (Shane, 2005).

Tobin L. Smith, a senior federal-relations officer for the Association of American Universities, said that a person's country of birth often provides no clue to political allegiance. Moreover, the report's recommendations would cost universities millions of dollars to inventory sensitive equipment, determine students' birthplaces, and study which foreigners were using which machines. "Our faculties don't want to say, 'Before you can work on this equipment I need to know where you were born,'" Smith said (Shane, 2005).

The proposed Defense Department rules would require contractors, including universities receiving research funding, to create separate security badges for foreign citizens and "segregated work areas" for research using export-controlled technology. "That's not really realistic in a campus environment, where students and researchers must share laboratories, equipment, and information," Mr. Smith said (Shane, 2005).

The number of new foreign students coming to the United States increased during the 2005-2006 school year, after several years of declines following 2001, according to a survey by the Institute of International Education. According to the survey, conducted by the institute and other education groups, the number of new international students at American colleges and universities increased 8 percent in one year, to 142,923. The State Department issued a record 591,050 student and exchange visas in the 12 months ending in September, a 14 percent increase over the previous year and 6 percent more than in the year leading up to the 2001 attacks. Allan E. Goodman, president of the Institute, attributed the increase to the easing of visa restrictions imposed after the terrorist attacks and to greater efforts by colleges to attract foreign students (Arenson, 2006).

The same organization also reported that the number of American students studying abroad hit a record 205,983 in 2004-5, an 8 percent increase over the previous year and more than double the number in the 1994-95 school year (Arenson, 2006).

GUILT BY ETHNICITY

The federal government's impediment of scholarship had reached a point by 2006 that potential for terroristic activity was sometimes being construed solely on ethnicity. Witness the case of Waskar Ari of Bolivia, who was denied a visa to assume an academic position in Nebraska, most likely because he is an Aymara Indian, an ethnicity he shared with Bolivia's new president, left-of-center (and avid critic of George W. Bush) Evo Morales.

On February 13, 2006, the American Historical Association (AHA) sent a letter to the Departments of State and Homeland Security expressing acute concern regarding the visa delay for Ari, who is an internationally known authority on religious beliefs and political activism among indigenous Bolivians. Ari was being prevented from filling a post as assistant professor of History and Ethnic Studies at the University of Nebraska–Lincoln (UNL) because he has been placed on a list of individuals under "conspicuous revision"—and subjected to extensive background checks due to alleged security concerns. Apparently, the months-long delay in Ari's visa had nothing to do with his background, except that he was a member of the same ethnic group as Morales. Scholars across the United States expressed alarm at the clumsy, ham-handed nature of this case.

UNL's request for an H-1B visa had been delayed by eight months, despite the university's payment of $1,000 for expedited (15-day) handling, by the time the AHA weighed in, and accounts began to appear in the press. The visa was eventually granted, after much press attention and many protests from the conservative state of Nebraska.

The AHA asserted that in "Dr. Ari's case . . . no perceptible grounds existed for such treatment. Under such circumstances, a fine scholar whose only apparent offense is his indigenous identity could be permanently excluded from U.S. academia" (Jones, 2006). The AHA appealed to the Department of State and the Department of Homeland Security to reconsider the decision to subject Dr. Ari to conspicuous revision, and asked that he be granted the visa requested by the UNL, which had hired him to begin working there in the fall of 2005. Linda Kerber, Barbara Weinstein, and James Sheehan, the three most recent presidents of the AHA, authored the letter to Secretary of State Condoleezza Rice asking her to reconsider Ari's visa status.

The letter also was sent to Nebraska senators Chuck Hagel and Ben Nelson as well as Rep. Jeff Fortenberry, who represents Lincoln. The letter argued that Ari is a political moderate. "In the absence of any connection to extremist groups, we fear Dr. Ari is being subject to 'conspicuous revision' solely due to his indigenous identity. Rather than being a question of national security, this appears to be a case of racial profiling," they wrote (Hansen, 2005). What's more, Ari's student visa was revoked with no explanation just as it was about to expire. Queried by a reporter for the *Chronicle of Higher Education*, a State Department representative said the visa had been canceled under "a terrorism-related section of U.S. visa laws" (Hord, 2005, 3-B).

Ari was the first member of his ethnic group to complete a PhD in the United States, earned in history at Georgetown University in the fall of 2004. Ari served as a consultant on social and economic issues confronting the Aymara community with various organizations (the World Bank, the Inter-American Development Bank—not notably terrorist groups), and had worked as a visiting assistant professor at Western Michigan University and a postdoctoral fellow at the University of Texas. "Considered alongside other similar recent cases, I believe that this represents a very disturbing trend in our society as well as a direct attack on academic freedom," said Patrick D. Jones, assistant professor of history at UNL (Hord, 2006, 3-B).

According to an account in the Lincoln [Nebraska] *Journal-Star*, "The unexplained delay baffles history colleagues, frustrates UNL's immigration expert, and angers opponents of the U.S. Patriot Act, who see the case of Waskar Ari as more evidence that it's used arbitrarily to punish those with no connection to terrorism." "It would have to be unimaginable circumstances for someone from Bolivia to be classified as a security risk," says Barbara Weinstein, the president-elect of the American Historical Association (Hansen, 2006).

The UNL History Department regarded Ari as "a prize catch after he turned down several other job offers" (Hansen, 2006).

CHEMISTRY EXPERTISE A "THREAT?"

As Ari's case surfaced, the *Washington Post* carried reports that a U.S. consulate in India had refused a visa to a prominent Indian scientist, a decision that provoked intense protests in that country just as President Bush was preparing to visit. The scientist, Goverdhan Mehta, said that the U.S. consulate in the south Indian city of Chennai told him that his expertise in chemistry was deemed a "threat" (Vedantam, 2006, A-11). Facing outrage in India, the U.S. Embassy in New Delhi issued a highly unusual statement of regret. Within two days, the visa was approved, but not before the security-trauma of the U.S. State Department had caused a major problem. Mehta told Indian newspapers that his dealing with the U.S. consulate was "the most degrading experience of my life" (Vedantam, 2006, A-11).

The consul's nervousness was something of a public-relations disaster in the world of international science. Mehta was a former director of the Indian Institute of Science and served as a science adviser to India's prime minister, as well as president of the International Council for Science, a Paris-based organization comprising the national scientific academies of a number of countries (Vedantam, 2006, A-11). Mehta's prominence raised the diplomatic profile of the case, which especially angered Indians because he had previously visited the United States "dozens of times" (Vedantam, 2006, A-11).

Mehta said that after traveling 200 miles, waiting three hours with his wife for an interview, and being accused of deception, he was outraged when his accounts of his research were questioned and he was told he needed to fill out a detailed questionnaire. The consulate told Mehta that his visa application had been denied, and then instructed him to submit additional information, according to an official at the National Academy of Sciences, who saw a copy of the document. Mehta said in a written account obtained by the *Washington Post* that he had been humiliated, accused of "hiding things" and being dishonest, and told that his work is dangerous because of its potential applications in chemical warfare (Vedantam, 2006, A-11). Mehta denied that his work has anything to do with weapons. He said that he would provide his passport if a visa were issued, but that he would do nothing further to obtain the document: "If they don't want to give me a visa, so be it" (Vedantam, 2006, A-11).

"I indicated that I have no desire to subject myself to any further humiliation and asked that our passports be returned forthwith," Mehta wrote. The consular official, Mehta added, "stamped the passports to indicate visa refusal and returned them." After the U.S. government reversed itself and granted Mehta's visa the taint of insult lingered. He said travel plans had been canceled; he declined a visiting professorship at the University of Florida in Gainesville. He said the issuance of a visa would not change his decision.

The treatment of Mehta boiled over in India not only because of his eminent position, but because several other scientists there had reported similar humiliation at the hands of U.S. consular officials. Several, including biochemist Govindarajan Padmanaban and C.N.R. Rao, also a science adviser to India's prime minister, said they would no longer even apply for visas to visit the United States. Samir Brahmachari, director of the Institute of Genomics and Integrative Biology at Delhi, said he was body-searched at a New York City airport in 2005 despite his diplomatic passport. He cut off all collaborative research in the United States, looking instead to China, Japan, and Taiwan (Jayaraman, 2006, 901).

Visa rejections or delays for foreign academics after the September 11, 2001, attacks have led to widespread complaints by U.S. universities and scientific organizations, but the incident involving Mehta occurred as the overall situation was improving, said Wendy White, director of the Board of International Scientific Organizations. The board was established by the National Academy of Sciences, and had helped about 3,000 scientists affected by the new policies. "This leaves a terrible impression of the United States," said White, who has seen a copy of the consulate's letter to Mehta. In an interview February 22, 2006, she added that top scientists had worked with senior State Department officials to reverse the decision before Bush's visit next week. "We want people to know the U.S. is an open and welcoming country" (Vedantam, 2006, A-11).

LOST IN THE BACKLOG

Even for skilled workers who are not controversial, the path to a visa for employment in the United States has become an incredible gauntlet, a fact that troubles many employers in the physical sciences and engineering, where U.S. citizens at the PhD level are scarce. Concerns regarding terrorism and an incredibly inept bureaucracy has caused backlogs for many people ranging in the decades. Skilled laborers' visas, even for employees whose employers are eager to keep them, usually have to pass through three layers of approval that can cost tens of thousands of dollars in legal and other fees. The first step is usually the Labor Department, which, as of 2006, had a backlog of 235,000 cases. Next, the Citizenship and Immigration Service, which following the September 11, 2001 attacks has required the FBI to check applications, had a backlog of 180,000 files. Third, the State Department, which actually issues the visas, in 2006 was requiring a wait of one to five years for even the most highly sought PhD-level scientists (Kronholz, 2006, A-1).

Roughly half of the PhD-level engineers, life scientists, computer and mathematics scientists, and physical scientists were foreign-born in 2006; U.S. universities graduated only two-dozen PhDs in meteorology, for example (Kronholz, 2006, A-13). Most of the skilled workers are from India and China, but the government will allow only 7 percent of green cards to be issued to any one country's nationals. All of this is directing skilled workers to countries such as Great Britain and Canada, where immigration is much less onerous, raising concern for the competitiveness of U.S. sciences and engineering.

REFERENCES

"Academia Assailed: Conservatives Seek Balance." Censorship News: National Coalition Against Censorship Newsletter, No. 97(Spring, 2005):1. http://www.ncac.org.

Alam, M. Junaid. "Columbia University and the New Anti-Semitism." March 16, 2005. Unpublished paper. Cf: fouda@bu.edu.

"Ali al-Tamimi." Wikipedia, the Free Encyclopedia. http://en.wikipedia.org/wiki/Ali_al-Tamimi. Accessed August 24, 2006.

Anderson, Stuart. "America's Future is Stuck Overseas." New York Times, November 16, 2005. http://www.nytimes.com/2005/11/16/opinion/16anderson.html.

Arenson, Karen W. "A Decline in Foreign Students Is Reversed." New York Times, November 13, 2006. http://www.nytimes.com/2006/11/13/education/13students.html.

Bartlett, Thomas. "The Most Hated Professor in America." Chronicle of Higher Education, April 18, 2003, A-56. http://chronicle.com/free/v49/i32/32a05601.htm.

Berman, Morris. Dark Ages America: The Final Phase of Empire. New York: W. W. Norton, 2006.

"The Bollinger Whitewash." [Editorial] New York Sun, November 19, 2004. http://www.campus-watch.org/article/id/1374.

Cohen, Jodi S. "Northwestern University Rips Holocaust Denial: President Calls Prof an Embarrassment but Plans no Penalty." Chicago *Tribune*, February 7, 2006. http://www.lexis-nexis.com.

De Genova's Web page. Columbia University site. http://www.columbia.edu/cu/anthropology/fac-bios/de_genova/faculty.html, Accessed December 22, 2005.

Doumani, Beshara, ed. *Academic Freedom after September 11.* New York: Zone Books, 2006.

Dwyer, Timothy. "Prosecution Called 'Overzealous;' Guilty Verdict in Terror Case Angers Muslims Who Know Lecturer." *Washington Post*, April 26, 2005. http://www.washingtonpost.com/wp-dyn/content/article/2005/04/26/AR2005042601548_pf.html.

Eisenberg, Arthur. "New York Civil Liberties Union: Letter to Columbia University President Lee Bollinger in Defense of Academic Freedom." December 20, 2004, in Beshara Doumani, *Academic Freedom after September 11.* New York: Zone Books, 2006, 298–308.

Feiden, Douglas. "Hate 101: Climate of Hate Rocks Columbia University." *New York Daily News*, November 21, 2004. http://www.nydailynews.com/front/story/254925p-218295c.html.

Fisk, Robert. "Since When Did 'Arab' Become a Dirty Word? In Australia They're Even Trying to Prevent Hanan Ashrawi from Speaking." London *Independent*, November 4, 2003.

Genova, Nicholas de [Letter to the Editor]. Columbia *Spectator*, March 27, 2003. On History News Network. http://hnn.us/articles/1396.html.

Goldberg, Michelle. "Osama University?" Salon.com, November 6, 2003. http://salon.com/news/feature/2003/11/06/middle_east/index_np.

Hansen, Matthew. "Government Blocks Professor from Teaching at U.N.L." Lincoln [Nebraska *Journal-Star*, February 18, 2005, n.p.

Hord, Bill. "Scholar's Visa Delay Puzzles U.N.L. Officials." Omaha *World-Herald*, February 23, 2005, 3-B.

Horowitz, David. "Moment of Truth (For the Anti-American Left). Horowitz on the Aftermath of the De Genova Remarks." FrontPageMagazine.com, March 31, 2003. http://www.freerepublic.com/focus/f-news/880445/posts.

Hsu, Spencer S. "Former Florida Professor to Be Deported." *Washington Post*, April 18, 2006, A-3.

Jaschik, Scott. "Blackballed at Yale." *Inside Higher Education*, June 5, 2006. http://inside-highered.com/news/2006/06/05/cole.

Jayaraman, K.S. "Frosty U.S. Policy Leaves Indian Science Cold." *Nature* 439(February 23, 2006):901.

Johnson, Haynes. *The Age of Anxiety: McCarthyism to Terrorism.* Orlando, FL: Harcourt, 2005.

Jones, Arnita A. [Executive Director American Historical Association] American Historical Association Letter on Visa Denial. February 13, 2006. http://www.historians.org/press/2006_02_13_VisaDenial.cfm.

Kronholz, June. "For Dr. Sengupta, Long-term Visa is a Long Way Off." *Wall Street Journal*, June 27, 2006, A-1, A-13.

Lichtblau, Eric. "Not Guilty Verdicts in Florida Terror Trial Are Setback for U.S." *New York Times*, December 7, 2005. http://www.nytimes.com/2005/12/07/national/nationalspecial3/07verdict.html.

Lichtblau, Eric. "Professor in Terror Case May Face Deportation." *New York Times*, December 8, 2005, A-34.

Maharidge, Dale. *Homeland*. New York: Seven Stories Press, 2004.

O'Reilly, Bill. "The O'Reilly Factor." Fox News, December 21, 2005 http://www.lexis-nexis.com.

O'Reilly, Bill. "The O'Reilly Factor." Fox News, February 7, 2006 http://www.lexis-nexis.com.

Packer, George. "Keep Out." Talk of the Town. *The New Yorker*, October 16, 2006, 59–60.

Rothschild, Matthew. "Muslim-American Running Back off the Team at New Mexico State." *The Progressive* Media Project. McCarthyism Watch. November 18, 2005. http://progressive.org/mag_mc111805.

Rothschild, Matthew. "Stopping Ideas at the Border." *The Progressive,* November 2006, 16–17.

Rudyard Kipling to Nicholas de Genova. Accessed December 22, 2005. http://www.omdurman.org/leaflets/tommy.html.

Russo, Sara. "Columbia Prof. Expresses Desire for 'A Million Mogadishus.' " *Accuracy in Academia.* No date. Accessed December 22, 2005. http://www.academia.org/campus_reports/2003/apr_2003_2.html.

Schwartz, Susie. "CAN Fights Zionist Smear Campaign at Columbia University," by a Columbia student, *Left Hook*, December 17, 2004. http://lefthook.org/Ground/Birch012805.html.

Shane, Scott. "Universities Say New Rules Could Hurt U.S. Research." *New York Times*, November 26, 2005. http://www.nytimes.com/2005/11/26/education/26research.html.

Smolla, Rod. "Prosecuted, Not Persecuted: Why a Muslim Scholar Probably Crossed the First Amendment Line" *Slate*, July 27, 2005. http://www.slate.com/id/2123452.

Steinhauer, Jennifer. "Nineteen Months More in Prison for Professor in Terror Case." *New York Times*, May 2, 2006. http://www.nytimes.com/2006/05/02/us/02islamic.html.

Vedantam, Shankar. "Scientist's Visa Denial Sparks Outrage in India." *Washington Post*, February 23, 2006, A-11. http://www.washingtonpost.com/wp-dyn/content/article/2006/02/22/AR2006022202446_pf.html.

Wilder, Gary. "Civil Liberties and Academic Freedom." Historians Against the War. 2003. http://www.historiansagainstwar.org/freedom/genova.html.

Coda: Doing Well in an Apocalypse

While some readers of this book may be asking by now whether any author or scholar who offends established interests can escape being trussed up in his or her own private Star Chamber in today's America, rest assured that some people draw large audiences, sell many books, and even receive grants testifying to their genius—all the while engaging in Marxist analysis in the United States, even in the era of George W. Bush.

Meet Mike Davis, social commentator and urban theorist, who first became known (notorious to some) for his investigations of social class structures in his native Southern California in two books, *City of Quartz* (1990) and its sequel, *The Ecology of Fear* (1998). Born in 1946 in Fontana, California, Davis's education was punctuated by stints as a meat cutter, truck driver, and a Students for a Democratic Society (SDS) activist, before SDS dissolved. He briefly studied at Reed College in the mid-1960s but did not begin his academic career in earnest until the early 1970s, when he earned BA and MA degrees in History from the University of California, Los Angeles ("Mike Davis," n.d.). Davis has contributed to the British monthly *Socialist Review*, the organ of the Socialist Workers Party of Great Britain. He is a member of the Socialist Workers Party of Ireland. What kind of ideological Disneyland are we talking about here? Perhaps a country with a Constitution that protects freedom of expression?

Davis moved to London in 1981, where he became an editor of *New Left Review* and completed his political transformation into a Marxist. By the late 1990s, in his early 50s, Davis was teaching urban theory at the Southern California Institute of Architecture, having also become a sought-after speaker on the lecture circuit (Turenne, 1998). In 1998, he also received a $315,000 MacArthur Foundation "genius" grant for "exceptionally talented and creative people." He also received a Getty Fellowship.

"For someone who claims to have been functionally illiterate when he entered UCLA in 1973, Mike Davis has done quite well for himself," wrote Brant Bingamon in the Texas *Observer*. "A self-described Irish-California Marxist who has worked as a butcher, truck driver, protest organizer, and itinerant academic, Davis writes the kind of books that are routinely lauded as brilliant, passionate, and gripping—the perfect combination of rage, studious detail, and brilliant synthesis" (Binghamon, 2001).

Indeed. Davis is an engaging writer who is fast on his intellectual feet, a specialist in (as some said back in the 1960s) making lemonade from lemons—evidence that a self-avowed Marxist, with verve, writing talent, and a thick skin, can do just fine, thank you, even in a capitalistic empire that is rapidly graying at the temples.

Davis's methodology has improved over the years. For a time, he seemed to confuse fiction with fact and lazy "gonzo" journalism with rigorous scholarship. Poet and environmentalist Lewis MacAdams revealed that Davis once invented a conversation with him, complete with a vivid outdoor setting, for a cover story in the *LA Weekly* (Turenne, 1998).

The non-interview with Lewis MacAdams proved to have well-exercised legs, graduating from the *LA Weekly* to much larger East Coast venues, despite the fact that MacAdams himself didn't seem that upset about it. Sue Horton, editor of *LA Weekly*, said simply, "What Mike did was wrong. He shouldn't have done it." Davis says the same thing: "Yeah, it was a mistake" (Wiener, 1999).

Veronique de Turenne wrote in *Salon* that "faking one interview doesn't put Davis in the league of notorious fiction writers like former *New Republic-Wunderkind* Stephen Glass but Davis, for a while, faced accusations that reached beyond a single journalistic lapse. For a time, a chorus of critics claimed that Davis's scholarship and reporting are so inaccurate and biased as to border on the deceitful, that he sift[ed] and pick[ed] his facts to fit his dark Marxist vision. But unlike journalistic outcasts like Glass and Boston *Globe* columnists Mike Barnicle and Patricia Smith whose fast and loose dealings with reality led to disgrace and dismissal, some critics moaned that Davis paid no career-rending price for his freewheeling ways" (Turenne, 1998). Never dependent on an academic job or a state salary, Davis quickly broadened his scope and left his critics in the dust.

LOS ANGELES'S URBAN CONDITION

Davis's *Ecology of Fear* has been described as "a 484-page haymaker aimed at the soft white underbelly of Los Angeles . . . a chronicle of apocalypse, a study of a racially Balkanized city beset by natural plagues of biblical proportions: world-record rains, devastating fires, consuming floods, whirling tornadoes and disease-crazed squirrels." Davis described Los Angeles's power structure as a "police state rife with class warfare, ruled by corrupt politicians and planners bent on preserving an all-white status quo" (Turenne, 1998). He foresaw widespread violence in

Los Angeles two years before the 1992 riots that followed the police beating of Rodney King, earning points for prescience.

Davis's two early books on Los Angeles' urban condition, noted an entry in Wikipedia, "are open to criticism due to numerous errors, many of which are openly contradicted by the footnotes he cites. One example is his citation of an essay written by him about Bunker Hill [a Los Angeles neighborhood] in another book to support his Bunker Hill chapter in *Ecology of Fear*. However, the dates and events given in *Ecology of Fear* dramatically differ from the dates and events given in the essay, even though his name appears on both. Many scholars have published critiques of his work challenging his conclusions, which are sometimes fanciful" ("Mike Davis," n.d.)

Ward Churchill, whose every move over the last 35 years has been scrutinized, suggested I take a look at Davis's career. I came away thinking that skins are thicker in Los Angeles than in Denver, or perhaps Mike Davis just hadn't (as of this writing) been introduced as cannon fodder for the likes of Bill O'Reilly and Rush Limbaugh. Perhaps Davis just hasn't yet met the wrong people—or perhaps just hasn't properly engaged the scions of the Second Amendment (*a la* Mike Bellesiles), or come up with the kind of two-word weapon of mass verbal destruction ("Little Eichmanns" or "Million Mogadishus," for example) that provides a buzzword billboard for right-wing bloggers and talk-show hosts. He has, amazingly, engaged a left-wing audience while usually evading the right-wing lynch mob.

This is not to say that Davis has not been attacked. By the time Los Angeles' establishment was done with Davis, the history faculties of the University of California at Los Angeles and the University of Southern California rejected his applications for faculty jobs, but he did get a job at the State University of New York at Stony Brook. Later, Davis returned to California in a tenure-track line at the University of California—Irvine, after most academics dismissed his errors as minor. In between, he wrote a seminal historical study, *Late Victorian Holocausts: El Nino Famines and the Making of the Third World* (2001). Kenneth Pomerantz, president of the World History Association at the time and department chair at UC-Irvine when Davis was hired, said "He combines political economy, meteorology, and ecology with vivid narratives to create a book that is both a gripping read and a major conceptual achievement" (Wiener, 2004, 116). This book also has been cited in climate-change literature (Linden, 2006).

THESIS AND ANTITHESIS

Ecology of Fear (1998) portrayed Los Angeles as an apocalypse theme park with a doom-inducing geography prone to drought, flood, and earthquake. This book was a subject of favorable reviews, and spent 12 weeks on the Los Angeles *Times'* nonfiction bestseller list, rising briefly to Number One. As with Churchill's Jim Paine and Vincent Carroll, and Michael Bellesiles's James Lindgren (et al.) approving attention soon drew its antithesis: critics willing to spend many hours checking every nook and cranny of his work, holding it to a very exacting standard of politically honed accuracy.

In this case, Davis's self-appointed nemesis was Brady Westwater (an acquired name; his name of record is Ross Ernest Shockley), a Malibu realtor, "an almost laughably perfect occupation for a Davis nemesis—and third-generation Angeleno who has cast himself as *Ecology of Fear's* post-publication fact-checker and Davis' personal tormentor" (Turenne, 1998). Getting down to cases, one chapter in *Ecology of Fear* is titled "The Case for Letting Malibu Burn," which is less about Malibu real estate than dangers of fire faced by poor people living in the inner city of Los Angeles. Davis contrasts inner-city fire dangers with the amount of public money spent to protect high-income residents of Malibu from the threat of brush fires.

Expressing his love for the flora and fauna of the Los Angeles basin, not to be confused with his monetary interest in collection of commissions for sales of its real estate, Westwater became obsessed with holding Davis's scholarly feet to the counterfactual fire. Westwater's faxes and e-mails challenging Davis became familiar fare in editors' offices in and near Los Angeles, accusing Davis of wholesale fabrication. A casual Westwater fax could run to dozens of dense pages. Westwater's exacting deconstruction of Davis began with the back of *Ecology of Fear*, where Davis is said to have been born in Los Angeles. Not true, said Westwater. Davis really was born in Fortuna, a suburb of Los Angeles. Davis, however, had written of his Fortuna birthplace openly in *City of Quartz's* last chapter, so he was hardly hiding it. This was, to Westwater, evidence of fraud. Regardless of its trivial nature, this allegation shortly graduated to headline fodder in such estimable journalistic venues as *The Economist*.

Westwater took issue with assertions in *Ecology of Fear* about the ferocity of El Nino-provoked rainfalls, as well as the frequency of wildfires in the Los Angeles Basin. When Westwater found factual errors by Davis, he milked them avidly with anyone who would listen. In *City of Quartz*, for example, Davis admitted that he identified Howard Ahmanson, a right-leaning Christian, as Jewish. Jill Stewart, a columnist for the alternative weekly *New Times* Los Angeles, in an essay titled "Peddling Fear," presented Westwater's allegations as fact. She matched Davis's pugilistic style jab for jab, calling him a "city-hating socialist raised in a remote desert town so small it no longer exists" (Turenne, 1998). My, oh my.

Many thousands of earnest scholars who labor in relative obscurity, sculpting every endnote with utmost care, might envy Davis's quick ascent to fame despite his early devil-may-care attitude toward verifiable facts. Life at the top of the best-seller list can quickly become very rough, however. As with other scholars who have become household words for their controversial ideas, fame can be a tough taskmaster. Not long after Davis's *Ecology of Fear* hit Number One, the *New York Times*, *The Economist*, the *Los Angeles Times*, and other publications took a large measure of interest "in opponents who zero in on a few errors in the footnotes, manufacture other mistakes and denounce the book as 'fiction' and the author as a 'fraud,'" even as *Ecology of Fear* "got many strong reviews, from the *New York*

Times Book Review to *BusinessWeek*, which called it "compelling" and "persuasive." Davis, wrote Jon Wiener in *The Nation*, "Has been a passionate historian and analyst of the underside of a city built on public relations and mythologized from its inception as a kind of dreamwork in the desert" (Wiener, 1999).

For a time, feeding Mike Davis through a critical meat-grinder seemed to have become a matter *du jour* of journalistic fashion. *Ecology of Fear* was panned by one critic in the Los Angeles *Times* as "self-promoting, city-trashing rot." The *New York Times* quoted critics who declared that there was "something pathological" in how Davis has "twisted the facts." *The Economist*, usually the home of astutely measured words, called this book "Fake, phony, made-up, crackpot, bullshit" (Wiener, 2004, 107). *Salon*, the online magazine, has published three attacks on Davis; *New Times LA,* a free weekly, has published four; *Suck*, the Webzine of *Wired* magazine, published two (Wiener, 1999).

By 1999, with *Ecology of Fear* 17 weeks on the Los Angeles *Times* best-seller list, it presented a fat target. Wiener wrote that "the voices of the L.A. establishment, whose policies Davis has excoriated for years . . . are striking back—with a vengeance. At heart, it's a battle over who gets to define Los Angeles: the downtown boosters and their journalistic friends, deeply invested in selling the city as a sunny paradise, or Davis, who argues that developers have placed the city at risk of social and environmental disaster . . ." (Wiener, 1999).

Writing in *The Nation*, Jon Wiener commented that most of the objections to *Ecology of Fear* came down to endnote mistakes—a 484-page book with 831 endnotes could provide any trivia buff with *some* ammunition. No one accuses the *New York Times*, America's newspaper of record, of fraud because every day it runs a "Corrections" column, said Wiener (1999). In 1998, the *Times* ran 2,130 corrections, an average of six per day. Some of the corrections are nearly silly. I recall reading one day that a *Times* writer with a definitely right-coast take on geography had written that a certain art show was being held "two hours west of Los Angeles," which was corrected, upon a glance at a map, to "east." Two hours west of Los Angeles by most kinds of transport would have placed the art show in the Pacific Ocean.

Veronique de Turenne wrote in *Salon* that, while Davis said there are 2,000 gangs in Los Angeles, there are actually only 1,850 (Turenne, 1998). Davis countered that "The missing gangs are in Orange County. She's talking about Los Angeles County, while I was talking about the Census Bureau's Los Angeles Standard Metropolitan Statistical District, which includes Orange County" (Wiener, 1999).

Joel Kotkin, oft-described "urban policy expert," also was called upon as an expert witness of Davis's error-prone ways. Kotkin has been a research fellow at the Reason Foundation, a libertarian think tank, and a senior fellow at the Pepperdine Institute for Public Policy. When he is not holding Davis's feet to the fire, Kotkin has been busy rooting out supposed Communist influence in Los Angeles labor unions, most notably the AFL-CIO. Also, according to Wiener, Kotkin has described sweatshops as examples of immigrant entrepreneurialism on the opinion pages of the *Washington Post* and *Los Angeles Times*.

Davis zeroes in on the Los Angeles *Times* in *City of Quartz* for its role, during the early twentieth century, as part of syndicates that monopolized the subdivision of Hollywood, the San Fernando Valley, and much of northeastern Los Angeles (Wiener, 1999). Before authoring the book, Davis had contributed occasional opinion pieces to the Los Angeles *Times*. As previously mentioned, *Ecology of Fear* was the subject of a less-than-flattering review in the *Times*. After *City of Quartz* was published, the newspaper found Davis too "gloomy" to be "the pre-eminent analyst of Los Angeles' soul." It objected in particular to his description of Los Angeles as a place "where the future has turned rancid." *The Economist* made a similar argument: Davis's success "lies in the fact that the New York publishing establishment has a weakness for books that portray the upstart city of the West, its chief cultural rival, in the worst possible light" (Wiener, 1999).

For all its local acidity, the deconstruction of Davis seemed rather tepid next to the visceral national explosions over Churchill, de Genova, and Bellesiles, among others. Davis early weaned himself of academia when necessary, and thus avoided right-wingers' complaints that he was just one more Marxist professor sucking a tax-funded teat, with allied demands that left-of-center professors leave their rights to profess more or less at the door of public institutions. Unable to go for the economic jugular, Davis's critics were forced to confine their attacks on him to the marketplace of ideas, with his ideological curb appeal initially somewhat limited by its local focus. Nevertheless, Los Angeles, the second-largest urban area in the United States, is, in addition to all of its local distinctions, a very appropriate laboratory to study race and class distinctions in the twenty-first-century United States.

Davis also enjoyed some support. D. J. Waldie, author of a book on Lakewood, a suburb of Los Angeles, was very critical of Davis's work on occasion, but agreed with him on some central points: that Los Angeles is been compelled by geography to become among the most segregated large urban areas in the United States. In the ecological dimension, the city is no paradise. Risks of earthquake, drought, and fire are real. Even rainfall, which is usually rare in Los Angeles, can arrive in damaging deluges. "For a nonscientist, Davis has done an excellent job of synthesizing the state of the field," said Lisa Grant, who teaches earthquake science at UC Irvine. "I was impressed by his chapter [on earthquakes]. He has the right sources, and I didn't find any inaccuracies in the footnotes." Richard Walker, chairman of the geography department at University of California-Berkeley, agreed: "Most of what Mike is saying is completely accepted wisdom among scholars who work in the area of environmental hazards. . . . Extreme events, so-called natural disasters, are predictable, inevitable and inevitably made worse by human activity. The character of human activity is absolutely critical to the human losses" (Wiener, 1999).

DAVIS GOES WORLDWIDE

Davis's critique of Los Angeles has been only one part of his prolific, evolving critique of the modern urban landscape. Davis is so stylistically agile, and so prolific, that any single critic seemed to have had trouble keeping up with him. Davis's cognitive map quickly broadened from the Los Angeles basin, to Las Vegas, in "House of Cards—Las Vegas: Too Many People in the Wrong Place, Celebrating Waste as a Way of Life" (Davis, 1995a) and back, again to the human provocations of wildfires in Malibu:

> Fire in Malibu has a relentless, staccato rhythm. The rugged coastline is scourged by a large fire, on average, every two and a half years, and at least once a decade a blaze in the chaparral grows into a terrifying firestorm consuming hundreds of homes in an inexorable march across the mountains to the sea. In one week . . . ten homes and 14,000 acres of brush went up in smoke. And it will only get worse. Such periodic disasters are inevitable as long as private residential development is tolerated in the fire ecology of the Santa Monicas. Make your home in Malibu, in other words, and you eventually will face the flames. (Davis, 1995b, 229)

Davis broadened his scope from the city to California's prison system, in "Hell Factories in the Field: A Prison-Industrial Complex":

> The road from Mecca follows the Southern Pacific tracks past Bombay Beach to Niland, then turns due south through a green maze of marshes and irrigated fields. The bad future of California rises, with little melodrama, in the middle distance between the skeleton of last year's cotton crop and the aerial bombing range in the Chocolate Mountains. From a mile away, the slate-gray structures resemble warehouses or perhaps a factory. An unassuming road sign announces Calipatria State Prison. California has the third-largest penal system in the world, following China and the United States as a whole: 125,842 prisoners at last official count. (Davis, n.d.)

Davis also has extended his point of view to urban areas worldwide in *Dead Cities: And Other Tales* (2002), and, most recently, in *Planet of Slums* (2006). In the long range, Davis's critics hardly laid a hand on him. Instead, the growing class divisions of the Bush years seemed to enlarge and enrich his critique. Over the years, Davis's scope has broadened to ecological distress worldwide from *Ecology of Fear's* focus on the Los Angles basin. The urban crisis spawned by race, poverty, government incompetence, and Hurricane Katrina in New Orleans were made to order for Davis, who wrote them up on both sides of the Atlantic (Davis, 2005; Davis and Fontenot, 2005). In "Catastrophic Economics: The Predators of New Orleans," he looked at the devastation of Hurricane Katrina in New Orleans through his familiar lens of urban catastrophe that falls most heavily on the nonwhite poor. This time, however, his point of view was daily fare in national newspapers and evening television. In some respects, Davis and mainstream analysis have merged:

> After the criticism of his disastrous handling [of] the Katrina disaster, President George Bush promises a reconstruction programme of $200bn for areas destroyed by the hurricane. But the first and biggest beneficiaries will be businesses that specialise in profiting from disaster, and have already had lucrative contracts in Iraq; they will gentrify New Orleans at the expense of its poor, black citizens. (Davis, 2005)

In *Planet of Slums* (2006), Davis, who was by then married and living in San Diego, took his purview of urban apocalypse worldwide, sketching a trenchant portrait of the slums that now house a billion people, a figure that is increasing by 25 million a year. Up next to this, the dysfunctions of Los Angeles seemed mere child's play:

> Avilla Miseria outside Buenos Aires may have the worst *feng shui* in the world: is built in a flood zone over a former lake, a toxic dump, and a cemetery. Then there's the barrio perched precariously on stilts over the excrement-clogged Pasig River in Manila, and. . .in Vijayawada that floods so regularly that residents have door numbers written on pieces of furniture. In slums the world over, squatters trade safety and health for a few square meters of land and some security of tenure. They are pioneers of swamps, floodplains, volcano slopes, unstable hillsides, desert fringes, railroad sidings, rubbish mountains, and chemical dumps—unattractive and dangerous sites that have become poverty's niche in the ecology of the city. Cities have absorbed nearly two-thirds of the global population explosion since 1950, and are currently adding a million babies and migrants each week (Davis, 2006, 121).
>
> Dhaka, Kinshasa, and Lagos today are each approximately forty times larger than they were in 1950. According to the *Financial Times*, China in the 1980s alone added more city dwellers than did all of Europe (including Russia) during the entire nineteenth century. In this process of rampant urbanization, the planet has become marked by the runaway growth of slums, characterized by overcrowding, poor or informal housing, inadequate access to safe water and sanitation, and insecurity of tenure. United Nations researchers estimate that there were at least 921 million slum dwellers in 2001 and more than 1 billion in 2005, with slum populations growing by a staggering 25 million per year. (Davis, *Orion*, 2006)

"This book," wrote Amitabh Pal of *Planet of Slums* in *The Progressive*, "is not for the faint-hearted." One subsection is titled "Living in Shit," describing sanitation problems in urban slums, which cost the lives of 30,000 people, on average, each day. Davis offers this description of Baghdad's Sadr City:

> In Baghdad's giant slum of Sadr City, hepatitis and typhoid epidemics rage out of control. American bombing wrecked already overloaded water and sewage infrastructure, and as a result raw sewage seeps into the household water supply. Two years after the U.S. invasion, the system remain[ed] broken, and the naked eye can discern filaments of human excrement in the tap water. (Pal, 2006, 43; Davis, 2006, 144)

By late 2006, Davis was cruising along on a MacArthur "genius" grant, teaching at the University of California at Irvine, with barely a scar showing from long-ago attempts by the Los Angeles real-estate establishment to mug him, proof that a Marxist prophet of doom can do right well in George W. Bush's United States, with a deft sense of the moment, a prolific pen, and a headline-writer's sense for a provocative title. That news should hearten all of us. The vibrancy of American democracy may not be dead yet.

REFERENCES

Binghamon, Brant. "A Hunger for Imperialism." Review, *Late Victorian Holocausts*. Texas *Observer*, November 23, 2001. http://www.texasobserver.org/showArticle. asp?ArticleID=496.

Davis, Mike. *City of Quartz: Excavating the Future of Los Angeles*. London: Routledge, Chapman & Hill, 1990.

Davis, Mike. "House of Cards—Las Vegas: Too Many People in the Wrong Place, Celebrating Waste as a Way of Life." *Radical Urban Theory: Writings on the Modern Urban Condition*. No date. Accessed January 3, 2006. From *Sierra Magazine* 80:6 (November/December, 1995):36–42 (Davis, 1995a). http://www.rut.com/mdavis/housecards.html.

Davis, Mike. "Let Malibu Burn—A Political History of the Fire Coast." *Radical Urban Theory: Writings on the Modern Urban Condition*. No date. Accessed January 3, 2006. http://www.rut.com/mdavis/letmalibuburn.html, from *The Nation* 260:7(February 20, 1995b):229.

Davis, Mike. *Ecology of Fear: Los Angeles and the Imagination of Disaster*. New York: Metropolitan Books, 1998.

Davis, Mike. *Late Victorian Holocausts: El Niño Famines and the Making of the Third World*. Oxon, UK: Verso, 2001.

Davis, Mike. *Dead Cities and Other Tales*. New York: The New Press, 2002.

Davis, Mike. "Catastrophic Economics: The Predators of New Orleans." *Le Monde Diplomatique* (English Edition), October 2, 2005.

Davis, Mike and Anthony Fontenot. "Hurricane Gumbo." *The Nation*, November 7, 2005. http://www.thenation.com/doc/20051107/davis.

Davis, Mike. "Slum Ecology: Inequity Intensifies the Earth's Natural Forces." *Orion*, March/April, 2006. http://www.oriononline.org/pages/om/06-2om/Davis.html.

Davis, Mike. *Planet of Slums*. New York: Verso, 2006.

Davis, Mike. "Hell Factories in the Field: A Prison-Industrial Complex." No date. Accessed January 3, 2006. http://www.rut.com/mdavis/hellfactories.html.

Linden, Eugene. *The Winds of Change: Climate, Weather, and the Destruction of Civilizations*. New York: Simon & Schuster, 2006.

"Mike Davis." *Wikipedia: The Free Encyclopedia*. No date. Accessed January 2, 2006. http://en.wikipedia.org/wiki/Mike_Davis_scholar.

Pal, Amitabh. "Architects of Shantytowns." [Review, Mike Davis, *Planet of Slums*, 2006]. *The Progressive*, June 2006, 42–44.

Turenne, Veronique de. "Is Mike Davis's Los Angeles All in His Head?" *Salon*, December 7, 1998. http://www.rut.com/mdavis/salon1.html.

Wiener, Jon. "LA Story: Backlash of the Boosters." *The Nation*, February 22, 1999. http://www.thenation.com/docprint.mhtml?i=19990222&s=wiener.

Wiener, Jon. *Historians in Trouble: Plagiarism, Fraud, and Politics in the Ivory Tower*. New York: The New Press, 2004.

Selected Bibliography

"Academia Assailed: Conservatives Seek Balance." *Censorship News: National Coalition Against Censorship Newsletter.* 97:1(Spring, 2005). http://www.ncac.org.

"AIM Fire: The American Indian Movement Targets *The Rocky.*" Denver *Westword*, December 15, 2005, n.p. (in LEXIS).

Alam, M. Junaid. "Columbia University and the New Anti-Semitism." March 16, 2005. Unpublished paper. [fouda@bu.edu].

"Ali al-Timimi." Wikipedia, the Free Encyclopedia. http://en.wikipedia.org/wiki/Ali_al-Tamimi. Accessed August 24, 2006.

Anderson, Stuart. "America's Future Is Stuck Overseas." *New York Times*, November 16, 2005. http://www.nytimes.com/2005/11/16/opinion/16anderson.html.

Antlfinger, Carrie. "UW [University of Wisconsin] Instructor Compares Bush to Hitler" Associated Press, October 11, 2006 (in LEXIS).

Apuzzo, Matt. "Professor Points to Politics as Yale Fails to Renew Contract." Associated Press, October 23, 2005 (in LEXIS).

Arenson, Karen W. "When Scholarship and Politics Collided at Yale." *New York Times*, December 28, 2005, B-1.

"The Bancroft and Bellesiles." History News Network. December 14, 2002. http://hnn.us/articles/1157.html.

Banerjee, Neela and Anne Berryman. "At Churches Nationwide, Good Words for Evolution." *New York Times*, February 13, 2006. http://www.nytimes.com/2006/02/13/national/13evolution.htm.

Barbassa, Juliana. "Philosophy of Design Class Cancelled." Associated Press, January 17, 2006 (in LEXIS).

Bartlett, Thomas. "The Most Hated Professor in America." *Chronicle of Higher Education*, April 18, 2003, A-56. http://chronicle.com/free/v49/i32/32a05601.htm.

Bartlett, Thomas. "Religion Class Sparks Debate in Kansas." *Chronicle of Higher Education*, December 9, 2005, 11.

Bellesiles, Michael A. *"The Origins of Gun Culture in the United States, 1760–1865,"* *Journal of American History* 83 (1996): 425–455.

Bellesiles, Michael, ed. *Lethal Imagination: Violence and Brutality in American History.* New York: New York University Press, 1999.

Bellesiles, Michael. *Revolutionary Outlaws: Ethan Allen and the Struggle for Independence on the Early American Frontier.* Charlottesville: University Press of Virginia, 1995.

Bellesiles, Michael A. *Arming America: The Origins of a National Gun Culture.* New York: Knopf, 2000.

Bellesiles, Michael. "Exploring America's Gun Culture." *William and Mary Quarterly* 59(2002): 241–268.

"Bellesiles's Response to the Emory Report." History News Network, November 2002. http://hnn.us/articles/1072.html.

Berman, Morris. *Dark Ages America: The Final Phases of Empire.* New York: W. W. Norton & Co, 2006.

Bernard, Harold W., Jr. *Global Warming: Signs to Watch For.* Bloomington: Indiana University Press, 1993.

Binghamon, Brant. "A Hunger for Imperialism." Review, Mike Davis, *Late Victorian Holocausts. Texas Observer.* November 23, 2001. http://www.texasobserver.org/showArticle.asp?ArticleID=496.

Blumenthal, Ralph. "Evolution's Backers in Kansas Start Counterattack." *New York Times,* August 1, 2006. http://www.nytimes.com/2006/08/01/us/01evolution.html.

Bogus, Carl T. and Michael A. Bellesiles, eds. *The Second Amendment in Law and History: Historians and Constitutional Scholars on the Right to Bear Arms.* New York: The New Press, 2001.

"The Bollinger Whitewash." [Editorial] *New York Sun,* November 19, 2004. http://www.campus-watch.org/article/id/1374.

Bowen, Mark. *Thin Ice: Unlocking the Secrets of Climate in the World's Highest Mountains.* New York: Henry Holt, 2005.

Boyle, Francis. "The Racist Mascot from Urbana-Champaign: Why You Should Boo Illinois." *CounterPunch,* March 30, 2005. http://www.counterpunch.org/boyle03302005.html.

Brennan, Charlie. "Churchill Says U.S. a Fascist State; Hundreds Turn Out to Hear Professor Speak in Wisconsin." *Rocky Mountain News,* March 2, 2005, 4-A.

Brennan, Charlie. "N.Y. College Official Quits Post Over Speaking Flap." *Rocky Mountain News,* February 12, 2005, 4-A.

Brennan, Charlie. "Churchill Finds Fans at Calif. Fest; C.U. Professor Gives Keynote Address at Anarchist Book Fair." *Rocky Mountain News,* March 28, 2005, 4-A.

Brennan, Charlie. "Tribe Clarifies Stance on Prof.; Milder Statement Explains Churchill's 'Associate' Label" *Rocky Mountain News,* May 21, 2005, 16-A.

Brennan, Charlie. "Professor's Evaluations Drop." *Rocky Mountain News,* June 29, 2005, 22-A.

Brennan, Charlie. "2004 Work Nets Churchill a Raise." *Rocky Mountain News,* July 2, 2005, 4-A.

Brennan, Charlie. "Churchill Report Looms; Faculty Panel Could Release Its Findings as Early as Today." *Rocky Mountain News,* August 19, 2005, 4-A.

Buencamino, Manuel. "Coming Catastrophe?" *BusinessWorld,* June 14, 2004, 21.

Burnett, Sara. "C.U. Panel: Fire Prof.; Churchill Should be Cut Loose, Say Six of Nine Who Cast Secret Ballots." *Rocky Mountain News,* June 14, 2006. http://www.rockymountainnews.com/drmn/education/article/0,1299,DRMN_957_4773332,00.html.

"Bush Says Administration Has Not Changed Stance On Global Warming." *The Frontrunner*, August 27, 2004 (in LEXIS).

Caplis, Dan and Craig Silverman. "Churchill's Active Advocacy of Violence Demands his Firing." *Rocky Mountain News*, March 5, 2005, 13-C.

Caplis and Silverman Home Page, November 12, 2005. www.khow.com/hosts/caplis-silverman.html.

Capriccioso, Rob. "David Horowitz vs. Ward Churchill." *Inside Higher Education*, April 7, 2006. http://insidehighered.com/news/2006/04/07/debate.

Carroll, Vincent. "On Point: Teacher on the Fringe." *Rocky Mountain News*, March 3, 2006, 38-A.

Carroll, Vincent. "On Point: Ward's World: Fade-out." *Rocky Mountain News*, May 18, 2006, 44-A.

"Censoring Truth." [editorial] *New York Times*, February 9, 2006. http://www.nytimes.com/2006/02/09opinion/09thu2.html.

Chapman, Matthew. "God or Gorilla: A Darwin Descendant at the Dover Monkey Trial." *Harpers*, February 2006, 54–63.

"Churchill Inquiry Hits Another Wall." *Rocky Mountain News*, November 5, 2005, 14-C.

Churchill, Ward. *A Little Matter of Genocide: Holocaust and Denial* in *the Americas, 1492 to the Present.* San Francisco: City Lights Books, 1998.

Churchill, Ward. "Some People Push Back: On the Justice of Roosting Chickens." 2001. http://www.kersplebedeb.com/mystuff/s11/churchill.html, n.d. (accessed February 3, 2005).

Churchill, Ward. "Press Release." January 31, 2005. Via e-mail forward.

Churchill, Ward. "Excerpts from Ward Churchill's May 16, 2005 Letter to the Standing Committee on Research Misconduct." May 16, 2005.

Churchill, Ward. "Statement of Ward Churchill. September 9, 2005."

Churchill, Ward. "Summary of Fallacies in the University of Colorado Investigative Committee Report of May 9, 2006." May 20, 2006.

Clark, Elizabeth. "Committee Chosen for Inquiry; Five Profs Will Review Churchill Allegations." Boulder *Daily Camera*, November 2, 2005. http://www.dailycamera.com/bdc/buffzone_news/article/0,1713,BDC_2448_4205615,00.html.

Cockburn, Alexander. "The Year of the Yellow Notepad." *The Nation*, April 8, 2002. http://www.thenation.com/doc/20020408/Cockburn.

Cohen, Jodi S. "Northwestern University Rips Holocaust Denial: President Calls Prof an Embarrassment but Plans No Penalty." Chicago *Tribune*, February 7, 2006 (in LEXIS).

Cohn, D'Vera. "This Year, It's Winter That's in Hibernation; One of the Warmest Januaries on Record Calls People Outdoors." Washington *Post*, January 31, 2006, B-1.

Cole, Jonathan R. "Academic Freedom Under Fire." *Daedulus* 135:2(2005), 1–13.

Cooperman, Alan. "Floating Ice May Explain How Jesus Walked on Water, Researchers Say." Washington *Post*, April 6, 2006, A-3.

Coyle, Patrick X. "Activist Challenges the 'Peoples Republic of Chapel Hill.'" *Libertas*, Winter 2006, 23.

Coyle, Patrick X. "The X-Files: Answers to Your Activism Questions." *Libertas*, Winter 2006, 6.

Cramer, Clayton E. and Dave Kopel. "Disarming Errors." *National Review*, October 9, 2000, 54–55.

Cramer, Clayton E. "Firearms Ownership and Manufacturing in Early America." April 4, 2001. http://www.claytoncramer.com.

Creamer, Beverly. "Outspoken Prof Critical of U.S." Honolulu *Advertiser*, February 23, 2005. n.p.

Culotta, Elizabeth and Elizabeth Pennisi. "Breakthrough of the Year: Evolution in Action." *Science* 310 (December 23, 2005):1878–1879.

Culotta, Elizabeth. "Is ID [Intelligent Design] on the Way Out?" *Science* 311 (February 10, 2006):770.

Curtin, Dave, Howard Pankratz, and Arthur Kane. "Questions Stoke Ward Churchill's Firebrand Past." Denver *Post*, February 13, 2005, A-1.

Davey, Monica and Ralph Blumenthal. "Evolution Fight Shifts Direction in Kansas Vote." *New York Times*, August 3, 2006. http://www.nytimes.com/2006/08/03/us/03evolution.htm.

Davis, Mike. "Hell Factories in the Field: A Prison-Industrial Complex." No date. Accessed January 3, 2006. http://www.rut.com/mdavis/hellfactories.html.

Davis, Mike. *City of Quartz: Excavating the Future of Los Angeles*. London: Routledge, Chapman & Hill, 1990.

Davis, Mike. "Let Malibu Burn—A Political History of the Fire Coast." *Radical Urban Theory: Writings on the Modern Urban Condition*. No date. Accessed January 3, 2006. From *The Nation* 260:7 (February 20, 1995), 229. http://www.rut.com/mdavis/letmalibuburn.html.

Davis, Mike. "House of Cards—Las Vegas: Too Many People in the Wrong Place, Celebrating Waste as a Way of Life." *Radical Urban Theory: Writings on the Modern Urban Condition.* No date. Accessed January 3, 2006. From *Sierra Magazine* 80:6 (November/December, 1995):36–42. http://www.rut.com/mdavis/housecards.html.

Davis, Mike. *Ecology of Fear: Los Angeles and the Imagination of Disaster.* New York: Metropolitan Books, 1998.

Davis, Mike. *Magical Urbanism: Latinos Reinvent the U.S. Big City.* Oxon, United Kingdom: Verso, 2000.

Davis, Mike. *Late Victorian Holocausts: El Niño Famines and the Making of the Third World.* Oxon, United Kingdom: Verso, 2001.

Davis, Mike. *Dead Cities: And Other Tales.* New York: The New Press, 2002.

Davis, Mike. "Catastrophic Economics: The Predators of New Orleans. *Le Monde Diplomatique* (English Edition), October 2, 2005.

Davis, Mike and Anthony Fontenot. "Hurricane Gumbo." *The Nation*, November 7, 2005. http://www.thenation.com/doc/20051107/davis.

Davis, Mike. *Planet of Slums.* Oxon, United Kingdom: Verso, 2006.

Davis, Mike. "Slum Ecology: Inequity Intensifies the Earth's Natural Forces." *Orion*, March/April, 2006. http://www.oriononline.org/pages/om/06-2om/Davis.html.

Dean, Cornelia. "Helping Out Darwin's Cause With a Little Pointed Humor." *New York Times*, December 27, 2005. http://www.nytimes.com/2005/12/27/science/27evol.html.

De Genova, Nicholas de. [Letter to the Editor] *Columbia Spectator*, March 27, 2003. History News Network. http://hnn.us/articles/1396.html.

De Genova, Nicholas. Web Page, Columbia University. http://www.columbia.edu/cu/anthropology/fac-bios/de_genova/faculty.html. Accessed December 22, 2005.

Derby, Samara Kalk. "Churchill Defends 9/11-Nazi Link; Indian Issues Get Little Attention in U.W. Speech." *Capital Times* (Madison, Wisconsin), March 2, 2005, 3-A.

"The Dirty Thirty: Ranking the Worst of the Worst." Bruin Alumni Association. January 9–24, 2006. http://www.uclaprofs.com/profs/profsindex.html.

Doumani, Beshara. *Academic Freedom After September 11*. Cambridge, MA: MIT Press, 2006.

Dowdeswell, Julian A. "The Greenland Ice Sheet and Global Sea-Level Rise." *Science* 311 (February 17, 2006):963–964.

Dwyer, Timothy. "Prosecution Called 'Overzealous'; Guilty Verdict in Terror Case Angers Muslims Who Know Lecturer." Washington *Post*, April 26, 2005. http://www.washingtonpost.com/wp-dyn/content/article/2005/04/26/AR2005042601548_pf.html.

"Editors' Report: The Churchill Episode: Two Unfortunate Currents." *Indian Country Today*, February 10, 2005. http://www.indiancountry.com/content.cfm?id=1096410338.

Eilperin, Juliet. "Debate on Climate Shifts to Issue of Irreparable Change." Washington *Post*, January 29, 2006, A-1.

Eilperin, Juliet. "Censorship Is Alleged at NOAA; Scientists Afraid to Speak Out, NASA Climate Expert Reports." Washington *Post*, February 11, A-7.

Eilperin, Juliet. "Climate Researchers Feeling Heat from White House." Washington *Post*, April 6, 2006, A-27.

Eisenberg, Arthur. "New York Civil Liberties Union: Letter to Columbia University President Lee Bollinger in Defense of Academic Freedom." December 20, 2004, in Beshara Doumani, *Academic Freedom after September 11*. New York: Zone Books, 2006, 298–308.

Elliott, Dan. "Associated Press Interview: Professor Says He Won't Back Down from Sept. 11 Comments, but Is Weary of Fight." Associated Press, March 18, 2005 (in LEXIS).

Elliott, Dan. "Indian or Not? Churchill Committee Faces Daunting Task." Associated Press, March 25, 2005 (in LEXIS).

"Expand Focus of Churchill Probe; Don't Ignore New Revelations." [editorial] *Rocky Mountain News*, June 4, 2005, 14-C.

Feiden, Douglas. "Hate 101: Climate of Hate Rocks Columbia University." *New York Daily News*, November 21, 2004. http://www.nydailynews.com/front/story/254925p-218295c.html.

Fisher, Ian and Cornelia Dean. "In 'Design' vs. Darwinism, Darwin Wins Point in Rome." *New York Times*, January 19, 2006. http://www.nytimes.com/2006/01/19/science/sciencespecial2/19evolution.html.

Fisk, Robert. "Since When Did 'Arab' Become a Dirty Word? In Australia They're Even Trying to Prevent Hanan Ashrawi from Speaking." London *Independent*, November 4, 2003.

Flynn, Kevin, David Montero, and Charlie Brennan. "Heritage, Writings Split Indian Activists." *Rocky Mountain News*, February 12, 2005, 4-A.

Flynn, Kevin. "Churchill Inquiry Sent to Higher Level; Panel Recommends Further Investigation of Seven Complaints." *Rocky Mountain News*, August 23, 2005, 4-A.

"Fools on the Hill." *Capital Times* (Madison, Wisconsin), February 28, 2005, 6-A.

Forrest, Barbara and Glenn Branch. "Wedging Creationism into the Academy." *Academe* 91:1(2005):37–41.

Forrest, Barbara and Paul R. Gross. *Creationism's Trojan Horse: The Wedge of Intelligent Design*. Oxford, United Kingdom: Oxford University Press, 2004.

Frank, Joshua. "An Interview with David Graeber. Without Cause, Yale Fires an Acclaimed Anarchist Scholar." *Counterpunch*, May 13, 2005. http://counterpunch.org/frank05132005.html.

Gelbspan, Ross. *The Heat Is On: The High Stakes Battle Over Earth's Threatened Climate*. Reading, MA: Addison-Wesley Publishing Co., 1997.

Gibson, John. "The Big Story with John Gibson." Fox News Network, June 29, 2005 (in LEXIS).

Goddard Institute for Space Studies. "Global Temperature Trends: 1998 Global Surface Temperature Smashes Record." 1999. http://www.giss.nasa.gov/research/observe/surftemp.

Goers, Peter. "I'm a Heathen; I Won't Repent." *Sunday Mail* (South Australia), November 27, 2005, 42.

Goldberg, Michelle. "Osama University?" Salon.com, November 6, 2003. http://salon.com/news/feature/2003/11/06/middle_east/index_np.

Golden, Daniel. "In Religious Studies, Universities Bend to View of the Faithful; Scholar of Mormon History, Expelled from Church, Hits a Wall in Job Search." *Wall Street Journal*, April 6, 2006, A-1, A-8.

Goodman, Amy. "Ward Churchill Defends His Academic Record and Vows to Fight to Keep His Job at University of Colorado." Democracy Now. National Public Radio. September 27, 2006. http://www.democracynow.org/article.pl?sid=06/09/27/146255.

Goodstein, Laurie. "Judge Bars 'Intelligent Design' From Pa. [Pennsylvania] Classes." *New York Times*, December 20, 2005. http://www.nytimes.com/2005/12/20/education/20cnd-evolution.html.

Goodstein, Laurie. "California Parents File Suit Over Origins of Life Course." *New York Times,* January 11, 2006. http://www.nytimes.com/2006/01/11/national/11design.html.

Grace, Erin. "Concealed-Carry Absolutes Are a Moving Target." Omaha *World-Herald*, July 16, 2006, A-1, A-2.

Greenhouse, Linda. "Supreme Court Weighs Military's Access to Law Schools." *New York Times*, December 7, 2005. http://www.nytimes.com/2005/12/07/politics/07scotus.html.

Gruber, Ira D. "Of Arms and Men: *Arming America* and Military History." *William and Mary Quarterly* 59(2002):217–222.

Gugliotta, Guy. "'Link' Between Fish and Land Animals Found; Discovery Called Key Evidence Of Vertebrates' Ocean Origins." Washington *Post*, April 6, 2006, A-3.

Gutierrez, Barry. "The Churchill Files: A *News* Investigation of the Charges Before a C.U. Panel Reveals Strong Evidence of Possible Misconduct by Professor." *Rocky Mountain News*, June 4, 2005, 1-A.

Hagopian, Elaine C., ed. *Civil Rights in Peril: The Targeting of Arabs and Muslims.* Chicago: Haymarket, 2004.

"Hall of Fame: *Vanity Fair* Nominates Dr. James Hansen." *Vanity Fair*, May 2006, 106.

"Hamilton College Raises $5.44M [Million] Despite Uproar." Albany *Times-Union*, July 28, 2005, B-3.

Hansen, James, D. Johnson, A. Lacis, S. Lebedeff, P. Lee, D. Rind, and G. Russell. "Climate Impact of Increasing Atmospheric Carbon Dioxide." *Science* 213 (August 28, 1981):957–966.

Hansen, James E. "The Greenhouse, the White House, and Our House." Typescript of a Speech at the International Platform Association, Washington, D.C., August 3, 1989.

Hansen, James E. "Climatic Changes: Understanding the Global Warming." In Robert Lanza, ed., *The Health and Survival of the Human Species in the 21st Century*. Santa Fe, NM: Health Press, 1996, 173–190.

Hansen, James E., M. Sato, R. Ruedy, A. Lacis, K. Asamoah, K. Beckford, et al. "Forcings and Chaos in Interannual and Decadal Climate Change." *Journal of Geophysical Research* 102(D22), November 27, 1997, 25, 679–25, 720.

Hansen, James E. "Dangerous Anthropogenic Interference: A Discussion of Humanity's Faustian Climate Bargain and the Payments Coming Due." Presentation on October

26, 2004 in the Distinguished Public Lecture Series at the Department of Physics and Astronomy, University of Iowa. Iowa City. Transcript.

Hansen, James E. "Is There Still Time to Avoid 'Dangerous Anthropogenic Interference' with Global Climate? A Tribute to Charles David Keeling." A Paper Delivered to the American Geophysical Union, San Francisco, December 6, 2005. http://www.columbia.edu/~jeh1/keeling_talk_and_slides.pdf.

Hansen, Jim. On the Edge: Greenland Ice Cap Melting at Twice the Rate It was Five Years ago, Says Scientist Bush Tried to Gag." London *Independent*, February 26, 2006, 1.

Hansen, James E. "The Case for Action by the State of California to Mitigate Climate Change." Expert Report, Submitted to United States District Court of California–Fresno, in Regard to Case No.: 1:04-CV-06663 REC LJO. *Central Valley Chrysler-Jeep, Inc. vs. Catherine E. Witherspoon; Automobile Manufacturers vs. California Air Resources Board.* May 5, 2006. Graphic exhibits: ftp://ftp.giss.nasa.gov/outgoing/california/california_figs_2may06.pdf.

Hansen, Matthew. "Government Blocks Professor from Teaching at U.N.L." Lincoln [Nebraska] *Journal-Star*, February 18, 2005, n.p.

Harjo, Suzan Shown. "Why Native Identity Matters: A Cautionary Tale." *Indian Country Today*, February 10, 2005. http://www.indiancountry.com/content.cfm?id=1096410335.

Healy, Patrick D., Kirk Johnson, and Michelle York. "College Cancels Speech by Professor Who Disparaged 9/11 Attack Victims." *New York Times*, February 2, 2002, C-17.

Held, Tom. "Churchill Speech Protested." Milwaukee *Journal Sentinel*, February 12, 2005, 3.

Herdy, Amy. "CU [Colorado University] Prof. Plans Tough Defense; Moves to Oust Him 'Vicious'; Ward Churchill Says Race and Politics Are Motivating a Review of His Academic Credentials." Denver *Post*, March 31, 2005, A-1.

Herdy, Amy. "CU [Colorado University] Students' Vote Favors Churchill, but Award Withheld." Denver *Post*, May 27, 2005, B-1.

Hertsgaard, Mark. "While Washington Slept." *Vanity Fair*, May 2006, 200–207, 238–243.

Hirsch, Arthur. "Science, Faith Clash in Class; Some Biology Teachers Are Among Evolution's Challengers." Baltimore *Sun*, November 27, 2005, 1-A.

"Historian Welcomes Plug from Bin Laden." Washington *Post* in Omaha *World-Herald*, January 22, 2006, 13-A.

Hoffer, Peter. *Past Imperfect: Facts, Fiction and Fraud, American History from Bancroft and Parkman to Ambrose, Bellesiles, Ellis and Goodwin.* New York: PublicAffairs, 2004.

Hoffheiser, Chuck. "Previous Hot Theory was Global Cooling." Letter to the Editor. *Wall Street Journal*, June 19, 2001, A-23.

Hofstadter, Richard and Walter P. Metzger. *The Development of Academic Freedom in the United States.* New York: Columbia University Press, 1955.

Holden, Constance. "Darwin's Place on Campus is Secure—but not Supreme." *Science* 311 (February 10, 2006):769–771.

Holden, Constance. "Court Revives Georgia Sticker Case." *Science* 312 (June 2, 2006):1292.

Hord, Bill. "Scholar's Visa Delay Puzzles U.N.L. Officials." Omaha *World-Herald*, February 23, 2005, 3-B.

Horowitz, David. "Moment of Truth (For the Anti-American Left. Horowitz on the Aftermath of the De Genova Remarks." FrontPageMagazine.com, March 31, 2003. http://www.freerepublic.com/focus/f-news/880445/posts.

Horowitz, David. *The Professors: The 101 Most Dangerous Academics in America.* Washington, D.C.: Regnery Publishing, 2006.

"How the Bellesiles Story Developed." History News Network, October 25, 2002. http://hnn.us/articles/691.html.

Howell, Ron. "Radicals Speak Out At Columbia 'Teach-In,'" *Newsday*, March 27, 2003.

Hsu, Spencer S. "Former Florida Professor to Be Deported." Washington *Post*, April 18, 2006, A-3.

Hughes, Jim. "Bill Targeting Tenure Advances." Denver *Post*, February 24, 2005, B-1.

"Inhofe Calls Global Warming Warnings a Hoax." Associated Press Oklahoma State and Local Wire, July 29, 2003 (in LEXIS).

Italie, Hillel. "Challenges to Library Books on the Rise in 2004." Associated Press, September 1, 2005 (in LEXIS).

Ivins, Molly. "Ignoring Problem Works—For a While." Charleston (West Virginia) *Gazette*, June 28, 2003, 4-A.

Janofsky, Michael. "Professors' Politics Draw Lawmakers Into the Fray." *New York Times*, December 25, 2005. http://www.nytimes.com/2005/12/25/national/25bias.html.

Jaschik, Scott. "Blackballed at Yale." *Inside Higher Education*, June 5, 2006. http://insidehighered.com/news/2006/06/05/cole.

Jayaraman, K.S. "Frosty U.S. Policy Leaves Indian Science Cold." *Nature* 439 (February 23, 2006):901.

Johansen, Bruce. "A Rap Session with 'Hero Hank.'" *University of Washington Daily*, March 6, 1970, n.p.

Johansen, Bruce E., ed. *Enduring Legacies: Native American Treaties and Contemporary Controversies*. Westport, CT: Praeger, 2004.

Johansen, Bruce E. "Letter from Lublin: The New Poland." *Current History*, November 2005, 390–397.

Johansen, Bruce E. "Parting Words from Member of Churchill Probe Panel." *Rocky Mountain News*, November 10, 2005. http://www.rockymountainnews.com/drmn/editorials/article/0,2777,DRMN_23964_4225837,00.html.

Johansen, Bruce E. "Nebraska Professor Asserts That David Horowitz Missed Him on List of Dangerous Professors." Inter-activist Information Exchange, September 30, 2006. http://info.interactivist.net/article.pl?sid=06/02/08/1417212.

Johnson, Haynes. *The Age of Anxiety: McCarthyism to Terrorism*. Orlando, FL: Harcourt, 2005.

Johnson, Kirk and Michelle York. "Incendiary in Academia May Now Find Himself Burned." *New York Times*, February 11, 2005. http://www.nytimes.com/2005/02/11/national/11professor.html.

Johnson, Kirk. "University President Resigns at Colorado Amid Turmoil." *New York Times*, March 8, 2005. http://www.nytimes.com/2005/03/08/national/08colorado.html.

Johnson, Kirk. "Anti-Darwin Bill Fails in Utah." *New York Times*, February 28, 2006. http://www.nytimes.com/2006/02/28/national/28utah.html.

Johnson, Kirk. "University of Colorado Chancellor Advises Firing Author of Sept. 11 Essay." *New York Times*, June 27, 2006. http://www.nytimes.com/2006/06/27/education/27churchill.html June 27, 2006.

Jones, Arnita A. [Executive Director American Historical Association] American Historical Association Letter on Visa Denial. February 13, 2006. http://www.historians.org/press/2006_02_13_VisaDenial.cfm.

"Judge Rules Against 'Intelligent Design' in Class." *New Scientist*, December 20, 2005. http://www.newscientist.com/article.ns?id=dn8493.

Jurgensen, John. "The Weather End Game: The Climate-change Disaster at the Heart of 'Day After Tomorrow' May Be Overplayed, but the Global-warming Threat Is Real." Hartford *Courant*, May 27, 2004, D-1.

Kane, Arthur. "Clashes with Churchill Found [in] C.U. [Colorado University] Records Show Several Complaints about Prof's Behavior." Denver *Post*, February 17, 2005, B-1.

Karen, Mattias. "U.S. Nobel Science Winners Worry about Bush Policies Toward Research." Associated Press, December 8, 2005 (in LEXIS).

Kennedy, Donald. [Editorial] *Science* 310 (December 23, 2005):1869.

Kennedy, Donald. "Acts of God?" *Science* 311 (January 20, 2006):303.

Kennedy, Donald. "The New Gag Rules." Editorial. *Science* 311 (February 17, 2006):917.

Klepper, David. "Professor Resigns Chairmanship after Religion Course Controversy." Kansas City *Star*, December 8, 2005. n.p. (in LEXIS).

Koebensky, Jessica and Roger Custer. "Comedy, Tragedy, and Today's College Classroom." *Libertas*, Winter 2006, 7–9.

Kohn, Alfie. "Professors Who Profess: Making a Difference as Scholar-Activists." *Kappa Delta Pi Record*, Spring 2003. http://www.findarticles.com/p/articles/mi_qa4009/is_200304/ai_n9210167.

Kolbert, Elizabeth. "Firebrand: Phyllis Schlafly and the Conservative Revolution." *The New Yorker*, November 7, 2005, 134–138.

Kolbert, Elizabeth. *Field Notes from a Catastrophe: Man, Nature, and Climate Change.* New York: Bloomsbury, 2006.

Kramer, Martin. *Ivory Towers on Sand: The Failure of Middle Eastern Studies in America.* Washington, D.C.: Washington Institute for Near East Policy, 2001.

Kristof, Nicholas D. "Hubris of the Humanities Fuels Shortcomings in Science, Math." *New York Times* in Omaha *World-Herald*, December 27, 2005, 7-B.

Kronholz, June. "For Dr. Sengupta, Long-term Visa Is a Long Way Off." *Wall Street Journal*, June 27, 2006, A-1, A-13.

Krugman, Paul. "Enemy of the Planet." *New York Times*, April 17, 2006.

Kurtz, Howard. "Steady as He Goes; In the Anchor Chair, Bob Schieffer Buoys CBS." Washington *Post*, March 6, 2006, C-1. http://www.washingtonpost.com/wp-dyn/content/article/2006/03/05/AR2006030501190_pf.html.

Labash, Matt. "The Ward Churchill Notoriety Tour: The Worst Professor in America Meets His Adoring Public." *The Weekly Standard*, April 25, 2005, n.p. (in LEXIS).

Laughlin, Meg. "Plea May Let U.S. Deport Al-Arian." St. Petersburg [Florida] *Times*, April 15, 2006, A-1.

Lawler, Andrew. "NASA Mission Gets Down to Earth." *Science* 269(1995):1208–1210.

Lawrence, Jill. "Intelligent Design Is Religion, Judge Says." *USA Today*, December 21, 2005, 1-A, 3-A.

Lawrence, Jill. "ID [Intelligent Design] Ruling May Have Ripples." *USA Today*, December 23, 2005, 5-A.

Lee, Jeannette J. "Churchill Defends His Views in Hawaii; Hundreds Hear CU [Colorado University] Prof's Speech; 20 Students Protest." Associated Press, February 23, 2005 (in LEXIS).

Lemann, Nicholas. "Fear Factor: Bill O'Reilly's Baroque Period." *The New Yorker*, March 27, 2006, 32–38.

"Let Science Win." (Editorial), Omaha *World-Herald*, August 9, 2006, 6-B.

Lichtblau, Eric. "Not Guilty Verdicts in Florida Terror Trial Are Setback for U.S." *New York Times*, December 7, 2005. http://www.nytimes.com/2005/12/07/national/national special3/07verdict.html.

Lichtblau, Eric. "Professor in Terror Case May Face Deportation." *New York Times*, December 8, 2005, A-34.

Linden, Eugene. *The Winds of Change: Climate, Weather, and the Destruction of Civilizations*. New York: Simon & Schuster, 2006.

Lindgren, James. "Fall From Grace: *Arming America* and the Bellesiles Scandal (Part 1)." History News Network, August 27, 2002. http://hnn.us/articles/930.html, Excerpted from *Yale Law Journal* 111(June 2002):2195–2249.

Lindgren, James and Justin L. Heather. "Counting Guns in Early America." *William and Mary Law Review* 43 (April 2002):1777–1842.

Locke, Michelle. "Christians Throw the Book at University." Associated Press in Omaha *World-Herald*, January 7, 2006, 3-E.

Lott, John. *More Guns, Less Crime: Understanding Crime and Gun Control Laws*. Chicago: University Of Chicago Press, 1998.

MacPherson, Myra. *"All Governments Lie": The Life and Times of Rebel Journalist I.F. Stone*. New York: Scribner, 2006.

Maharidge, Dale. *Homeland*. New York: Seven Stories Press, 2004.

Main, Gloria. "Many Things Forgotten: The Use of Probate Records in *Arming America*." *William and Mary Quarterly* 59:1 (January 2002):212–216.

Malcolm, Joyce. [Book review, Bellesiles, *Arming America*], Texas *Law Review* 79(2001):1657.

McKibben, Bill. "Too Hot to Handle; Recent Efforts to Censor Jim Hansen, NASA's Top Climate Scientist, Are only the Latest; As His Message Grows More Urgent, We Ignore Him at Our Peril." Boston *Globe*, February 5, 2006, E-1.

Merced, Michael de la. "Bellesiles Resigns as Fraud Investigation Ends: External Panel Asserts Guilt in July; Main Report Released Today." *Emory Wheel*, October 25, 2002, 1.

Mekhennet, Souad and Dexter Filkins. "British Law Against Glorifying Terrorism Has Not Silenced Calls to Kill for Islam." *New York Times*, August 21, 2006. http://www.nytimes.com/2006/08/21/world/europe/21london.html.

Merritt, George. "Giuliani Weighs in About CU [Colorado University]; Former NYC [New York City] Mayor Says School Can Overcome Controversies." Denver *Post*, April 4, 2005, B-1.

Michaels, Patrick J. "Kyoto Protocol: A Useless Appendage to an Irrelevant Treaty." Testimony of Patrick J. Michaels, Professor of Environmental Sciences, University of Virginia, and Senior Fellow in Environmental Studies at Cato Institute before the Committee on Small Business, United States House of Representatives, Washington, D.C., July 29, 1998. http://climatechangedebate.com/archive/09-18_10-27_1998.txt.

Mieszkowski, Katharine. "Bush: Global Warming Is Just Hot Air." Salon.com, September 10, 2004 (in LEXIS).

"Mike Davis." Wikipedia: The Free Encyclopedia. No date. Accessed January 2, 2006. http://en.wikipedia.org/wiki/Mike_Davis_(scholar).

Milburn, John. "University Cancels Class on Creationism after Professor's Comments." Associated Press, December 1, 2005 (in Lexis).

Morgan, Edmund S. "In Love with Guns." *New York Review of Books*, October 19, 2000, 30.

Morello, Lauren. "Warming's Toll Could Exceed $10 Trillion, NASA's Hansen Warns." Greenwire Spotlight 10:9, April 14, 2006 (in LEXIS).

Morris, William, ed. *The American Heritage Dictionary of the English Language.* Boston: Houghton-Mifflin, 1969.

Morson, Berny. "Prof. Takes Giant Leap to Tenure; C.U. [Colorado University] Was Anxious to Add Minorities, Former Officials Say." *Rocky Mountain News*, February 18, 2005, 6-A.

Morson, Berny. "1993 Essay Also Raises Questions; Churchill Says Pieces Credited to Others Are Actually His Work." *Rocky Mountain News*, June 7, 2005, 16-A.

Morson, Berny. "Christian Group Targets Churchill; Demons Destroying Prof., Minister Tells Abortion Protesters." *Rocky Mountain News*, July 20, 2005, 6-A.

Morson, Berny. "Bennish in New Spotlight; Calif. Activist Wants to Run Newspaper Ads Criticizing Teacher." *Rocky Mountain News*, March 22, 2006, 6-A.

Nance, John J. *What Goes Up: The Global Assault on Our Atmosphere.* New York: William Morrow and Co., 1991.

"An Open Letter from the Department of Ethnic Studies, University of Colorado at Boulder to the Board of Regents, President Betsy Hoffman and Interim Chancellor Phil DiStefano." N.d.

O'Reilly, Bill. "Left Is Crowded at Many Colleges." Omaha *World-Herald*, February 5, 2005, B-7.

O'Reilly, Bill. "Networks Ignore Churchill Story." The O'Reilly Factor. Fox News Network. Transcript, February 11, 2005 (in LEXIS).

O'Reilly, Bill. "The O'Reilly Factor: Interview with White Nationalist David Duke." February 24, 2005 (in LEXIS).

O'Reilly, Bill. "The O'Reilly Factor." Transcript, Fox Broadcasting, March 2, 2005 (in LEXIS).

O'Reilly, Bill. "The O'Reilly Factor: Ward Churchill Charged with Plagiarism." Fox News Network, March 11, 2005 (in LEXIS).

O'Reilly, Bill. "The O'Reilly Factor: Is Jane Fonda a Traitor?" Fox News Network, April 5, 2005 (in LEXIS).

O'Reilly, Bill. "The O'Reilly Factor." Fox News, February 7, 2006 (in LEXIS).

O'Reilly, Bill. "The O'Reilly Factor." Transcript, Fox News Network, June 26, 2006 (in LEXIS).

O'Reilly, Bill. "The O'Reilly Factor." Fox News. Transcript. October 12, 2006 (in LEXIS).

Overbye, Dennis. "Philosophers Notwithstanding, Kansas School Board Redefines." *New York Times*, November 15, 2005. http://www.nytimes.com/2005/11/15/science/sciencespecial2/15evol.html.

Owens, Bill. [Letter to the Editor] Denver *Post*, February 1, 2005. http://www.denverpost.com/Stories/0,1413,36%257E53%257E2686241,00.html#.

Packer, George. "Keep Out." Talk of the Town. *The New Yorker*, October 16, 2006, 59–60.

Pal, Amitabh. "Architects of Shantytowns." [Review, Mike Davis, *Planet of Slums*, 2006]. *The Progressive*, June 2006, 42–44.

Parsons, Michael L. *Global Warming: The Truth Behind the Myth.* New York: Plenum Press/Insight, 1995.

Pennisi, Elizabeth. "Fossil Shows an Early Fish (Almost) out of Water." *Science* 311 (April 7, 2006):33.

Phillips, Kevin. *American Theocracy: The Peril and Politics of Radical Religion, Oil, and Borrowed Money in the 21st Century.* New York: Viking, 2006.

Post, Robert C. "Academic Freedom and the 'Intifada Curriculum.'" *Academe* 89:3(2003): 16–20.

Powell, Michael. "Judge Rules Against 'Intelligent Design': Dover, Pa. [Pennsylvania], District Can't Teach Evolution Alternative." Washington *Post*, December 21, 2005, A-1.

Powell, Michael. "Advocates of 'Intelligent Design' Vow to Continue Despite Ruling." Washington *Post*, December 22, 2005, A-3. http://www.washingtonpost.com/wp-dyn/content/article/2005/12/21/AR2005122101959_pf.html.

"Professor Apologizes for E-mail about New Class," Associated Press, November 29, 2005 (in LEXIS).

"Professor Who Compared 9-11 Victims to Nazis Taught in S.D." Associated Press, February 23, 2005 (in LEXIS).

" 'Radical' U.C.L.A. Professors Targeted by Alumni Group" January 18, 2006. Associated Press (in LEXIS).

Rakove, Jack N. "Words, Deeds, and Guns: *Arming America* and the Second Amendment." *William and Mary Quarterly* 59(2002):205–210.

Rave, Jodi. "Reporter's Notebook: Controversial C.U. [Colorado University] Professor Stretches Truth." Billings *Gazette*, February 6, 2005. http://www.billingsgazette.com/index.php?display=rednews/2005/02/06/build/nation/67-reporters-notebook.inc.

Regalado, Antonio. "Skeptics on Warming Are Criticized." *Wall Street Journal*, July 31, 2003, A-3, A-4.

"Religion Professor Says University Hasn't Supported Him." Associated Press, December 10, 2005 (in LEXIS).

"Religious Studies Professor Withdraws Intelligent Design Class, Cites Controversy." University of Kansas Press Release, December 1, 2005. http://www.news.ku.edu/2005/December/Dec1/course.shtml.

Remnick, David. "Ozone Man" [Talk of the Town]. *The New Yorker*, April 24, 2006, 47–48.

Revkin, Andrew C. "Study Proposes New Strategy to Stem Global Warming." *New York Times*, August 19, 2000, A-13.

Revkin, Andrew. "Climate Expert Says NASA Tried to Silence Him." *New York Times*, January 29, 2006, A-1.

Revkin, Andrew. "NASA Chief Backs Agency Openness." *New York Times*, February 4, 2006. http://www.nytimes.com/2006/02/04/science/04climate.html.

Rignot, Eric and Pannir Kanagaratnam. "Changes in the Velocity Structure of the Greenland Ice Sheet." *Science* 311 (February 17, 2006):986–990.

Rivedal, Karen. "In the Eye of the Storm: UW [University of Wisconsin] Whitewater Prepares for Speech by Controversial Colorado Professor." Wisconsin *State Journal* (Madison), February 24, 2005, A-1.

Rivedal, Karen. "Churchill Says Media Misrepresented Him; He Says All Americans Culpable for Abuses Overseas." Wisconsin *State Journal* (Madison, Wisconsin), March 2, 2005, A-1.

Roat, Ron. "Dumbing Down 101." Evansville (Indiana) *Courier-Press*, May 12, 2006. http://www.courierpress.com/ecp/news_columnists/article/0,1626,ECP_747_4693818,00.html.

Robin, Ron T. *Scandals and Scoundrels: Seven Cases That Shook the Academy*. Berkeley: University of California Press, 2004.

Rosse, Joseph, chair; Sanjai Bhagat, Mark Bradburn, Harold Bruff, Judith Glyde, Steven Guberman, Bella Mody, Linda Morris, Uriel Nauenberg, Ron Pak, and Cortlandt Pierpont. "Report and Recommendations of the Standing Committee on Research Misconduct

Concerning Allegations of Research Misconduct by Professor Ward Churchill." June 13, 2006. http://denver.rockymountainnews.com/pdf/churchillfinalreport.pdf.

Rossing, Barbara R. *The Rapture Exposed: The Message of Hope in the Book of Revelation.* Boulder, CO: Westview Press, 2004.

Roth, Randolph. "Guns, Gun Culture, and Homicide: The Relationship Between Firearms, the Uses of Firearms, and Interpersonal Violence." *William and Mary Quarterly* 59(2002):223–240.

Rothschild, Matthew. "Muslim-American Running Back off the Team at New Mexico State." *The Progressive* Media Project. McCarthyism Watch. November 18, 2005. http://progressive.org/mag_mc111805.

Rothschild, Matthew. "Stopping Ideas at the Border." *The Progressive*, November 2006, 16–17.

Rudoren, Jodi. "Ohio Expected to Rein In Class Linked to Intelligent Design." *New York Times*, February 14, 2006. http://www.nytimes.com/2006/02/14/education/14evolution.html.

Rudyard Kipling to Nicholas de Genova. Accessed December 22, 2005. http://www.omdurman.org/leaflets/tommy.html.

Ruse, Michael. *Darwinism and Its Discontents.* New York: Cambridge University Press, 2006.

Russo, Sara. "Columbia Prof. Expresses Desire for 'A Million Mogadishus.'" Accuracy in Academia. No date. Accessed December 22, 2005. http://www.academia.org/campus_reports/2003/apr_2003_2.html.

Saito, Natsu. Statement in Defense of Ward Churchill. Distributed by e-mail. Boulder, Colorado, March 21, 2005.

Saito, Natsu Taylor. "Update on University of Colorado's Investigation of Ward Churchill." Via e-mail. September 10, 2005.

Saito, Natsu Taylor. "Resignation." May 1, 2006. Transmitted to author by e-mail May 16, 2006.

Schlafly, Phyllis. "The Outrages Taxpayers and Parents Pay For." Copley News Service, Washington Wire, March 22, 2005 (in LEXIS).

Schrecker, Ellen. [Review, Wiener, *Historians in Trouble*] in *Academe* (American Association of University Professors) May 2005. http://www.aaup.org/publications/Academe/2005/05so/05sobr.htm.

Schuck, Peter. "Fighting on the Wrong Front." *New York Times*, December 9, 2005. http://www.nytimes.com/2005/12/09/opinion/09schuck.html?pagewanted=print.

Schuman, Sharon. "Picked on by Their Profs." *The Sunday Oregonian* (Portland, Oregon), October 30, 2005, E-1.

Schwartz, Susie. "CAN Fights Zionist Smear Campaign at Columbia University," by a Columbia student, *Left Hook*, December 17, 2004. http://lefthook.org/Ground/Birch012805.html.

Seals, David. "Nicaragua: What's Ward Churchill Got Against You?" in Marijo Moore, ed. *Eating Fire, Tasting Blood: Breaking the Great Silence of the American Indian Holocaust.* New York: Thunder's Mouth Press, 2006, 182–198.

Shane, Scott. "Universities Say New Rules Could Hurt U.S. Research." *New York Times*, November 26, 2005. http://www.nytimes.com/2005/11/26/education/26research.html.

Shermer, Michael. *Why Darwin Matters: The Case Against Intelligent Design.* New York: Times/Henry Holt, 2006.

Shulman, Seth. *Undermining Science: Suppression and Distortion in the Bush Administration.* Berkeley: University of California Press, 2006.

Singer, S. Fred. "Global Warming Whining." Washington *Times* April 16, 1999. http://www.cop5.org/apr99/singer.htm.

Singer, S. Fred. *Hot Talk/Cold Science: Global Warming's Unfinished Debate.* Oakland, CA: Independent Institute.

Smallwood, Scott. "Inside a Free-speech Firestorm." *Chronicle of Higher Education*, February 18, 2005, 10.

Smallwood, Scott. "Aloha, Ward Churchill." *Chronicle of Higher Education*, March 4, 2005, 48.

Smallwood, Scott. "In a Clash of Academic-Freedom Titans, Civility Reigns." *Chronicle of Higher Education* 52:33(April 21, 2006): n.p. (in LEXIS).

Smolla, Rod. "Prosecuted, Not Persecuted: Why a Muslim Scholar Probably Crossed the First Amendment Line." *Slate*, July 27, 2005. http://www.slate.com/id/2123452.

"Some Faculty Reviewing C.U. Professor's Future Have Spoken Publicly on Case." Associated Press, March 27, 2005 (in LEXIS).

Southin, John. "Creationism, Intelligent Design Aren't Scientific Theories." [Letter to the Editor] *The Brockville Recorder and Times* (Ontario), November 30, 2005, A-6.

Spencer, Jim. "Whom Does Churchill Work for?" Denver *Post*, February 11, 2005, B-1.

Speth, James Gustave. *Red Sky at Morning: America and the Crisis of the Global Environment.* New Haven: Yale University Press, 2004.

Stevens, William K. "The Oceans Absorb Much of Global Warming, Study Confirms." *New York Times*, March 24, 2000, A-16.

Stone, Geoffrey R. *Perilous Times: Free Speech in Wartime from the Sedition Act of 1798 to the War on Terrorism.* New York: Norton, 2004.

Stout, David. "Supreme Court Upholds Campus Military Recruiting." *New York Times*, March 6, 2006. http://www.nytimes.com/2006/03/06/politics/06cnd-scotus.htm.

Sprengelmeyer, M.E. "Churchill, Horowitz on Their Best Behavior; Liberal Professor, Conservative Author Keep Discourse Civil." *Rocky Mountain News*, April 7, 2006, 4-A.

Steinhauer, Jennifer. "Nineteen Months More in Prison for Professor in Terror Case." *New York Times*, May 2, 2006. http://www.nytimes.com/2006/05/02/us/02islamic.html.

"Summary of the Emory Report on Michael Bellesiles." History News Network. November 2002. http://hnn.us/articles/1069.html.

Talbot, Margaret. "Darwin in the Dock: Intelligent Design Has Its Day in Court." *The New Yorker*, December 5, 2005, 66–77.

"Talking Points Memo"; Top Story: Interview with Hamilton College Students Jonathan Rick, Matthew Coppo. The O'Reilly Factor [Transcript] Fox News Network, February 1, 2005 (in LEXIS).

"There They Go Again." Review and Outlook. *Wall Street Journal*, January 28, 2005, W-11.

Thomas, Cal. "Study's Results Hardly Shocking; College Faculties Lean Leftward." Omaha *World-Herald*, April 11, 2005, 7-B.

Turenne, Veronique de. "Is Mike Davis's Los Angeles All in His Head?" *Salon*, December 7, 1998. http://www.rut.com/mdavis/salon1.html.

"Unsatisfying End to Bennish Affair; What Was the Punishment?" (Editorial) *Rocky Mountain News*, March 11, 2006, 12-C.

Vanlandingham, James. "Capitol Bill Aims to Control 'Leftist' Profs; The Law Could Let Students Sue for Untolerated Beliefs." University of Florida *Alligator*, March 23, 2005. http://www.alligator.org/pt2/050323freedom.php.

Vaughan, Kevin and Felix Doligosa, Jr. "High School in Turmoil over Teacher's Remarks; Controversial Lecture Thrusts Overland into National Spotlight." *Rocky Mountain News*, March 3, 2006, 4-A.

Vedantam, Shankar. "Eden and Evolution: Religious Critics of Evolution Are Wrong about Its Flaws; But Are They Right that It Threatens Belief in a Loving God?" Washington *Post Sunday Magazine*, February 5, 2006, W-8. http://www.washingtonpost.com/wp-dyn/content/article/2006/02/03/AR2006020300822_pf.html.

Vedantam, Shankar. "Scientist's Visa Denial Sparks Outrage in India." Washington *Post*, February 23, 2006, A-11. http://www.washingtonpost.com/wp-dyn/content/article/2006/02/22/AR2006022202446_pf.html.

Waldrep, Christopher and Michael Bellesiles. *Documenting American Violence: A Sourcebook*. New York: Oxford University Press, 2006.

Weiss, Rick. "NASA Sets New Rules On Media: Employees May Discuss Findings, Agency Says." Washington *Post*, March 31, 2006, A-10.

Wesson, Marianne, chair. Report of the Investigative Committee of the Standing Committee on Research Misconduct at the University of Colorado at Boulder Concerning Allegations of Research Misconduct Against Professor Ward Churchill. May 9, 2006. www.colorado.edu/news/reports/churchill/churchillreport051606.html.

"What About Us?" (Editorial) *New York Times*, July 28, 2006. http://www.nytimes.com/2006/07/28/opinion/28fri2.html.

Whoriskey, Peter. "Warning Label on Darwin Sows Division in Suburbia; Parents in Cobb County, Ga., Clash Over Sticker in Textbooks." Washington *Post*, December 11, 2005. http://www.washpost.com.

Wiener, Jon. "L.A. Story: Backlash of the Boosters." *The Nation*, February 22, 1999. http://www.thenation.com/docprint.mhtml?i=19990222&s=wiener.

Wiener, Jon. "Fire at Will." *The Nation*, November 4, 2002. http://www.thenation.com/doc/20021104/wiener.

Wiener, Jon. *Historians in Trouble: Plagiarism, Fraud, and Politics in the Ivory Tower.* New York: The New Press, 2004.

Wiley, John K. "Controversial Colorado Prof Visits Eastern Washington University." Associated Press, April 5, 2005 (in LEXIS).

Wills, Garry. "Spiking the Gun Myth" *New York Times*, September 10, 2000, Book Review, 1.

Woodwell, George M. and Fred T. MacKenzie, eds. *Biotic Feedbacks in the Global Climate System: Will the Warming Feed the Warming?* New York: Oxford University Press, 1995.

York, Michelle. "Professor Quits a Post Over a 9/11 Remark." *New York Times*, February 1, 2005. http://www.nytimes.com/2005/02/01/nyregion/01hamilton.html.

Younge, Gary. "Bush U-turn on Climate Change Wins Few Friends." London *Guardian*, August 27, 2004, 18.

Vaughan, Kevin and Felix Doligosa Jr. "High School in Turmoil over Teacher's Remarks; Controversial Lecture Thrusts Overland into National Spotlight." *Rocky Mountain News*, March 3, 2006, 4-A.

Index

About the Author

BRUCE E. JOHANSEN is Fredrick W. Kayser Research Professor of Communication and Native American Studies at the University of Nebraska, Omaha. He is the author of dozens of books; his publishing efforts are concentrated in Native American studies and in environmental issues.